The Slave Ship *Clotilda* and the Making of AfricaTown, USA

The Slave Ship *Clotilda* and the Making of AfricaTown, USA

Spirit of Our Ancestors

Natalie S. Robertson

Westport, Connecticut
London

Library of Congress Cataloging-in-Publication Data

Robertson, Natalie S.
  The slave ship Clotilda and the making of AfricaTown, USA : spirit of our ancestors / Natalie S. Robertson.
    p. cm.
  Includes bibliographical references and index.
  ISBN 978–0–275–99491–4 (alk. paper)
1. Slaves—Alabama—History—19th century. 2. West Africans—Alabama—History—19th century. 3. West Africans—Alabama—Biography. 4. Slaves—Alabama—Biography. 5. Clotilda (Ship) 6. Slave trade—Alabama—Mobile—History—19th century. 7. Slavery—Alabama—History—19th century. 8. Mobile (Ala.)—History—19th century. I. Title.
E445.A3R63 2008
306.3′620899660761—dc22   2007044010

Library of Congress Catalog Card Number: 2007044010
ISBN-13: 978–0–275–99491–4

First published in 2008

Praeger Publishers, 88 Post Road West, Westport, CT 06881
An imprint of Greenwood Publishing Group, Inc.
www.praeger.com

Printed in the United States of America

∞

The paper used in this book complies with the Permanent Paper Standard issued by the National Information Standards Organization (Z39.48–1984).

10 9 8 7 6 5 4 3 2 1

To my loving family, to the *Clotilda* Africans who have crossed over into ancestorhood, to their spirited descendants who carry on their West African legacies, and to all African-Diasporans who have yet to decipher their specific geographical and cultural origins—all of Africa is yours to claim.

Table of Contents

Acknowledgments

This book is the culmination of an extraordinary 15-year, trans-Atlantic research odyssey made possible with the generous support of many people, academic institutions, and funding agencies on both sides of the Atlantic. First and foremost, I must acknowledge the influence of those ancestral voices who generated, and sustained, the momentum of this great story, having informed, and shaped, the writing from the beginning to a new beginning—reciprocity (360°).

In the secular realm, several organizations have contributed to the success of this project in its formative years, including the CIC (Committee on Institutional Cooperation) that funded my feasibility study in AfricaTown in 1992 at the behest of Dr. Allen F. Roberts. I received additional encouragement and support from other academic mentors at the University of Iowa, including Dr. Christopher R. Roy, Dr. Michael W. Harris, Dr. Jacqueline Bolden, Dr. Darwin T. Turner, Dr. Salome Raheim, Dr. James Giblin, Drs. Janice and William Welburn, and Dr. Lauren Rabinowitz.

The success of my field work in AfricaTown, however, depended heavily on the assistance of Mrs. Vernice Stone, Mrs. Aurelia Craig, and Mr. Henry C. Williams, who acclimated me to the community by introducing me to several of the *Clotilda* descendants, including Lorna Woods, Mary Pogue, Ivory Hill, Vernetta Henson, and Israel Lewis, whose insight into the perspectives and practices of their ancestors strengthened this story beyond measure. One cannot overlook the contributions of ancestors John Smith, former mayor of Prichard, Alabama, and State Senator Michael A. Figures, Esq., who fought valiantly, and tirelessly, to bring political recognition and respect to the history and the heritage of AfricaTown, in the face of hostile opposition.

Numerous librarians and archivists, at both the state and national levels, have contributed their expertise to this project at various stages of its development. Thanks to Lendal Jones and Sheryl Somathilake of the Genealogy and Public History branch of the Mobile Public Library; Carol Ellis, Barbara

Asmus, and Scotty Kirkland of the University of South Alabama Archives; Coll'ette King and June Curran of the Mobile Probate Archives; Christine Cramer of the Minnie Mitchell Archives (Historic Mobile Preservations Society); and Donna Wells of the Moorland-Spingarn Research Center, Howard University. A special thanks also to Cathy Williamson of the Mariner's Museum (Newport News, Virginia) and to Walter B. Hill Jr. and Kim Y. McKeithan of the National Archives (College Park, Maryland, and Washington, DC).

The feasibility study established the historiographical baseline for field research in the Republic of Benin in 1994, undertaken with a travel fellowship from the Stanley Foundation (University of Iowa). My research agenda in the Republic of Benin was a success, in large measure, due to the assistance of my interpreter, Martine F. de Souza, who gave me room and board in her family's compound and who introduced me to so many fascinating, knowledgeable, and wise people, including her mother, Eulalie, who helped me to maintain my health during my first visit to West Africa. I would like to thank Dr. Joseph Adande (Art Historian, Université Nationale du Benin) who served as my academic mentor and who introduced me to stalwart historians who helped shape this project by providing me with critical insight into various aspects of Fon culture, such as Sylvain C. Anignikin, a senior lecturer in the Department of History at the Université Nationale du Benin. Thanks also to Dr. Elisée Soumoni, professor of history at Université Nationale du Benin, for his intellectual leadership and for the warm reception that he held for me at his house in Benin. This project benefits immensely from archival and art historical data that has been collected from important repositories in Benin, such as the Musée Historique de Ouidah (director, Ayadokoun Mizehoun Dorothé); the Musée Historique d'Abomey (docent, Jean Gauthier Amidi); the Archives Nationale Du Benin, Porto Novo; and the Zoungboji Village Museum, Whydah.

Secondary data sources can never substitute for primary ones. The former needs elucidation by the latter. That is particularly true within the methodological framework of this trans-Atlantic, interdisciplinary, and cross-cultural research that benefits from the insight of indigenous scholars and peoples who are the authorities on their history and culture. The discourse on, and about, African peoples and their histories have been controlled largely by Westerners, with little consideration given to the perspectives of indigenous scholars. This project endeavored to begin the process of correcting that problem by raising the profiles, and drawing on the expertise, of Fon indigenes. In that regard, Supreme Chief Dagbo Hounon enhanced my knowledge of Vodun relative to Fon culture and politics. Primarily, the research agenda in

Whydah aimed to tap the knowledge of Fon indigenes who descended from persons who controlled the supply side of the trans-Atlantic slave trade. Towards that end, the contributions made by Supreme Chief Dah Akolemin Dossou Agaja Kakanakou and Chief Lohotogbe Nongloakou Gankpe, whose descendants regulated slave sales and exports at Zoungboji, are invaluable.

The writing has been strengthened by indigenes who are capable of excavating and articulating indigenous knowledge by esoteric means and methods that are not readily available, or apparent, to outsiders. Therefore, a special thank you is extended to Nobel Laureate Wole Soyinka, before whom I had the honor of presenting my research at Gorée Institute in Senegal, as a component of a faculty seminar made possible by Dr. Cynthia Spence at Spelman College and the United Negro College Fund/Mellon Foundation in 2002. Dr. Soyinka's constructive criticisms confirmed that my research agenda was on course, in terms of the investigative angles that I was pursuing relative to Yoruba history, culture, and politics in the nineteenth century. Dr. Soyinka enhanced my understanding of the epistemological dimensions of Yoruba culture. I am also grateful for the assistance of Dr. Babatunde Agiri, an historian at Norfolk State University, who contributed valuable information regarding Yoruba political and military history in the nineteenth century.

The intellectual contributions of both Soyinka and Agiri helped prepare me for my subsequent expedition to Yorubaland in southwestern Nigeria in 2003 and 2004, undertaken with a National Endowment for the Humanities Faculty Research Award. I appreciate the hospitality shown to me by Ferdinand and Victoria Addo in Lagos, prior to my arrival in Ibadan in 2003. Thanks to Dr. Olutayo Adesina, former head of the Department of History at the University of Ibadan, who provided me with official letters of invitation and academic affiliation; administrative assistance; and lodging in Ibadan. Thanks also to his wife, Kemi, for her hospitality and research assistance in Ibadan as well as in Oyo. Interviews with prominent Yoruba scholars, active and retired, of the University of Ibadan further strengthened my knowledge of Yoruba cultural, political, and economic history, including Dr. I. A. Akinjogbin, Dr. Bolanle Awe, and Dr. G. O. Oguntomisin. Sam Odularu, Head of the Kennith Dike Library, and archivists at the National Archives of Nigeria (Ibadan), helped shape my research agenda by introducing me to important source material within their respective collections and repositories. Thanks also to Dr. Foluke Ogunleye and Dr. Biodun Adediran, at the University of Ife, for their scholarly advice and support.

When one's health fails, so does everything else. Without the medical aid of the very wise Sesan Fadare, MD, of the University College Hospital (Oyo

State), I could not have completed my 2003 research agenda, whose focus was to tap the knowledge bases of Oyo-Yoruba indigenes who descended from titled political officials, military personnel, and merchants who launched slave raids, had intimate knowledge of slave trade routes, and who sold African captives at coastal ports during the nineteenth century. Interviews with the *ilari*, a cadre of titled, royal messengers at the *Afin* (Royal Palace) in Oyo, yielded primary data on the history of the Oyo Empire as a slave-raiding powerhouse and as a source of captives, many of whom were evacuated to coastal slave ports such as Badagry that was controlled by members of the Mobee family. Insight into the manner in which Africans were processed for export at Badagry, or transshipped to adjacent ports such as Whydah, was provided by ViaVoh Mobee, curator of the Mobee Family Museum, and by John Babatunde Ajose, curator of the Badagry Heritage Museum.

As a National Endowment for the Humanities Scholar, I returned to Nigeria in 2004 to expand my research agenda into the Middle Belt region. If the voices of indigenous scholars have been ignored by outsiders, the problem becomes more acute in the interior of Africa where geographical, linguistic, cultural, and gender barriers can undermine the best efforts to tap indigenous knowledge. I was able to mitigate some of those problems due to the cultural savvy, political astuteness, diplomacy, and street wisdom of Olayinka Adekola, who served tirelessly as my interpreter, research assistant, and protocol agent in Nigeria. I am eternally grateful for the matchless hospitality of his wife, Olubunmi, who is truly a "gift from God." Olayinka's assistance was invaluable, particularly in the Middle Belt where my research agenda focused on the manner in which slave raids were launched and the spatial arrangements of the trade routes along which captives were evacuated to the coast.

Geographically, culturally, and linguistically, the Middle Belt is vastly different from southwestern Nigeria. Contributing to my understanding of these differences were significant individuals such as Professor Joseph Jemkur, the authority on the archaeology of the Middle Belt region, at the University of Jos. I appreciate his willingness to confer with me in his office, on short notice and without prior introduction or a formal invitation. In the Middle Belt, my research activities were concentrated in southern Kaduna, where Simon Yohanna, a professor at Kaduna State College of Education, helped me secure a guide in the person of Mr. Sati Baba. As the royal secretary in the Kaninkon Chiefdom, Sati provided impeccable guidance and service. He afforded me direct access to Malam Tanko Tete (Tum Nikyob I), the Supreme Chief of Kaninkon who shared his perspectives on slave raiding in that area. One of the true values of this research is that it yields primary data that is rarely obtained by outsiders. Obtaining such information was imperative, if the project was to elucidate the cultural origins of that portion of the *Clotilda* cargo that was comprised of captives from the Middle Belt. Regarding those origins, I am extremely appreciative of the information imparted by Dr. S. N. Sani and Mr. Emmanuel I. Galadima of the Jaba Chiefdom as well as Mr. Tobias Nkom Wada, the *Agwam* of the Takad Chiefdom.

This research assumes greater significance when it is shared with the larger public on both sides of the Atlantic. Thanks to Barbara White, dean of the Advanced Studies in England Program, associated with University College, Oxford, for acknowledging the value of my work and for inviting me to disseminate it to a wider audience via my course entitled "A Semiotic Exploration of the Triangular Slave Trade," taught in Bath in 2006. Thanks to Rachel Mulhearn, deputy head and curator of Maritime History, Merseyside Maritime Museum, for inviting me back to Liverpool to conduct additional research on the slave trade. Thanks to Dr. Toyin Falola, the Frances Higgenbothom Nalle Centennial Professor of History at the University of Texas at Austin, for allowing me to share my research results at the "Nigeria in the 20th Century" Conference (2002) and for inviting me to publish some of those results in the first *Encyclopedia on the Middle Passage* (2006). I am humbled by the professional support received from The Honorable L. Douglas Wilder, former governor of Virginia; Dr. Vonita Foster; and Dr. Gerald Foster of the United States National Slavery Museum. A very special thank you is extended to William Cosby, EdD, for his support and for the value lessons conveyed, and learned, through his exemplary contributions to the field of education and through the genius of "Old Weird Harold."

Certain individuals have contributed tremendously to my professional development with regards to this project, and beyond. Thanks to Dr. Roslyn A. Walker, former director of the Smithsonian's National Museum of African Art and my fellow Hamptonian, who cultivated my interest in African aesthetics in general, and in Yoruba material culture in particular, as a graduate intern. In that regard, I am also thankful to Jean Zeidler and Mary Lou Hultgren, former directors of the Hampton University Museum. I must recognize my Hampton University mentors who supported me throughout this scholarly endeavor, including Dr. Kanata Jackson, Professor Nelly McCrae, Dr. Charles Amissah, Professor Robert Watson, Dr. Ayuba Sarki, and Dr. Tyrone Ferdinance. Thanks also to numerous Hampton University students for their unwavering support. Finally, special thanks to my editors, Elizabeth A. S. Demers and Elizabeth Potenza, and to my literary agent, Sha-Shana N. L. Crichton, of Crichton & Associates, for recognizing the intrinsic value of this research and for helping to make its dissemination to a wider audience possible.

Any views, findings, conclusions, or recommendations expressed in this publication do not necessarily reflect those of the National Endowment for the Humanities, nor do they reflect those of any university, organization, institution, or library that has contributed support to this research.

CHAPTER 1

Prelude to Peril

The 1986 AfricaTown Folk Festival was the most significant one in the 136-year history of this small black community situated primarily in the Magazine Point-Plateau area, located three miles north of Mobile, Alabama. The festival is held annually to celebrate the town's West African roots, founded by African captives who were smuggled into Alabama, in the hold of the slaver *Clotilda*, on the eve of the Civil War. Attending the 1986 festival were numerous dignitaries, including U.S. Representative John R. Lewis, the Honorable Walter E. Fauntroy, Reverend Joseph Lowery, Reverend Jesse L. Jackson, Civil Rights activist Dick Gregory, and Alex Haley.[1] Joining them was an entourage of Beninese dignitaries, dancers, and drummers who had crossed the Atlantic to participate in this momentous occasion and to witness the historic Twinning Ceremony that officially recognized the trans-Atlantic link between AfricaTown and Whydah, a slave depot in the powerful Kingdom of Dahomey (currently called the Republic of Benin).

Among the Beninese nationals were Jean Vincent Adjovi and Archbishop Isidore De Souza who delivered the keynote address at the "Season of Prayers" ceremony that sanctified the festival's activities, including the grand Feast of Relatives and Friends. But, Archbishop De Souza's participation added a political dimension to this typically spiritual event, being a descendant of Dahomean slave dealers who profited from the trans-Atlantic slave trade.[2] The names De Souza and Adjovi are infamously linked to slave trading in Whydah, where they, and other Fon traders, sold more than two million Africans into the slave trade between 1641 and 1860.[3] Whydah was to Dahomey what Gorée and El Mina were to Senegal and Ghana respectively—the point of no return for millions of African captives whose fate was mortality, actualized or symbolized by perpetual enslavement for the economic, political, social, and psychosexual benefits of their foreign owners.

The *Clotilda* captives were among those Africans who were victimized by Dahomean slave dealers at Whydah during that period, although their victimization began at the point of capture in the West African interior where they were captured. The *Clotilda* Africans' victimization did not begin, nor did it end, with the Dahomean slave dealers who cannot accept sole responsibility for their enslavement. In the second half of the nineteenth century, Americans, mainly Southerners, were the primary buyers of African captives at Whydah.[4] Thus, the *Clotilda* smuggling venture began its history as an American crime perpetrated by two Yankee shipbuilders who successfully financed, and launched, a trans-Atlantic smuggling voyage in violation of federal anti-importation laws that failed to curb the trafficking in black flesh during the slave trade's "illegal" period.

Slave smugglers were aided and abetted by U.S. consuls serving duty in Havana and Cape Verde, veritable smugglers' dens where vessels were fitted out and provisioned for trans-Atlantic voyages. In specific cases, U.S. consuls provided false registries, bills of sale, and American flags to smugglers who manipulated them to mask the true intent of their voyages, allowing them to avoid having their vessels seized by authorities at sea. Federal complicity in smuggling activities, negligent enforcement of anti-importation laws, and the high demand for African laborers in the South's cotton belt comprised the nexus of factors that contributed to the success of numerous smuggling ventures during the illegal period.

This book chronicles the trans-Atlantic smuggling episode of the *Clotilda*, one of the last slavers to enter U.S. territory on the eve of the Civil War, and it dramatizes the plight of her captives from their points of capture in West Africa to their place of disembarkation in Alabama in 1860. Trapped in a strange, hostile land, and with no prospects for returning to West Africa, 30 of the 110 captives who comprised the *Clotilda* cargo founded their own "Affriky town," known today as AfricaTown. Although they were physically severed from continental Africa, the *Clotilda* Africans, like other captives who were forced to transverse the Atlantic in the filthy, fetid bowels of slave ships, arrived in the Americas endowed with indigenous traditions that allowed them to supersede the treachery of slavery. This is the story of the knowledge, skills, and wisdom that those spirited West Africans employed to triumph over their tragic ordeal as captives in the United States. Indeed, overcoming adversity is, by far, the most powerful dimension of the Black Experience.

That same indomitable spirit propels the *Clotilda* descendents who are endeavoring to preserve AfricaTown's historical, cultural, and architectural integrity. AfricaTown contains several sites that speak to their ancestors' presence in that place. Union Baptist Church, for example, was founded by Cudjo Kazoola, who was a member of the *Clotilda* cargo and a founding father of AfricaTown. Located on Bay Bridge Road, the church is one of the cornerstones of AfricaTown's landscape and legacy. In the tradition of the Black Church as an institution, it has served a myriad of functions for AfricaTown's residents for more than 130 years. Located in close proximity to Union Baptist Church is Plateau Cemetery, established in 1878, where Cudjo, some of his shipmates, and many of their descendants are interred. A chimney that represents the last remnant of a house that was built by the *Clotilda* captive named Gumpa was spared by new construction that widened Bay Bridge Road, the main thoroughfare. But, the new construction demolished the "home-house" of Martha and Mary, twin granddaughters of Cudjo. Increasingly, AfricaTown is threatened by encroachment.

Less conspicuous than the physical destruction, but equally threatening to AfricaTown and its residents, is the industrial waste emitted and deposited by paper and lumber companies that operate on the community's periphery. Although the effects of pollution on AfricaTown have not been measured, the residents feel that their quality of life is eroding. AfricaTown continues to be a semi-agricultural community where some of the *Clotilda* descendants, like their creative, industrious ancestors, cultivate their own fruit and vegetable gardens. Therefore, the descendants are not only fighting to save Africa-Town itself, but they are struggling to preserve the agricultural traditions that they inherited from their forebears. The descendants consider their West African folk ideas and practices to be as important to their existence now as they were to the survival of their ancestors. By keeping their West African folk traditions alive, they have retained the knowledge and wisdom of their ancestors as well as some of the important cultural threads that tie them to specific places and peoples in Benin and Nigeria.

This study explores the extent to which the *Clotilda* descendants continued to implement the West African traditions that they inherited from their ancestors. Refuting the notion that ignorance, shiftlessness, and immorality are the sum of the Black Experience in America, AfricaTown's rich legacy of struggle and triumph over adversity allows it to stand as a microcosm for understanding the development of African America that was forged by adaptive, tenacious, and talented Africans and their descendants who persevered in the face of slavery and oppression. This is also an account of my experiences, encounters, and observations as I travel to Mobile, Benin, and Nigeria in search of pertinent information that would further elucidate AfricaTown's emergence in connection with the *Clotilda* smuggling venture.

My international research odyssey began in 1992, when I applied for, and received, a small research grant from the CIC (Committee On Institutional Cooperation) that facilitated my first trip to Mobile for the purposes of conducting a feasibility study. Visiting Mobile for the first time, I felt as if I had traveled back to the nineteenth century. The city is a virtual time capsule that memorializes Jim Crow, its residents still visibly segregated along racial lines. Many blacks continue to occupy menial labor positions, while whites control the commercial machinery. Solidifying that point was one observation that I made while dining in a "Soul Food" restaurant in downtown Mobile, near the site of the old slave market at St. Louis and Royal streets. The food was prepared by blacks, but the money was tendered by whites. Although such racial juxtapositions are not peculiar to Mobile, they are magnified tenfold in the Deep South, where the Confederate flag continues to wave proudly as a seditious symbol that threatens the national security of the United States.

The ghosts of slavery haunt Mobile, walking the halls of the Augustine Meaher House and other antebellum mansions embellished with verandas of cast iron produced by highly skilled Africans whose ancestors practiced metallurgy before Greece and Europe were born, lurking in their basements that served as sleeping quarters for house slaves and holding pens for *bozale,* or newly arrived, unseasoned Africans destined for local and interior markets. To one extent or another, directly or indirectly, the history of slavery is alive in Mobile's architecture, cemeteries, museums, and libraries. It was at the Local History and Genealogy Division of the Mobile Public Library that I made one of the most fascinating discoveries of this entire research adventure, locating a legible copy of Captain William Foster's account of the *Clotilda's* voyage and of her daily experiences at sea.[5] I use the account to track the *Clotilda's* trans-Atlantic voyage from Mobile to Dahomey and to provide a rare glimpse into slave-trade protocol in Whydah, as an American slave buyer observed, and participated in, that process.

In 1994, with funding from the Stanley Foundation and PASALA (Project for the Advanced Study of Art and Life in Africa), I took my first trans-Atlantic flight to Whydah to interview descendants of Dahomean slave dealers who sold the *Clotilda* Africans to Captain Foster. In Whydah, I resided in the De Souza compound. I often considered the irony surrounding my residency there, as I, a descendant of slaves, was now sharing a house with descendants of some of the most prominent slave dealers in the history of the trans-Atlantic trade. My residency there was necessary, however, in order to gain insight into the contributions that their ancestors made to the supply side of the trade. Arguably, scholars have ignored indigenous perspectives as valid interpretations of African history, politics, and culture, even when their studies warranted, or demanded, the inclusion of Africans' opinions. This study's interdisciplinary approach does not repeat that egregious intellectual mistake, representing a shift towards a new paradigm that incorporates, and respects, indigenous perspectives as chroniclers of African history in general, and of slave-trade protocol in particular. Purposefully, it exceeds the limitations of conventional, conformist scholarship that talks about, and around, Africans, instead of conversing with them.

Many people outside of the continent of Africa fail to realize, or refuse to recognize, the fact that Africans developed and maintained highly stratified, sophisticated, and prosperous societies, economies, and political institutions. Dahomey is no exception, having devised and implemented a slave-trade protocol to sell Africans as commodities. The data that I collected via interviews with descendants of Dahomean slave dealers was cross-checked by conducting semiotic analyses of artifacts in the Dahomean king's palace in Abomey and in the Portuguese trading factory in Whydah, both of which exist currently as museums. Within this study's quantum, interdisciplinary framework that capitalizes on the interconnectedness of phenomena, African artifacts and historic sites are valued and utilized as "texts" that yield a wealth of information about their producers and about the milieu out of which they emerged.

Significant to Whydah's history is the village of Zoungboji that doubled as a garrison and as a processing center for Africans bound for the Atlantic trade. It is located on the "Route of Slaves" that leads from the beach, to the city of Whydah, and beyond. Manacles and other artifacts preserved by the village museum remind visitor's of Zoungboji's infamous connection to the slave trade. I placed some of the manacles around my neck, in order to experience being shackled in that way. Doing so revealed the inhumanity of the slave trade and the suffering of millions of Africans for whom Zoungboji served as their last sight of a West African village. Within the process of slave trading, point of departure rarely indicated place of capture. In fact, most Africans were captured 200 miles, or more, into the West African interior. Subsequently, they were evacuated over various routes to coastal markets. Since Badagry (Nigeria) served as an important transit point for the *Clotilda* Africans during their evacuation to Whydah, some attention is given to the manner in which indigenes implemented trade protocol in that slave depot.

During the nineteenth century, Fon warriors of Dahomey engaged in a protracted war with their Yoruba neighbors in Nigeria. Although previous writers have attempted to link the *Clotilda* Africans to Yoruba culture, such generalizations do not fully explain their heterogeneous geographical and cultural origins. The ability to trace origins back to specific places and peoples in West Africa depends heavily on the availability of sufficient data to facilitate the search. Tracing the *Clotilda* Africans' origins has been a 15-year endeavor. In order to elucidate those origins, names, languages, folk traditions, and other ethnographic data have been analyzed within the contexts of political, military, and cultural events in Benin and Nigeria in the second half of the nineteenth century. These analyses are supported by data that I collected via interviews with village chiefs, scholars, and indigenes in southwestern and central Nigeria. Consequently, this research sheds new light on the *Clotilda* Africans' geographical and cultural origins, revealing that they were captured in separate raids; they fell into Dahomean possession via different circumstances; most of them hailed from Yoruba cultures in southwestern Nigeria; some of them were taken from cultures in central Nigeria; two of them hailed from Benin; and one of them was a Fon national from Dahomey itself.

Ultimately, this study aims to metaphysically reconnect Cudjo and some of his shipmates back to their West African ancestral homelands by delineating their geographical and cultural origins to degrees of specificity that have not been reached by previous investigators.[6] Towards this goal, I have also tapped the historical memory of third, fourth, and fifth-generation descendants of the *Clotilda* Africans via a series of interviews with them in AfricaTown. They have yielded valuable information about their ancestors and about their relationships with them. Collecting data via the interview is a challenging pursuit, particularly when the researcher is an "outsider." Trust is difficult to establish with individuals who rightfully question the researcher's motives. My ability to establish a rapport with the residents of AfricaTown was facilitated tremendously by Mrs. Aurelia Craig. She introduced me to Mrs. Vernice Stone, who provided me with room and board during my subsequent visits to AfricaTown. Residing in Mrs. Stone's house offered several advantages, affording me direct access to people in the community. It was also there that I experienced the essence of southern comfort and hospitality, being given generous quantities of hoe cakes, collard greens, and fried fish, served with thought-provoking, soul-searching, spirit-renewing stories about life in AfricaTown.

Mrs. Stone became so interested in my research that she arranged some of my interviews with people in the community. Of course, there is no better way to connect with residents than to meet them in church. In addition to being the spiritual nucleus of the black community, churches are "clearing-houses" for various kinds of information. I attended four churches in Africa-Town, including Union Baptist Church. On each occasion, Mrs. Stone introduced me to several *Clotilda* descendants who were willing to share information concerning their experiences with their ancestors. Yet, collecting data was not easy. Some descendants declined my invitation to participate in this study, forcing me to consider the sensitive nature of my work. Indeed, history is personal and painful, often filled with memories of past horrors that continue to plague, even torture, the minds, bodies, and souls of descendants throughout the African diaspora.

Local residents who knew AfricaTown's founding mothers and fathers filled voids in the data that were left by some of the descendants. Even when old age was attempting to steal their fondest memories of their childhood experiences, the senior members of the community were able to recall their interactions with Cudjo and his shipmates. Mrs. Stone introduced me to Mr. Richard Edwards, a resident of AfricaTown, who, after learning the nature of my visit, proceeded to tell me about another investigator who came to AfricaTown in 1927. The investigator, who rented a room in a house on Kent Hill, in Magazine Point, introduced herself as "Zora."[7] That investigator, whom Edwards described as tall, and wearing a long dress, was none other than Zora Neale Hurston, the renowned African American anthropologist, folklorist, and ancestor.

Alabama was one of several stops on her journey through the Gulf states in search of folk material, funded by a $1,400 research fellowship.[8] The literary world is immeasurably enriched by Hurston's work because she conscientiously endeavored to collect primary material from blacks who had been viewed by other writers as being devoid of intellect and culture. She, however, preferred to document the experiences of "the average, struggling, non-morbid Negro," who, in her opinion, "was the best-kept secret in America."[9] The average, struggling Negro was not to be demeaned as such, but venerated as the true keeper of *black-folk* lore. Hurston found the keepers of these folk heritages in various work camps, such as the road camp in which Mr. Edwards was working when she first arrived in AfricaTown in 1927. He had vivid memories of Hurston, who collected a folk expression from him when he was only 15 years old.[10]

Ordinary, "regular" folk constituted the subject matter for Hurston's most profound and provocative writings. As an anthropologist, she understood that inferiority was a status that American society had assigned to blacks. She understood further that the discipline of anthropology, to which she was intimately connected, led efforts to ground racialist assumptions in science.

Working against pervasive pseudoscientific propaganda that aimed to vilify blacks by depicting them as subhuman, Hurston endeavored to reveal the intelligence of black peoples, as it is reflected in their artistic, folkloric, and technical traditions. Her interpretive ability was extraordinary. Interpreting black culture was her strength. Preserving, respecting, and honoring black culture was her spirituality. It is in this extensive black-folk heritage that much of America's popular culture is rooted.

Black-folk material continues to create wealth for many non-blacks throughout the world. Understanding this, Hurston had a political agenda attached to her work. She was cognizant of the important relationship between collecting culture and taking ownership of cultural productions, for ownership is political and lucrative. Ownership empowers one with the ability to place a culturally correct interpretation on that which one owns. This holds true for folklore, artifacts, literature, film, and other cultural productions. In this case, however, what African-descended peoples own are African-derived ideas and practices that demand an interpretation that will elucidate their significance for America's intellectual and cultural histories, highlighting the genius of their creators. As Hurston asserted, "research is formalized curiosity. It is poking and prying with purpose."[11] Her purpose was to raise and validate the voices of the ancestors through their descendants.

Hurston's endeavors to collect and preserve the rich cultural and intellectual heritages of black folks led her to Cudjo who, in the summer of 1927, was the last survivor of the *Clotilda's* cargo. She spent a considerable amount of time interviewing him, publishing some of the data that she collected in an article entitled "Cudjo's Own Story Of The Last African Slaver."[12] She returned to AfricaTown to collect additional material from him in December. That data was published in two works, the autobiographical *Dust Tracks on a Road* and "The Last Slave Ship."[13] Hurston focused her investigations on Cudjo for the same reason that other investigators concentrated on him: he was the most outspoken member of the *Clotilda* group. "I found him a cheerful, poetical old gentleman, in his late nineties, who could tell a good story," Hurston recalled.[14]

Cudjo could do more than tell a good story, however. He was a griot who possessed the ability to articulate ideas in dramatic, allegorical fashion. It was this communication style that drew Hurston and others to him. She recalled an instance in which Cudjo became very emotional while recounting the events that separated him from his African homeland:

> Cudjo's eyes were full of tears and memory of fear when he told me of the assault on his city and its capture...His other great sorrow was that he had lost track of his folks in Africa...After seventy-five years, he still had that tragic sense of loss.

That yearning for blood and cultural ties. That sense of mutilation. It gave me
something to feel about.[15]

Collectively, Cudjo's stories, and his narrative style, were endowed with an
emotive force that caused an emotional reaction in Hurston. In one way or
another, he seems to have impressed, influenced, or motivated all persons
who interfaced with him.

In addition to possessing a seductive, captivating narrative style, Cudjo had
a tremendous capacity for recalling vast amounts of information, as another
writer noted:

His memory of dates and facts seems to be more accurate and reliable than the
memory of some of the captains of finance who have recently testified before the
senate committees. You would hardly expect such a tenacious memory in an
unlettered man direct from the jungles of Africa.[16]

These comments reflect a persistent desire to equate Africa with savagery and
primitivism, although historiography and archaeology confirm that East
Africa is the genesis of humankind and civilization; that Khemetic Africans
trained Greeks in the faculties of arts and sciences; that North Africans
(called Blackamoors) ruled and influenced the Iberian Peninsula (Spain and
Portugal) from 711 to 1492; that East and West Africans explored the New
World prior to Cristobal Colon (Christopher Columbus); and that the rise
and fall of the West African kingdom of Ghana predates the organization
and emergence of the European nation-states. Indeed, blacks hail from sophisticated, well-organized societies that exemplified erudition, not ignorance.

To label Cudjo as "unlettered" is also to overlook, or ignore, the genius that
is contained in oral traditions as chroniclers of phenomena and as vehicles for
education in Africa. Africans who use verbal arts as their primary mode
of communication also possess astonishing capacities for memorizing vast
quantities of information,[17] without dependency on written records. Because
Cudjo hailed from West Africans who are masters of the spoken word, it
was not difficult for him, even as a nonagenarian, to recall the circumstances
that led to his capture and forced migration to Alabama. Psychologically,
enslavement was the landmark event that explained his presence in Africa-
Town, supporting the notion that "memory is active—the present is not
disassociated with the past."[18] Quantumly, memory connects past events with
contemporary phenomena.

Cudjo's enslavement, his separation from his home and family, was a tragic
event that provoked his memories rather than suppressed them. Cudjo never
forgot details about his African home because the oppressive conditions
under which he arrived, and lived, in Alabama forced him to contemplate

and compare the nature and quality of his life before he was thrown into the hold of the slaver *Clotilda*. The captives' historical memory was reinforced by their application of their West African folk traditions in AfricaTown and by their continuous discussions about Africa. Motivated by the hope of being discovered and returned to Africa, Cudjo seized every opportunity to call attention to his plight by sharing information with investigators. Therefore, whenever possible, I allow his voice to assist in the narration of this story. Invoking ancestral voices is both the essence of black spirituality and the salvation of black peoples.

One of the earliest descriptions of AfricaTown can be found in "Little Africa: The Last Slave Cargo Landed In The United States," published in 1897.[19] This article contains useful ethnographic data about the *Clotilda* Africans, but it also references a Dahomean village located in what is described as "the Exposition." Given the date of the article, this exposition is likely to have been the Chicago World's Columbian Exposition (1893) in which a "Dahomean Village" had been installed along the midway, as a component of a racist exhibit meant to demonstrate the supposed savagery of African peoples. Using the article's date as a chronological marker and as a cultural baseline, however, the *Clotilda* Africans were still speaking and applying their West African languages and traditions 37 years after they arrived in Alabama. The words "Little Africa" reflect that reality. As a group of partially acculturated Africans in Mobile County during the second half of the nineteenth century, the *Clotilda* Africans, like the Dahomeans on display at the Chicago World's Columbian Exposition, constituted an exhibit of *primitifs* in the minds of many spectators who remained curious about their origins and about the perilous events that brought them out of Africa and into Alabama in 1860.

CHAPTER 2

Voyage of the Slaver Clotilda

The *Clotilda* Africans were smuggled into Mobile, Alabama, in violation of the 1794 and 1807 Slave Trade Acts that criminalized the importation of any negro, mulatto, or person of color from any foreign kingdom, place, or country into the United States for the purposes of holding, selling, or disposing of such persons as slaves.[1] The 1807 act further states that violators would be guilty of a high misdemeanor, punishable by not more than 10, but not less than five, years in prison. Effective January 1, 1808, this legislation helped to usher in the "illegal" period in the Atlantic slave trade. American citizens smuggled Africans into the United States beyond the threshold of the Civil War. The rise of cotton as the dominant cash crop and the admission of new slave states to the Union comprised the factors that increased the demands for African laborers. American smugglers endeavored to meet those demands, defying all federal antismuggling laws implemented to end the illegal traffic on land and at sea.

Slave smuggling became a lucrative industry, the criminality of which increased the prices for Africans relative to the real or perceived "risks" associated with obtaining, transporting, and delivering them to American markets. It staggers the mind when one conceives of the enormous profits that smugglers reaped from the sale of African men, women, and children during the illegal period. An African man who cost $50 on the West African coast, for example, was sold for as much as $2,500 in the Gulf states in 1860.[2] A cargo of

500 Africans could net a smuggler $1,250,000, *minus expenses*. Allied enterprises such as slave brokering (mortgaging, consigning, leasing, subletting, renting, jailing, auctioning, prostituting, and flogging), shipbuilding, lumber milling, and rum distilling continued to flourish during the illegal period. Like other crimes, smuggling did not occur in a vacuum. Contributing to its success were federal, state, and local government officials, who aided and abetted smugglers in their illegal activities.

Corruption, from the highest to the lowest levels, weakened antismuggling laws on some fronts and completely undermined them on others. The legislative basis for this corruption rests in the language of Article 1, Section 9 of the U.S. Constitution, constructed by slaveholders for slaveholders who demanded that the new government allow them to continue to import and enslave Africans. "In order to form a more perfect Union," and to appease their proslavery constituents who wielded tremendous electoral power, Congress agreed to give constitutional protection to the institution of slavery. The manner in which they accomplished this, however, represents a study in political connivance between the Constitution's drafters.

By design, the words *slave* and *slavery* were withheld from the text on the basis that it would be "wrong to admit in the Constitution the idea that there could be property in men."[3] This semantical manipulation was not meant to mask the existence of American slavery. Politically, economically, and socially, the nation was founded upon slavery. That Americans filled their personal, state, and federal coffers with profits from slavery was no great secret. In fact, property ownership, in the form of land and slaves, was the ticket to high office in America. James Madison, the Constitution's master architect, was born into a propertied family that owned 5,000 acres of land shackled to which were 100 or more slaves.[4] When he moved into the White House, President Madison brought his slaves with him. They, like their predecessors, were required to sleep in the basement and the attic, although "body servants" sometimes slept on the floor at the foot of their masters' beds. After President Madison died, Mrs. Madison sold his body servant, a black man named Paul Jennings, to Daniel Webster for $120. [5] President Madison was following in the tradition of Washington and Jefferson, who, collectively, owned more that 500 black men, women, and children. Indeed, the White House and the slave masters who occupied it were, simultaneously, symbols of the federal government and of the institution of slavery.

The phenomenon of catering to special interest groups is not new to American politics. In 1787, slaveowners comprised the most powerful special interest group in America. The special interest included importing, marketing, and holding black men, women, and children as slaves. Instead of being issued to mask the existence of slavery in the United States, therefore, Madison's instructions to withhold the words *slave* and *slavery* from the Constitution represented a legal strategy that would allow him to use certain articles to preserve slavery without giving explicit constitutional support to the institution. Madison and his colleagues aimed to conceal the proslavery bias and agenda of Article 1, Section 9 that permits states to regulate the *importation of such persons* (Africans fell into that amorphous category) *as they shall think proper to admit.*[6] In Article 1, Section 9, therefore, Congress codifies the right of each state to regulate slavery *up to* 1808, giving up federal regulatory power in the process.

By ceding regulatory power to the states, Congress not only diminishes the Constitution's political integrity and legal strength, but it violates that constitutional principle that requires the federal government to maintain complete sovereignty over the civil, military, and economic life of the states. Equally troublesome is the fact that Article 1, Section 9, unlike the Slave Trade Act of 1807, fails to explicitly define the criminality of, and the penalties for, smuggling in the post-1808 period, providing a constitutional loophole for states that used the omission as leverage to argue for rights to regulate importations *beyond* 1808. Article 1, Section 9 further undermined the 1807 Slave Trade Act because smugglers came to regard the article as their special device, a gift from Congress. These events proved ominous for the federal government, as W.E.B. Du Bois asserts:

> It was the plain duty of the Constitutional convention, in founding a new nation, to compromise with a threatening social evil only in case its settlement would thereby be postponed to a more favorable time: this was not the case in the slavery and the slave-trade compromises: there never was a time in the history of America when the system was a slighter economic, political, and moral justification than in 1787: and yet with this real, existent, growing evil before their eyes, a bargain largely of dollars and cents was allowed to open the highway that led straight to the Civil War.[7]

Slavery was so lucrative that Article 1, Section 9 did postpone abolishing the institution to a more "favorable" time, which was, in essence, 21 years beyond the date of the Constitutional Convention. That was the crux of the problem! Fully aware of the proslavery context out of which Article 1, Section 9 emerged, and completely cognizant of the article's origin as a concession to slave traffickers, states continued to use it as a political weapon to argue for states' rights to import Africans beyond 1808 and without interference by Congress. Article 1, Section 9 began its history as a gift to states, but it became a bogey for the federal government that would have to fight a fratricidal war to regain its power to regulate importations. Such would be the fate of a nation founded upon a pseudodemocracy in which American citizens *secured the blessings of liberty to themselves and to their posterity* on the backs of enslaved peoples.

In 1810, President Madison asserted, "it appears that American citizens are instrumental in carrying on a traffic in enslaved Africans equally in violation of the laws of humanity, and in defiance of those of their own country."[8] Madison was a member of that slaveowning class of Americans who violated the laws of humanity for the sake of profit. He was a separatist who thought of blacks as licentious, immoral, and predatory, a distorted, but a convenient, and useful, perception that is of the slaveowner's making and that haunts American society from 1776 to this very day. As for defying the laws of the nation, Madison set the stage for such defiance when he empowered his proslavery constituents with Article 1, Section 9. Rather than ending new importations, the article gave impetus to American slave traffickers who were keenly aware of the fact that its language was left open for them to interpret and use as they deemed necessary.

Since Article 1 Section 9 does not state explicitly that importations shall end in 1808, smugglers viewed their activities as violating neither the letter nor the *spirit* of that article. The American slaver *Constitution,* named for the very document that empowered smugglers, was overhauled with 84 Africans in her hold in 1818.[9] Her commander Henry Peckham, and her owners Daniel T. Walden and Maunsel White, residents of New Orleans, were acquitted of smuggling charges in Alabama, although they had violated the 1807 Act. Subsequently, Congress passed the Piracy Act of 1820 that defined fitting out ships for the slave trade, and importing Africans into the United States, as acts of piracy that are punishable by death. In that same year, however, Missouri was admitted to the Union as a slave state. As long as Congress continued to expand slavery into the new territories, smugglers would work to fill the demand for laborers. The *Gypsy,* owned by Timothy Meaher and William Foster, had slaves in her hold when she was overhauled by federal authorities in the 1830s.[10] Her owners were not arrested, convicted, and hanged as pirates pursuant to the Piracy Act. Instead, both men felt justified in demanding that the federal government pay them reparations in the amount of $400,000 for the "unlawful" destruction of the *Gypsy.*[11] Thus, smugglers remained steadfast in their belief that they had a constitutional right to import Africans, emboldened by the fact that, up to the 1830s, no smuggler had been hanged for violating the Piracy Act.

Various nations signed treaties for the mutual suppression of the illegal trade at sea. The Anglo-Spanish Treaty of 1815 also established Courts of

Mixed Commission, located in Sierra Leone and in Havana, to hear cases involving slave smuggling. Those smugglers who were apprehended managed to escape prosecution by paying fines, jumping bail, bribing magistrates, or having the prosecutor enter *nolle prosequi*. In other cases, captains successfully argued that their slavers had been wrongfully seized, although their apparatus and their cargo confirmed their involvement in smuggling. Condemned slavers were allowed to return to sea, sometimes under the same name. In 1842, the Webster Ashburton Treaty sanctioned the establishment of independent squadrons of U.S. and British naval vessels for the mutual suppression of slave smuggling. However, the treaty remained ineffective amid complaints by American captains who charged that the British officers were encroaching upon their national sovereignty.

Matthew C. Perry, commander of the first African Squadron (1843–44), undermined the treaty by instructing his men not to permit British and other foreign officers to search ships flying the American flag.[12] That the American flag offered protection against search and seizure soon became known to foreign smugglers who used it as a shield against search and seizure. The Webster-Ashburton Treaty, as well as Section 7 of the 1807 Slave Trade Act, provided for the issuance of prize money to officers who seized slave-laded vessels that were condemned and auctioned to the highest bidder. The quest for prize money, often supplemented by brandy and Cuban cigars, superseded the enforcement of antismuggling laws as the primary incentive for seizing slavers. For several hours, naval officers observed smugglers loading their vessels with the desired number of Africans. They permitted them to fill their ships, because an empty vessel yielded no prize money. In some cases, they allowed a seized slaver to refill her hold, in order to claim her as a prize for a second time.[13] Where the quest for prize money eclipsed the enforcement of antismuggling laws, slavers and smugglers escaped prosecution.

Great Britain's naval prowess allowed her to dominate the trans-Atlantic slave trade during the seventeenth and eighteenth centuries. Britain would like her legacy to record that, in the nineteenth century, she led humanitarian efforts to end the traffic in human flesh. The cumulative effects of abolitionism were not realized until the nineteenth century, because those persons who were calling for an end to the slave trade on humanitarian grounds lacked the political power to end it. Members of Parliament, like members of the U.S. Congress, who were endowed with such power also had financial interests in slavery and the slave trade. Efforts to successfully prosecute the few smugglers who were apprehended were undermined by the *quid pro quo*, proslavery relationships that existed between smugglers, politicians, law enforcement officers, consular agents, and judges, all fraternal members of the slavocracy. This conflict allowed slavery to flourish, a reality that trumped any claims of humanitarian abolitionism on behalf of both governments. While promoting abolitionism, Lord Palmerston, Britain's foreign affairs secretary, led efforts to force the Chinese to keep their ports open to the trade in opium to which many Chinese persons were already addicted. The opium trade paralleled the slave trade in that it destroyed the lives of other populations for the economic benefit of British and U.S. citizens whose ships carried opium across the seas.

Humanitarian abolitionism has to be distinguished from economic abolitionism, advocating the end of the slave trade out of concern for the slaves versus the need to industrialize. Great Britain abolished the slave trade in 1807. Yet, her role in the trade did not end; it transformed. Britain ceased to be the major purchaser of African captives, but she continued to protect the other dimension of her Atlantic niche as a supplier of rum, shackles, and other commodities to the illegal slave trade.[14] As Britain decreased her position as a major slave buyer, she also increased her role as a consumer of raw materials (minerals, fibers, lubricants) necessary for industrialization.[15] The demand for raw materials, however, increased the need for African laborers on both sides of the Alantic. African laborers were supplied by smugglers who, in turn, received much of their smuggling apparatus from the British. Because British textile industries depended so heavily upon cotton produced in the Gulf states, Palmerston and other members of Parliament encouraged their secession from the Union. In fact, several Confederate ships were British-built.

Any serious examination of slave smuggling activities after 1820 must consider Cuba's role as a port of call for American traffickers. Hundreds of illegal cargoes entered the Gulf states via Havana, where American vessels were provisioned and cleared for sail, despite the fact that they were fitted out for slaving. The persistence of smuggling after 1820 was due not merely to negligent enforcement of anti-importation laws or to Cuba's role as a smuggler's den, but to the criminal activities of American consuls stationed at Havana. In 1838, Rear Admiral George Elliot, of the British Squadron, detained the Portuguese slaver *Constitução* on the West African coast. Eduardo Roberto, the ship's commander, possessed blank registries bearing the signature of Nicholas P. Trist, the American consul at Havana.[16] Although the Portuguese government had no consul at Havana between 1838 and 1840, Trist was not authorized to clear the *Constitução* for sail because she had been fitted out for the slave trade after Portugal had abolished its participation in the trade in 1830. If the U.S. government was not aware of Trist's illegal activities, it was made aware of them in 1839 when British Commissioner R. Doherty and Judge H. W. Macauley, serving duty in the Court of Mixed

Commission in Sierra Leone, petitioned the United States to "discountenance the proceedings of their agents at Havana, Mr. N.P. Trist and Mr. J.A. Smith, who openly assist in the dispatch of vessels which, from their armament and force, they are perfectly well aware are intended to act as slavers or pirates, or both."[17]

Despite the warning, or, perhaps, in consequence of it, the federal government allowed Trist to maintain his post for another three years. He was serving duty when the slaver *Tecora* smuggled Sengbe and his fellow Mende captives into Havana in 1839. The captives were subsequently transferred to *La Amistad,* upon which they staged a successful revolt against their Spanish smugglers. Dr. Richard Robert Madden, a member of the Anglo-Spanish Commission to suppress smugglers, gave testimony in the *Amistad* case. Regarding the complicity of Havana officials in smuggling schemes, Madden testified that "Nicholas Trist, the American consul in Havana, was heavily involved and reaping tremendous financial benefits from the traffic."[18] Trist and Smith profited from the illegal slave trade by selling false bills of sale and blank registries to American and foreign smugglers, in direct violation of Section 3 of the 1807 Act that prohibited American citizens, not to mention government officials, from assisting slave smugglers.

Blank registries and false bills of sale were valuable paraphernalia of the smuggling industry, parts of elaborate schemes to mask a vessel's origin, ownership, and destination. Blank registries could be filled out to say that ships were American, Spanish, or Portuguese, whichever claim was legally expedient at the time, and depending upon the nationality of the authorities conducting the search of a slaver at sea. Andrew H. Foote, Commander of the U.S. Navy, observed that "two-thirds of the slavers on the African Coast claiming American nationality have been provided with these sea-letters."[19] To complete the ruse, foreign smugglers possessed American flags that had been obtained from Trist.[20] In 1839, British commissioners identified 12 vessels that were sailing under the American flag, but they were registered to Spanish or Portuguese owners.[21] Sailing under the American flag, the infamous slaver *Henriquetta* smuggled 3,040 Africans into Brazil during her career.[22]

Spanish vessels used the American flag for protection against seizure by British cruisers. In other cases, those vessels had dual registries only after being "sold" by an American to a Spaniard. This was part of an elaborate scheme to mask the identity of the original owners of slavers. Specifically, owners of American slavers granted power of attorney to captains who could "transfer ownership" of the vessel to foreigners who, in turn, smuggled slaves on behalf of American owners. To complete this ruse, Trist sold certificates verifying that power of attorney had been granted to the American captains.[23]

Trist and Smith also gave verbal instructions to captains, prior to their departure, regarding the course of action that they should take upon being overhauled at sea. The following instructions were given to Frederic Adolph Peterson, commander of the slaver *Catherine*, before he left Havana for West Africa in 1839:

> [T]he main thing for you to do on this voyage is to be ready in case you are boarded by a man of war, to show your log book, which must be regularly kept from the time you leave here. Your ship's papers, your charter paper for the voyage, your ship's roll, and instructions; and you are, in that event, to take all command with your American sailors, according to your roll—all the others are to be passengers. You are to be very careful that in any cross questions you do not commit yourself, and always stick to the same story. When the vessel is discharged, you must at once cut your register in two pieces—one piece you must enclose, direct and send to Messrs. Thomas, Wilson & Co., Baltimore—the other piece you will bring with you, and give me when you return here. You must be very particular about that, and do not let any thing pass and after the cargo is out, before you cut the register in two pieces, and be careful to keep them separate—throw one piece overboard if you are obliged to, by being boarded by a man of war.[24]

Peterson was a foreigner with American papers and an American crew. His registry, per the American consul's instructions, was to be cut in two pieces. One piece was to be returned to Trist or Smith, while the second half was to be returned to Messrs. Thomas, Wilson & Co., owners of the ship, agents acting on behalf of the owner, or insurers. The owner, agents, or insurers would accept the second piece as proof that the slaver had been seized. The second piece would also allow the first owner to file a claim against his insurance policy for the loss of the vessel, its apparatus, and cargo.

In 1841, Congress imputed malpractice to Trist for issuing blank registries and false bills of sale, bearing his signature and the seal of the United States, to American and foreign slave smugglers, in violation of the laws of the United States.[25] Speaking before Congress, Trist attempted to mask his culpability by claiming that he had been "born amidst black domestics," that he was "nursed by a black woman," and that his feelings towards blacks were "kindlier than those towards his own race."[26] He provides the classic, schizophrenic defense offered by racists who claim to have some affinity for black people while harboring contempt for them and contributing to their destruction. As the congressional hearing proceeded, Trist revealed his true feelings about blacks:

> The negro is decidedly, inherently, and irremediably inferior to the white man; although, possibly, he may not only be, as he is, comparatively inferior, but may

further prove to be positively and incurably incapable of improvement, except when in contact with, and in subjection to, some higher variety of species.[27]

Trist's statements and actions reveal that he experienced the same psychosexual conflict of other white supremacists who once sucked at the breasts of, and copulated with, the very people who they came to regard as vile, subhuman creatures.

This psychosexual conflict, in fact, was the bane of the slave master's existence. It is a conflict that occurred in all slave systems in which there was contact between Europeans and Africans. Barbinais explains the nature, and source, of this conflict in Brazil:

> Portuguese men native to Brazil prefer to have a black or mulatto woman rather than the most beautiful Portuguese woman, I often asked them why did they have such odd taste, but they themselves could not explain. I hazarded a guess, that as they were brought up and nursed by these women slaves, they imbibed this propensity along with the milk they fed on.[28]

Commenting on the nature of this relationship between white men and black women in the American South, Jefferson Davis said, "Every Southern man in his memory runs back to the negro woman who nursed him."[29] As one who was raised on Rosemont Plantation in Woodville, Mississippi, Davis would have intimate knowledge of that relationship. The taste for black flesh was acquired in infancy, and it was cultivated throughout adulthood. Despite romantic and propagandistic notions of a better life for those blacks working in the master's house, that house became a vertibale trap for servants who were vulnerable to attacks not only by the master, but by the master's son seeking his first sexual encounter.

Lusting for, and having sexual intercourse with, the very people that they loathed created a psychosexual dilemma for those whites who imagined themselves to be a separate, and superior, species but whose genetic heritage was, and continues to be, bound up with that of blacks. Nowhere on the American landscape is this psychosexual conflict more apparent than in the life of Thomas Jefferson. In *Notes on the State of Virginia*, Jefferson asserted that blacks were "dull-witted" and possessed a "disagreeable odor." Yet, he married the half sister of Sally Hemings (also called "Black Sal"), a slave concubine with whom he produced a child.[30] To say that they had sexual relations is a gross misunderstanding of the dynamics of those illicit affairs in which power rested with the master.

Enslavement represented a built-in opportunity to defile the black body with perverse sexual acts forced upon slave women and their offspring, who were, in many cases, the master's own children.[31] However, Jefferson's case is more acute because he was, and continues to be, idolized as a rational thinker. But, his private *sexcapades* with blacks were quite irrational, in the sense that they contradicted his public discourse. Recall, it was Jefferson who asserted that, "amalgamation produces a degradation to which no one . . . can innocently consent."[32] Yet, Jefferson flagrantly consented to the degradation, his "bi-racial" descendants existing as the indisputable evidence of his "race-mixing" in violation of Virginia's antimiscegenation laws. His sexual attraction to blacks helps to explain why, in theory, he supported the idea of manumitting slaves, but, in practice, he never freed his own. Desire and utilitarianism always increase the value of property.

The idea of race, as it is globally perceived and applied, has no biological basis in fact. Moreover, intelligence is not a condition of race, since the very notion of race is false. Racial categories are political and social constructions that emerged out of the strategic plan of Europeans to define themselves as white and superior to justify the enslavement, exploitation, and extermination of Africans and other groups whom they classified as Black-Brown-Red-Yellow and inferior, in the quest for world dominance and riches. When the colonists codified the enterprise of slavery on the basis of race, they could not predict the paranoia and schizophrenia that would develop in the American psyche in consequence of their actions. The problem for the Trists, the Jeffersons, the Randolphs, the Thurmonds, and others who fantasize that they descend from "pure white stock" is that no pure white stock ever existed among humans who trace their mitochondrial DNA to an African mother, nor does it exist for people who bear the historical, cultural, genetic, or phenotypical evidence of African influence in their surnames such as Braun, Brown, Ham(m), Melani, Blackman, and Schwarzeneggar (German-Dutch, meaning *swarthy-dark*, as in complexion. "Negar" is one in a series of references to dark skin, including "negre," "negros," "niger," and the derogatory *nigger*).[33]

The ancient, recent, and Southern ancestries of whites are traceable to blacks. In the United States, and in other countries that developed and cultivated institutions of slavery, it is extremely difficult, if not impossible, for whites to trace their genealogical heritages without discovering the proverbial *nigger in the wood pile*. Trist, like most proslavery white supremacists, argued that liberating blacks would result in racial amalgamation and intermarriage.[34] However, Trist need only refer to the sexual practices of his mentor, Thomas Jefferson, to see that both phenomena were occurring long before freedom came. That is, in part, why freedom came so late. Furthermore, when Trist married Virginia Jefferson Randolph, Jefferson's granddaughter,[35] it is highly probable that he married a woman who was of African descent, considering the degree of miscegenation in those families. After completing his legal training under Jefferson's tutelage, Trist accepted the consulship at Havana in 1833. He obtained that position by patronage, a system of appointing individuals to positions, not based upon merit, but as rewards for their loyalty to the political party in power.[36] Members of the ruling family, their friends, and business partners were given preference over others. As Jefferson's clerk, and as the friend of Andrew Jackson's nephew, Trist was socially and politically positioned to receive the consulship.

Patronage engendered corruption in the federal government. Consuls serving duty in Cuba and Cape Verde used their positions as covers for illegal activities that were profitable. The slave-smuggling industry, including sales of blank registries, American flags, and bribes, yielded $20 million annually in Cuba. In fact, the price of bribes and other favors (paid to government officials at Havana) were regularly factored into the overall expense of smuggling ventures at eight dollars per slave.[37] American consuls continued to prostitute the seal and the flag of the United States during the Buchanan administration. John R. Spears, a former U.S. Navy officer, summed up the federal attitude towards the abuse of the American flag as a cover for domestic and foreign smugglers:

> Neither James Buchanan nor James K. Polk, nor any other member of any administration from and including that of Andrew Jackson down to the Civil War, did anything that could in justice be called an effort to stop the use of the American flag for covering such atrocities. It is a significant fact that there was one slave-ship named *Martin Van Buren* and another named *James Buchanan*. It is a pity that these two slavers could not have been preserved in the navy yard of the American metropolis as monuments to the officials whose names they bore, and to remind the shuddering spectator that along with our days of magnificent glory we have had our age of infinite shame.[38]

In 1857, the slaver *James Buchanan* cleared Havana for West Africa, where she procured 300 Africans who were deposited in Cuba.[39] Buchanan favored slavery as a constitutionally protected right, and slave ships, such as the *James Buchanan* and the *P. Soule*, were symbols of the proslavery, Democratic platform.

Proslavery Democratic administrations subverted antismuggling efforts, allowing plantation owners to replenish their labor supplies and, ultimately, line their pockets with money. In fact, Buchanan, along with two of his colleagues, Pierre Soulé and John Y. Mason, secretly drafted the Ostend Manifesto that proposed annexing Cuba to the United States. The document outlines various strategies for completing the annexation. Buchanan, Mason, and Soulé argue that Spain made little or no money from Cuba; therefore,

Spain would benefit tremendously from the $120 million that the U.S. would offer for the island. In reality, Cuba made money for Spanish consuls who regulated business in its ports and for planters who owned *engenhos* or sugar plantation-mills that yielded profits in excess of $60 million.[40] Therefore, the $120 million that the United States offered Spain for Cuba was a trifling sum, considering the fact that the United States could recoup its investment in only two years.

The *modus operandi* of the U.S. government in this case, and in others, is to persuade its target group of the remunerative benefits of serving U.S. interests or capitulating to its demands while laying the political and military ground-work for forceful seizure of property. Reclassifying the target group or nation as an "enemy" that threatens its "freedoms," "peace," or "national security," has served as a pretext for invasions. Haunted by its historical memory of L'Ouverture's victory in Saint Domingue, the United States viewed the Africanization of Cuba via armed rebellion as a threat to its national security, in general, and to its slavocracy, in particular, arguing that Spain, which ruled the island from a distance, could not control the slave population. However, it was American citizens like John A. Quitman and Nathan Bedford Forrest, white supremacist members of the Knights of the Golden Circle (the prelude to the Ku Klux Klan) who led filibustering expeditions in Cuba in order to incite enslaved blacks to rise up against their Spanish masters, an event that, if successful, would leave Cuba vulnerable for seizure by the United States.

The Ostend Manifesto provided additional support for the forceful seizure of Cuba, if Spain refused to sell the island, through armed rebellion, making the following assertion regarding the "rights of slaves":

> Extreme oppression, it is now universally admitted, justifies any people in endeavoring to relieve themselves from the yoke of their oppressors. The suffer-ings which the corrupt, arbitrary, and unrelenting local administration necessarily entails upon the inhabitants of Cuba, cannot fail to stimulate and keep alive that spirit of resistance and revolution against Spain, which has, of late years, been so often manifested.[41]

Buchanan and his proslavery colleagues were not self-reflexive enough to admit their own corruption, nor did they encourage blacks in the United States to rise up against their American oppressors as they were encouraging them to do against their Cuba enslavers. In the case of Cuba, Buchanan, his proslavery colleagues, and the filibusters are not inciting the blacks to revolt out of humanitarian concern for the blacks themselves. They aimed to use them in a divide-and-conquer scheme to pit the slaves against their Spanish masters, in an effort to seize the island from the latter's control. Once this had been accomplished, the Americans intended to subdue the blacks because, as the drafters argued, "we should, however, be recreant to our duty, be unworthy of our gallant forefathers, and commit base treason against our posterity, should we permit Cuba to be Africanized and become a second St. Domingo, with all its attendant horrors to the white race, and suffer the flames to extend to our own neighboring shores, seriously to endanger or actually to consume the fair fabric of our Union."[42]

Lastly, Buchanan, Mason, and Soulé advocated seizing Cuba to avenge the insult to America's national honor via the abuse of the American flag by the Spanish consul. But, they have their own U.S. consul, Trist, to blame for that. In addition to acquiring the *engenhos,* its lucrative harbors, and its black population, the annexation of Cuba would ensure its elimination as Louisiana's major competitor in the sugar industry, of personal importance to Soulé, who owned plantations in Louisiana. Nicholas Trist owned sugar plantations in Lafourche Parish and in Adams Parish, Louisiana, in addition to the one that he owned in Havana.[43] Gulf state planters benefited significantly from the illegal slave cargoes that arrived in the South by way of Havana, where smugglers could readily obtain fraudulent registries, bills of sale, and flags of various nations, supplied, in large part, by Trist. His criminal activities not only aided and abetted slave smugglers, but they demonstrated the fact that those officials who were responsible for upholding the laws of the United States were also in the best position to violate those laws and profit from those violations.

Federal government officials and private citizens reaped enormous profits from slave smuggling and from affiliate enterprises such as shipbuilding. The majority of American slave ships were designed and constructed by northeasterners who, rather than owning large numbers of slaves, were more concerned with building schooner and clipper ships, and retrofitting merchant and whale ships, to transport African captives to North America. Cuban smugglers also used American ships built in New York and Baltimore during the second half of the nineteenth century. Trist's "official business necessarily concerned itself with Yankee skippers,"[44] shipbuilders, and ship-brokers who were linked economically to associate businessmen in Cuba and in the South. Instead of being completely embroiled in a sectional rivalry over the issue of slavery, as most people believe the North and the South to have been, northerners and southerners were partners in the enterprise of slave smuggling.

The first North American slave ships were built in the New England colonies, Rhode Island serving as the vanguard in ship construction. New Englanders were the premier shipbuilders and traders of the Atlantic. In that regard, New England mirrored Old England. In order to profit from the illegal trade, many Yankee skippers relocated to the Gulf states to engage in ship-building and slave smuggling. Timothy Meaher was one of those Yankees. A native of Whitfield, Maine, Meaher relocated to Mobile in 1836. In that same year, Congress passed a resolution stating that it had no authority over state slavery laws, further empowering the states with the legal instruments to regulate slavery after 1808.[45] That resolution, coupled with the extermination of Creek, Choctaw, and Chickasaw indigenes and the forced migration of their survivors to the other side of the Mississippi River, opened the way for white settlement in the Black Belt region, with nutrient-rich soil, extensive timberland, and navigable waterways. Its location in the heart of the Black Belt, and its hydrological connection to the Gulf of Mexico, made Mobile ideal for shipbuilding and cotton planting.

As a descendant of sailors and shipbuilders, Tim Meaher quickly engaged in both enterprises. He established his home three miles north of Mobile, on Telegraph Road that runs parallel to the Mobile River. In 1847, he built his shipyard at Meaher's Wharf, spanning 18 acres of land on the west bank of Chickasabogue Creek in Magazine Point. In fact, he owned considerable tracts of land between Three Mile Creek and the west bank of Chickasabogue Creek, known as Meaher's Hummock, where he operated a shipyard, a shingle yard, a blacksmith shop, and a plantation.[46] Because Chickasabogue Creek empties into the Mobile River, it was the perfect location in which to build, and from which to launch, oceangoing ships and steamboats. He built the *Sarah E. Meaher*, a three-masted schooner measuring 400 tons. She is credited with being the first American ship to sail up the Danube and hoist the American flag at Moldovia, under the command of Captain Ward L. Smith during Crimean War.[47] However, the majority of vessels built at Meaher's Shipyard were steamboats. In the first half of the nineteenth century, steamboats consti-tuted a major mode of transportation for people and commodities traveling between Mobile, Montgomery, and New Orleans. Tim Meaher built and oper-ated his shipyard and steamboat business in partnership with his brother James Meaher, under the name of J.M and T. Meaher. He had a second brother, Byrnes Meaher, who also was involved in the steamboat business. Among those steamboats that the Meahers built, owned, and operated were the *Waverly, Orline St. John, Czar, Southerner, Roger B. Taney, WM Bradstreet, William R. Hallet* (President of the Bank of Mobile), and *Southern Republic,* nominal symbols of the nexus between capital, political power, and slavery.

In copartnership with Cox, Brainard & Co., the Meaher brothers dominated the steamboat business in Mobile.[48] Tim Meaher operated his steamboats as weekly packets that transported people, supplies, pitch pine, and cotton from Montgomery to Mobile, with stops at Wetumpka. In April 1850, while plying the Alabama River, the *Orline St. John*, with Tim Meaher as commander, Byrnes Meaher, Tim's brother, as mate, and Ben Pierce as pilot, burned and sank at St. John Bar (Wilcox County) when pitch pine, placed too close to the furnace, combusted. There were 41 casualties. Some passengers were consumed by the flames, while others drowned in the river.[49] Steamboats were dangerous modes of transportation, but merchants depended heavily upon them to move their crops from field to market. During his career as a steamboat operator, one that span more than ten years, Meaher transported over 1.7 million bales of cotton from points of production to the Mobile Docks.[50] Many of these bales were produced on his plantation near his home on Telegraph Road.

By 1850, Alabama had surpassed Mississippi as the leading producer of cotton in the Black Belt. Collectively, Southern slave states produced 4.5 million bales of cotton in the middle of the nineteenth century.[51] Gulf state planters were in such great need of laborers that they called for a "re-opening" of the Atlantic slave trade. It is incorrect, however, to argue that they wanted to reopen the Atlantic slave trade, since, in practice, the trade was never completely closed. In the post-1808 period, Africans continued to be smuggled directly, or circuitously by way of Cuba, into the Gulf states. Planters, and persons engaged in allied enterprises, wanted to repeal all anti-importation laws that they viewed as infringements on their constitutional rights to "regulate slavery" or to make money as dealers in black flesh. They found support for their pro-importation agenda in the writings of Dr. Josiah C. Nott, the leading proponent of scientific racism in Alabama. In *Two Lectures on the Natural History of the Caucasian and Negro Races*, Nott argued that perpetual enslavement was the fate of blacks who constituted an alien species.[52] In this context, the term "alien" is the code word that marks blacks out for perpetual subjugation ("ethnic" became a code for genocide in Bosnia and elsewhere). Labeling is the first step in the process of rationalizing domination and genocide in the minds of enslavers and murderers.

Nott described his work as *niggerology.*[53] What that work amounted to was pseudoscientific explorations of the various ways to make black peoples fit the classification of *niggers*. Nott was to American white supremacists what Josef Goebbels was to Germany's Nazi regime—a propagandist whose racist views were used as justification for enslavement and genocide. Nott's writings provided an ideological support for slaveowners and other individuals who wanted to repeal anti-importation laws that not only threatened their "constitutional rights" to import African laborers, but jeopardized the master-slave relationship itself. Slave ownership was the gauge by which white men measured their status in Southern society, where masters were revered as "gentlemen" and as "upstanding" citizens.[54] Despite their Revolutionary cries and efforts to abolish titles of nobility, Americans cherished, and fought a civil war to preserve, the title of "master of slaves." The importance of owning black people as symbols of economic success and social status was expressed by the *Delta,* the leading proslavery newspaper of the South, that proclaimed, "we would re-open the slave trade that every white man might have a chance to make himself owner of one or more negroes."[55]

The ownership of black people was not only a value of American society, but slavery and race were codified in the colonial and state legislatures. Codification generated the dual consequence of reducing blacks to a permanent, perpetual position of slavery while further endowing whites with political and social power. Strategically, laws afforded debtors, prostitutes, thieves, killers, those who committed "unnatural or unspeakable crimes," and those considered the lowest individuals in English society, an opportunity to remake themselves in North America, to assume a "racial" identity, to obtain land, and, ultimately, to rise above their wretchedness through the subjugation and ownership of black men, women, and children. Baldwin summed up the phenomenon by saying that, "Europeans never imagined themselves as being white until they arrived in America and began to define themselves in relation to blacks; therefore, becoming white was a process."[56] Via codes and etiquette schools established to help rogues live out their fantasies of becoming royalty, something that they could never achieve without blue blood, English paupers became *white, superior, and privileged* in North America. These codes granted identity and status to mere dregs who quickly, and conveniently, redefined laziness as *leisure.* In pursuit of such leisure, many women would not breast-feed their own children. Instead, they shirked that important parental responsibility, leaving it to black slave-nannies.

Whites' dependency on blacks for their freedom to pursue leisure, their milk, their privileged status, and their identity was, and continues to be, a source of their hatred towards blacks. This hatred stemmed from fear associated with the threat of losing the very people on which they depended for so much socially, politically, and economically. Without blacks, whites had no standard against which they could measure their constructed superiority.[57] Socially, white skin lacked power without the black against which it can be compared. Without the slave, the slaveowner lost his master status. Anti-importation laws threatened to annihilate the master-over-slave relationship necessary to maintain identity and power. This looming threat, coupled with Congress' rejection of demands to repeal all federal anti-importation laws, made the year 1859 an extremely volatile one in the period of the "illegal" slave trade. Instead of repealing anti-importation laws, Congress strengthened them. Under the 1859 Act, no American ship could depart for Africa without notifying the district attorney whose responsibility it was to search the vessel to confirm that it was not fitted out for a slaving voyage.[58]

In 1819, Congress passed a law to give monetary rewards to American citizens who informed on smugglers. The 1859 Act increased the reward, giving informants $250 for each African captured as contraband. Moreover, Congress funded measures to regulate more closely ship registries, requiring Americans to consent to a right of search by American and British steamers patrolling the West African coast.[59] Southerners viewed the new legislation as further encroachment upon states' rights to regulate slavery. In protest, they began to smuggle Africans into the Gulf states as much for political revenge as for economic gain. They were "fighting for a principle," argued Charles Augustus Lafayette Lamar, who owned the *Wanderer*.[60] That principle entailed the right to import Africans "as they shall think proper to admit," without interference by the federal government. The *Wanderer*, first built for a wealthy member of the New York Yacht Club, was purchased by Lamar, who retrofitted the ship for slaving in 1858.[61] In that same year, she sailed under the command of Captain Semmes (the brother of Raphael Semmes, commander of the Confederate cruiser *Alabama*), and under the flag of the New York Yacht Club, to the Congo for 750 Africans who were smuggled into Georgia.

Sailing up the Great Ogeechee River by night, Semmes deposited the slaves on Lamar's plantation. He was paid $3,500 for his services.[62] The slaves were sold at $600–700 each. If all of the slaves survived the trans-Atlantic voyage, Lamar made from $450,000–525,000 on this particular slaving venture. Lamar was so successful as a smuggler that he aimed to expand his operations by purchasing a 1,750-ton steamer, *Vigo*, in which he would transport 2,000 Africans to Georgia.[63] The steamer possessed extraordinary storage capacity, and it could outsail men-of-war that might attempt to capture her as a prize. Had aircraft been available for use in the trafficking of slaves, he and other smugglers, no doubt, would have employed it to the detriment of the African continent that would have been depleted of its entire human population.

As the preeminent smuggler of Georgia, Lamar belonged to a cadre of slave traffickers who operated along the Gulf coast, including Jean Lafitte, a Louisiana pirate and slave smuggler, and the Texan James Bowie, maker of the "Bowie knife." James and his brothers ran a scheme that took advantage of loopholes in the 1819 law that rewarded citizen-informants. Specifically, they would purchase captives from Lafitte, act as "informants" against each other, collect the bounty from the U.S. marshall who seized the slaves, use a portion of the bounty to repurchase the captives; and sell them to the highest bidders at Galveston and other places.[64] Tim Meaher was the leading smuggler in Mobile. In December 1858, Meaher's ship *Susan* was overhauled by Lieutenant White, Commander of the Revenue Cutter *Mclleland* in Mobile Bay. In a letter to Attorney General Jeremiah S. Black, Robert H. Smith, collector of customs in the port of Mobile, recounted Lieutenant White's experience when he boarded the schooner *Susan* that had been fitted out for an illegal filibustering expedition to Nicaragua, into which Democrats were attempting to extend the institution of slavery.[65] White discovered that the *Susan* was transporting several armed men, and he ordered her captain, Harry Maury, to pull her into Dog River and anchor her for the duration of the night.

In defiance, the armed men surrouned, detained, and threatened Lieutenant White, who was released only when he gave orders to sink the *Susan*.[66] After conferring with the district attorney, the collector of customs prepared an affidavit for the arrest of the *Susan*'s captain and crew for violating neutrality laws and for resisting the revenue officer's orders. He also initiated the process for libeling the *Susan*, the first step towards claiming her as a prize. The responsibility of arresting the captain, crew, and passengers was placed in the hands of the U.S. marshal. His negligence, the letter suggests, allowed the *Susan* and her crew to escape unpunished. She escaped under the cloak of night and a heavy mist, carrying Lieutenant White, 240 armed men, rifles, and mini balls, but she became shipwrecked in the coral reefs of Honduras.[67]

The case of the *Susan* illustrates the degree to which proslavery men like Meaher endeavored to preserve the institution of slavery, even if preservation included extending it to Cuba, Nicaragua, and other areas off the shores of the U.S. mainland. Meaher and his proslavery Democrats also engaged in illegal filibustering expeditions in defiance of the U.S. government's attempts to end new importations of slaves into the U.S. mainland. Angered by the government's efforts to end illegal importations to the mainland and filibustering expeditions to offshore destinations, Meaher wagered a bet that he could smuggle, as he was purported to have said, "a ship full of niggers right into Mobile Bay under the Officer's noses."[68] Meaher boasted about bringing an illegal cargo of Africans into Mobile with a brazen defiance that characterized smugglers who were angered by the federal government's efforts to stop illicit importations. Captain David Martin, co-owner of the *Wanderer*, told the collector at the port of Savanna that he was going "after a cargo of niggers," inviting him to "kiss his ass" as he was leaving the port in route to West Africa in 1859.[69]

"Going after cargoes of niggers" or "blackbirding" was both the parlance and the sport of wealthy white men who made a mockery of local and federal authorities, in part because the authorities were their political puppets. With equal contempt, southern newspapers openly solicited smugglers to deliver slave cargoes to the Gulf states. The following is a typical solicitation that appeared in Alabama's *Camden Republic:*

> One thousand Africans wanted—any person wishing to contract for delivering one thousand or more Africans at any point between Savannah, Georgia, and Corpus Christi, Texas, will please address M.W.N. and Company.[70]

Due to the lucrative nature of the illicit trade, venture capitalists and smugglers jumped at opportunities to fill the demand for Africans. Veteran smugglers like Meaher knew how to avoid capture by federal and state authorities whose antismuggling efforts were, in the main, negligible. If caught, he did not fear being prosecuted and hanged under the conditions of the Piracy Act of 1820. After all, he had escaped prosecution once before in connection with his slaver *Gypsy.*

Meaher was also aware of the fact that, although some smugglers were captured after 1820, no one had hanged for the crime before 1860.[71] The *Wanderer* was seized and libeled in 1858, 1859, and 1860. Her captains were indicted under the 1820 Piracy Act in the first two cases, but they were acquitted in the presence of *prima facie* evidence that the *Wanderer* was engaged in smuggling.[72] The success of any slaving venture depended, in part, upon the investor's ability to secure, fit out, and provision a ship for a trans-Atlantic voyage. For this reason, slaving ventures were financed by affluent individuals, multiple investors, or banks. In Georgia, Lamar was a prominent financier in the tradition of his father Gazaway Bugg Lamar.[73] Meaher was a wealthy Irish-Catholic plantation magnate who owned lumber mills, a shipyard, several ships, and steamboats.

After 1820, the success of a smuggling venture also depended upon the craftsmanship and seaworthiness of the vessel employed. Efforts to apprehended slave-laded vessels at sea were undermined by advances in maritime technology in the form of schooners and clippers that were designed for speed, allowing smugglers not only to evade sluggish federal cruisers, but to "clip" or decrease the sail time between West Africa and North America. Schooners and clippers constituted the perfect technological response to the federal government's antismuggling efforts. Tim Meaher was known for building fast-sailing ships. In fact, the builders of the yacht *America* came to Mobile to study the Meaher brothers' shipbuilding techniques.[74] However, he used $35,000 to charter the schooner *Clotilda* to complete his

Timothy Meaher, shipbuilder and slaveowner, was a conspirator in the *Clotilda* smuggling crime. Mobile Public Library, Local History and Genealogy Division (1886). Courtesy of the Mobile Public Library. All rights reserved. Reprinted with permission.

trans-Atlantic smuggling venture, masterminded and financed by him.[75] The federal Register of Vessels lists David and William Foster, of D. & W. Foster, as the *Clotilda*'s original owners.[76] The Fosters hailed from a family of ship-builders and captains in Fisher's Grant, Pictou, Nova Scotia. Like the Meahers, they relocated to Mobile, where they could profit as shipwrights in a thriving slave smuggling industry. The 1860 Census for Mobile County lists William Foster's occupation as "shipbuilder"; he was 35 years of age; and he resided in the household of Jacob and Mary Vanderslice.[77]

The federal Register of Vessels describes the *Clotilda* as a two-masted schooner, with a 120 81/95 ton displacement. She was 86 feet in length, 23 feet in breadth, and 6 11/12 feet in depth, having a square stern, a Billet head, and no galleries.[78] *American Lloyds' Registry of American and Foreign Shipping* further describes the *Clotilda* as being constructed of white oak, with iron fastenings.[79] Shipwrights preferred to use oak for constructing hulls that needed to be durable enough to withstand passages on rough seas. Pine was

Captain William Foster commanded the slave ship *Clotilda* that smuggled 110 Africans into Mobile in 1860. Mobile Public Library, Local History and Genealogy Division (1890). Courtesy of the Mobile Public Library. All rights reserved. Reprinted with permission.

reserved for decking and masts. An abundance of oak and pine woods were readily available to shipbuilders in Mobile where the *Clotilda* was built and surveyed on November 19, 1855. When a vessel changes possession, a new registry must be filled out to reflect the property change. A second registry noted that the *Clotilda*'s ownership was *partially changed* in August 1857, with William Foster becoming her sole owner.[80] Her ownership partially changed again in November 1859. Since the full registry could not be found in the National Archives, the nature of the last change remains uncertain. The *Clotilda*'s fourth registry is filed in February 1860, revealing that James A. Wright, of Mobile, becomes a co-owner of the *Clotilda*, along with William Foster.[81]

In March 1860, Meaher and Foster "fitted-out in Chickasabogue, 3 miles north of city."[82] This is the location of Meaher's shipyard, a convenient location from which to launch a slaver, being only three miles from Mobile Bay and the Gulf of Mexico. The *Clotilda* had a trunk cabin, a centerboard, and one deck.[83] The centerboards could be raised to permit navigation in rivers and shallow waterways such as Chickasabogue Creek. The fact that the *Clotilda* only had one deck means she would need to be provisioned with lumber planks with which to construct a "sub-deck" or "slave deck" on which her captives would be stored. Lumber planks were readily available at Meaher's sawmill in Magazine Point, on Chickasabogue Creek. Within the context of the illegal slave trade, lumber planks were considered the "apparatus" associated with smuggling, and fitting out a vessel with large quantities of planks violated the 1807 Anti-Importation Act as well as the 1820 Piracy Act. Captain Foster, the *Clotilda*'s shipwright who would also serve as her commander, violated both laws by taking on board the *Clotilda* a large quantity of lumber planks with which to store captives as well as to hide the water casks, food, and manacles that would identify the *Clotilda* as a slaver.[84] In addition to 125 casks of water, the *Clotilda* was laded with 40 barrels of pork, 30 barrels of beef, 26 casks of rice, 25 barrels of flour, four barrels of bread, four barrels of molasses, and three barrels of sugar.[85]

Captain Foster also carried a cache of guns and cutlasses that would be attractive to Dahomean slave dealers in the city-port of Whydah, the *Clotilda*'s West African destination. American smugglers were well aware of Whydah's identity as a supplier of captives during the illegal period in the trade. As late as 1858, the *Daily Register,* Mobile's leading newspaper, announced that, "The King of Dahomey was driving a brisk trade in slaves, at from $50 to $60 each, at Wydah [Whydah]."[86] The slavers *Wanderer* and *Bogota* (New York) procured cargoes of slaves at Whydah in 1859. The low prices of Africans in Whydah attracted both American and European buyers who sold those same Africans at a tremendous markup in the Gulf states.

Various items have been accepted as payment for captives in West African ports, the nature and value of which fluctuated over time and in accordance with other market variables. American traders needed to take what Wright refers to as "the proper mix" of trade items to West Africa, to ensure a successful transaction.[87] For this reason, Tim Meaher ordered Captain Foster to carry with him diverse trade items that would be valuable to slave dealers in Whydah, including $9,000 worth of gold, 80 casks of "augident" [aguardente] rum, and 25 boxes of dry goods (beads and sundries).[88] Gold remained a popular trade item throughout the eighteenth and nineteenth centuries, alongside guns, tobacco, and rum. Aguardente rum, or "fire water," was a crude brandy that was produced primarily on sugar plantations in the West Indies and in Cuba, although New Englanders produced a considerable amount of cheap rum for the slave trade.[89]

Once the *Clotilda* had been sufficiently provisioned, Captain Foster picked up his crew. "Nine men for the mast, first and second mates, and myself made

12 in all on board," Foster wrote in his account.[90] Slave ship crews consisted, usually, of rascals and convicts who viewed trans-Atlantic voyages as opportunities to escape imprisonment or, in the case of black men traveling as crewmen, slavery.[91] Due to the risks associated with slaving ventures, captains concealed the true nature of the voyage until the crewmen had signed on or until the ship had set sail, and, in some cases, crewmen were forced, at gunpoint, to sign articles (contracts) for slaving voyages.[92] The *Clotilda*'s crew would discover the purpose of her voyage only after she set sail for Dahomey on the March 7, 1860.

Fair winds pushed the *Clotilda* across Mobile Bar, and she reached the island of Cuba by March 10. [93] Havana remained a haven for smugglers in the second half of the nineteenth century. At the time of the *Clotilda*'s smuggling voyage, it was still possible for a ship to clear U.S. customs as a "legal" vessel and sail to Havana, where it could be fitted out or provisioned for a slaving voyage. While serving duty in Havana on May 28, 1859, Her Majesty's Commissary Judge wrote, "The celebrated yacht 'Wanderer' arrived to-day from Savannah and will doubtless be got ready for her African expedition as soon as possible."[94] Addressing the Secretary to the Admiralty, Rear Admiral Sir F. Grey made the following comment regarding the *Wanderer*, in particular, and slave smuggling in the United States, in general:

> It is, therefore, conclusively proved that if the US acted vigorously in carrying out the engagements contracted by them in the Treaty of Washington, the slave trade could not flourish in the manner it now does; and it is to be hoped that the proceedings of the "Wanderer," which have shown that the disgraceful traffic in slaves is now no longer confined to Cuba, but has been introduced into the US territory itself, will rouse the people of those States to do a more just sense of what they owe both to humanity and to their Treaty engagements with Great Britain.[95]

However the plantation owners of "those States" were the beneficiaries of illegal cargoes, and they had no interest disfranchising themselves. Furthermore, there remained a strong economic relationship between Baltimore shipbuilders and Havana smugglers.

Smugglers found additional support in the negligence of law enforcement agents like Jeremiah S. Black, the attorney general in the proslavery Buchanan administration, who issued the following orders prohibiting American consuls from inspecting ships to determine whether or not they had been fitted out for slave smuggling:

> [T]he clearance of any Am.[erican] vessel from the Custom House at Havana...is prima facia evidence of the legality of the voyage—and consequently the Consul need take no further steps—than the ordinary one of exacting from the Master,

an oath that he is bound on a proper voyage & with a cargo in accordance with his clearance from the Custom House.[96]

Black's order gave impetus to the smuggling industry, providing a legal cover for the *Clotilda*'s illegal expedition. The slavers *Ardennes, Clara Windsor, Lyra, Falmouth, Mary J. Kimball, Mexina, Nancy,* and *Tecora* were cleared for sail from Cuba, after the *Clotilda* left that island. At Havana, smugglers could also obtain blank registries and bills of sale in the post-Trist era. In the tradition of most smugglers who operated during the illegal slave trade, Captain Foster possessed two ship registries.[97]

The *Clotilda* sailed past Havana to enter the Gulf Stream that would propel her into the Bermuda Triangle, where the ship began to drift off course. Captain Foster discovered that the performance of the *Clotilda*'s compass was being altered by the magnetic properties of the gold that he placed next to the instrument.[98] As he traveled through the Bermuda Triangle and in the direction of West Africa, however, Foster also had to consider, and calculate, the directional differences between the geographic equator versus the geomagnetic equator, the latter having a gravitational pull on vessels and their compasses. If he did not account for those differences, the *Clotilda* would continue to drift off course. Other factors that altered the course of ships included the velocity of the Gulf Stream and the weather. "Rough weather sprung main boom and [caused] other damages," wrote Captain Foster.[99] The Atlantic Ocean's multiple currents and winds combine to produce unpredictable, often turbulent, weather. Tropical storms produce gales of 32 to 63 miles per hour. Ship logs often document encounters with squalls (single or multiple thunderstorms) that can produce violent winds and rains feared by captains who understood their ability to destroy vessels and voyages. On March 17, just off Bermuda, the *Clotilda* was damaged further by a heavy gale that lasted nine days.[100] Her on-deck supplies were blown overboard, with the exception of two boats atop the midshipman's house and the cabin house; her boat davits and half the steering wheel were carried away; and her rudder head was split in three pieces.[101]

Many ships have met their doom in the Bermuda Triangle, sometimes called the Devil's Triangle. However, those shipwrecks have nothing to do with the actions of the devil, or those of some deep-sea monster that haunts the Atlantic, and more to do with the volatile, "monstrous" weather that devoured ships, their crews, and their cargoes.

As she sailed through the Sargasso Sea, the *Clotilda* continued to encounter a series of squalls. Her foresail detached from the bole, the rope having splintered.[102] On one front, the *Clotilda* was threatened by weather. On another, she was threatened by a Portuguese man-of-war that chased her for 10 hours, from 8:00 AM to 6:00 PM, on March 17.[103] Bermuda served as a depot where English, Spanish, and Portuguese ships obtained water, food, and other provisions. The Portuguese also transported Cape Verdean Africans to Bermuda for the purposes of slavery. European captains also called at Bermuda for black laborers who served duty as crewmen, cooks, and interpreters aboard their vessels.[104] Thus, Portuguese men-of-war would have been cruising between Bermuda and Cape Verde. With considerable damage trumped only by her speed, the *Clotilda* managed to outsail the Portuguese war ship. "The most exciting race I ever saw," wrote Captain Foster.[105]

Bermuda was a nautical landmark, a point of convergence for two ocean currents (the Gulf Stream and North Atlantic Current). The Gulf Stream propelled ships along Bermuda's western boundary. North of Bermuda, between 40° and 52° N, captains accessed the North Atlantic Current that propelled their vessels eastward in the direction of Cape Verde. On April 14, Captain Foster sighted the Cape Verdean island of Fogo. "While running to land at Fogo, we sighted a Portuguese Man of War running for us. We changed course to get away from her not wishing to be boarded so early on the voyage as he would follow us for capture," wrote Captain Foster.[106] His writings reveal that he was keenly aware of the illegality of the *Clotilda*'s voyage. On April 16, having eluded two Portuguese cruisers, and with a severely damaged vessel, Foster docked at Porto Praya [Praia] 14°55′ N and 23°31′ W.[107] There, the events of Captain Foster's treacherous journey were exacerbated when his crew mutinied. Having discovered that the *Clotilda* was a slaver, the crewmen demanded higher wages that were commensurate with the dangers associated with a smuggling venture. "I thought my voyage broken up. However I made a bargain with my crew to double their wages from first agreement in Mobile and they went to work cheerfully to repair the vessel," wrote Captain Foster.[108]

Throughout the trans-Atlantic trade, Praia played a major role as a port of call for European and American slavers in need of repair, provisions, or West African laborers for the whaling industry headquartered in New England. Upon arrival, Captain Foster made contact with the American consul. In 1860, William H. Marse was serving in that capacity. Dispatches from Praia reveal that Marse meticulously reported the various activities taking place on the island. Yet, he provided very little evidence of illegal slavers that frequented Praia during his tenure, reporting only the capture of the slaver *Falmouth* off the West African coast in June 1860. Her capture occurred four years after she was first seized and libeled in 1856. She was seized for the third time in 1862.[109]

In another instance, Marse refused to discharge crewmen who resisted duty on one particular slaver. Instead, they were forced back into service on that unidentified slaver that was cleared for sail to the Bight of Benin.[110] After quelling the mutiny aboard the *Clotilda* by promising to double the crewmens' wages, Captain Foster wrote that he "did not have any trouble with the American Consul notwithstanding his tact at guessing as to my whither bound, but [he] gave me clearance to trade on the coast of Africa and recommended to me to go to the island of Anabow [Anomabo] and sell my cargo as there was a famine on the island."[111] Captain Foster appears unfamiliar with the geography of the West Africa, for Anomabo is not an island. It is a slave depot in the region known to slave traders as the Gold Coast (Ghana). Perhaps, Captain Foster was making his first voyage to West Africa, only for the purposes of carrying out Meaher's bet. However, Foster was not unfamiliar with the illegal nature of his voyage, and to ensure the consul's cooperation, he *dashed* the consul's wife with the beautiful shawls, beads, and sundries that he reserved for such "emergencies" or situations that threatened the success of the voyage.[112] As a matter of course, captains used certain goods as "hush money" to bribe government officials.[113]

Factored into the budget of any smuggling venture, bribes and contraband were readily accepted by American consuls who were not salaried before 1856. In that year, Congress enacted legislation to define the parameters of the consular office; to pay consuls a regular salary; and to prohibit consuls from engaging in "private" or illegal business.[114] By 1856, however, bribery and other forms of corruption had become entrenched in the culture of the American consulate. Pleased with the items that Captain Foster had given his wife, the American consul "asked no questions" of Foster.[115] Instead, he allowed him to sail to the West African coast for a cargo of slaves, another blatant case of a federal government official aiding and abetting a slave smuggler in violation of the laws of the United States. In fact, British consuls complained that the American consuls at Praia consistently interfered in any efforts to apprehend American slave smugglers by refusing to arrest them or surrender them to British officials patrolling the West African coast.[116]

The proslavery agenda of the Constitutional Congress; the federal government's Atlantic policy that allowed smugglers to operate under the cover of protecting American merchant-ships and national sovereignty from British encroachment; the negligent enforcement of anti-importation laws; the apathy of the African Squadron that spent much of its time anchored at Cape Verde in 1860, under the direction of Isaac Toucey, the secretary of the navy and a proslavery Democrat; and the criminal activities of American consuls at Havana and Praia combined to facilitate Americans' participation in the illegal enterprise of slave smuggling. Having bribed the American consul, having appeased his mutinous crewmen, and having repaired the *Clotilda,*

Captain Foster weighed anchor in preparation for sail to the Kingdom of Dahomey in the Bight of Benin on April 22. Admittedly, Captain Foster had little knowledge of the current in Porto Praia, where the winds were very high during the month of April. Consequently, he crashed into a Portuguese man-of-war, as he attempted to maneuver the *Clotilda* out of the port of Praia. The *Clotilda* did not suffer any new damage, but the Portuguese warship was left without her bumpkins (a spar projecting from a ship's stern), rail, and main boom. "I thought she would intercept us with shot, but did not," wrote Foster.[117] After remaining in port for six days, the *Clotilda* set sail, once again, for Dahomey.

CHAPTER 3

The Dahomean Dimension

The *Clotilda* narrowly escaped further confrontation with the Portuguese cruiser in the Cape Verde Islands. At 14°55′ N, 23°31′ W, off the northwest coast of Africa, the *Clotilda* took advantage of the Canary Current that, along with the prevailing northeast trade winds that are strongest between November and May, pushed her further south. At 6°N, 13°W, the *Clotilda* entered the Guinea Current that flows parallel to the West African coast, from Sierra Leone to Whydah. Regarding the wind conditions as he sailed towards Whydah, Captain Foster wrote, "blowing a fine breeze at the time we were soon out of reach of guns...had fine breeze off the coast of Cape Palmas."[1] Throughout the history of the trans-Atlantic slave trade, Cape Palmas (Liberia) was another important nautical landmark, representing the point at which the West African coast breaks sharply towards the east and in the direction of the Whydah. With prevailing winds and a strong current, the *Clotilda* reached Whydah on May 15, 1860, at 4:00 PM.[2]

European slave traders divided the West African coast into sections that corresponded to the types of commodities found in those sections (i.e., Grain Coast or Rice Coast; Ivory Coast; Gold Coast; and Slave Coast). The city-port of Whydah, the jewel of Dahomey's political economy, was situated on the Slave Coast, so-called for the quantity and "quality" of captives sold there. Whydah was also known for its highly productive Fon slave raiders, whose warrior spirit is rooted in the history of their kingdom. The name Dahomey

(Danxome) means "in the belly of Dan."[3] According to Fon lore, chief Dan refused to relinquish his forest territory, "Dan-zunme," for the establishment of a Fon Empire. Consequently, Fon warriors killed him, and they established their kingdom on his abdomen.[4] The name Danxome (Dahomey), therefore, symbolizes and embodies the warrior spirit and military prowess of the Fon peoples who expanded their kingdom's geopolitical sphere of influence, and enriched its royal coffers, by sacking and vassalizing peoples on the periphery of the empire.

From 1727 to 1740, King Agadja focused his geopolitical agenda on giving the interior kingdom of Dahomey, with its royal seat, Abomey, being located some 17 kilometers from the sea, direct access to the economy of the Atlantic slave trade from which it derived considerable profits in the form of slave sales and customs duties. That some Africans sold other Africans into the trans-Atlantic slave trade surprises outsiders who question their willingness to market their own people. It must be pointed out, however, that Africans did not comprise a monolithic group devoid of political diversity and divisions. The Fon peoples of Dahomey, for example, engaged in a protracted war with Yoruba groups in territories currently called the Republic of Benin and Nigeria. Fon groups defined their Yoruba neighbors as "enemies," and they did not hesitate to sell their enemies, "traitors," and "undesirables" into the Atlantic slave trade.

The current ideological trend, however, is to blame Africans for the trans-Atlantic slave trade, in an attempt to release non-Africans from their culpability in the enterprise. But, the enslavement of Africans was a global enterprise. There are no peoples, governments, or religions that have not directly participated in that enterprise or that have not benefited indirectly from it. Portuguese kidnappers initiated the trans-Atlantic slave trade that became more organized with the religious, ideological, and financial support of the Catholic Crown of Spain, whose New World colonies demanded more labor after Europeans decimated indigenous peoples. Father Bartolomé de las Casas, who owned indigenous peoples as slaves, propositioned Pope Leo X to replace the indigenes with African laborers.[5] The Pope, also known as Giovanni di Lorenzo de Medici, was a member of a financial powerhouse in Italy. Therefore, he recognized Las Casas's proposition to enslave Africans as a lucrative venture. Subsequently, the Catholic Crown of Spain drafted and sold the *Asiento,* a license giving its purchasers permission to enslave more Africans than could be obtained by mere kidnapping. In order to meet their quotas for African captives, Europeans needed the cooperation of Africans. At best, these "cooperatives" remained tenuous, since Europeans instigated wars between African groups, and since Europeans supplied guns to execute those wars, in order to acquire African captives for their New World plantations.[6]

The fact that Europeans established forts and trade factories along the West African coast to manage the trade affairs of their respective nations and to make certain that their ships met their slave quotas must not be overlooked. Equally important is the fact that the trans-Atlantic slave trade was buyer-driven, due to the growth of cash crops in need of cheap labor in the Americas. Sellers would not have prospered without buyers who continued to call at West African slave-depots in violation of the anti–slave trade laws of the United States, England, France, Spain, and Portugal. This reality prompted Dahomey's King Glele to explain his role on the supply side of the trade by saying that, "he did not send slaves away in his own ships, but 'white men' came to him for them, and was there any harm in his selling? We ought to prevent the 'white men' from coming to him: if they did not come he would not sell."[7] Captain Foster arrived in Whydah during the reign of King Glele, who ascended to the throne on a nationalistic political platform that reinforced Dahomey's commitment to slave raiding *vis-à-vis* British pressure to end its participation in the slave trade in favor of increased production of palm products.[8]

Glele regarded British interference as an infringement upon Dahomey's sovereignty and its expansionist agenda facilitated, in large measure, by slave raiding. As buyers continued to come to Whydah to secure slaves, the Dahomeans endeavored to supply them. In the second half of the nineteenth century, Americans, many of whom were Southerners like Captain Foster, were the principal buyers of slaves in Whydah.[9] Most of the wealth that was derived from the commodification of African peoples was accumulated outside of the African continent. Ostensibly, the Africans were on the losing side of those "deals," selling other Africans for trinkets, inferior rum, and a trifling sum of $40–$100 on the West African coast when those same Africans were resold for $300–$3,500 in the Americas, Cuba, and the Caribbean. On the West African coast, the sale of a captive was a one-time event. The slave buyer-owner, on the other hand, owned every part of the slave—his body, his mind, and the products of those two. Slave ownership also yielded multiple streams of income from associative trades such as breeding, mortgaging, renting, and prostituting slaves. Slave sellers profited once, but slaveowners profited for the duration of the slave's life.

When measuring the extent of Africans' participation in the trans-Atlantic slave trade as sellers, it is important to note that not all Africans participated in the enterprise. Before the trans-Atlantic slave trade emerged, wars produced captives for domestic farms and for Xwetanu (the Annual Customs

Ceremony with humans sacrificed to the ancestors). Within Dahomey's diversified political economy, Xwetanu took precedence over slave sales. As King Kpingla asserted, "the few that can be spared from this necessary celebration we sell to white men."[10] Kpingla's statement indicates that the slave trade was of secondary importance behind Xwetanu. That may be so from a cultural-religious standpoint, but the slave trade occupied an important position in Dahomey's political economy, indicated by Kplinga's destruction of Ekpe and Badagry as Whydah's competitors in the trade in the eighteenth century.[11]

By the middle of the nineteenth century, Dahomey had earned a reputation as one of the most prolific slave-dealing nations on the Slave Coast. Africans who sold high volumes of slaves were, more often than not, warriors with the political organization and the military strength to make slave raiding and trading productive and profitable ventures. Speaking about the slave trade, Basil Davidson articulated the matter in this way:

> This business was always that of powerful men on either side, operating directly, or indirectly, through appointed agents, merchants, and captains; but it was increasingly, on the African side, an affair of chiefs and rulers who understood the value of monopoly and how to defend it.[12]

Dahomey's distinction as a major slave-dealing nation is due not only to its voluminous slave exports, but to its ability to facilitate the trade within the framework of a well-established political economy reinforced by a powerful military, necessary for capturing Africans in interior regions, moving them to coastal markets, warehousing them, processing them, and selling them to foreign buyers.

The systematic manner in which Fon peoples facilitated that process is one of the most extraordinary aspects of Dahomey's history, dispelling the myth that Africans lacked political organization. In Dahomey, Africans were sold in accordance with a specific slave-trade protocol that was devised by the king and implemented by his officials at the coast. The origin of this protocol corresponds, in large part, to the annexation of the city-port of Whydah, a military move that gave Dahomey direct access to the sea, thereby allowing Fon nationals opportunities to increase their participation in, and regulation of, international trade, particularly where slave sales were concerned. King Agadja initiated Dahomey's slave-trade protocol by designating several villages, along the main route leading from the shore to Whydah proper, as military garrisons. Secondly, he stationed Fon nationals at those garrisons, delegating to them the responsibilities of reporting the arrival and departures of foreign vessels; monitoring the movements of their captains while they were conducting trade in Whydah; collecting customs duties; and controlling slave exports.[13] Zoungboji was one of those villages.

Its location on the main road, approximately one kilometer from the shore, just beyond the river Djebadji, allowed Zoungboji to play a strategic role in regulating international trade and implementing Dahomey's slave-trade protocol. John McLeod, a slave ship surgeon who traveled to Whydah in the eighteenth century, provides a detailed description of the way in which Dahomean officials monitored the movements of foreign traders in Whydah in general, and at Zoungboji in particular:

> Were a dozen white people to send their names on the same morning, in a regular manner, by the interpreter to the viceroy, desiring a free pass to the beach, having business to perform on-board ship, that permission would, no doubt, be granted, and a polite answer returned. A different messenger would then be dispatched by the viceroy to the village between Grigwee and the sea, through which the party must pass, to give the Caboceer [slave-trading agent] of that place the distinguishing marks as they had been pointed out by the first messenger, of each individual who had really demanded a pass. On their arrival at this village, although they might be perfectly correct as to number, yet, should a person appear who had not asked for leave, but had come in the room of one who had done so, he would be instantly picked out as not being one of those described by the first messenger to the viceroy. On more occasions than one, during my stay, interlopers were detected, who though they might pass in the throng at Kakeraken's Kroom, and, with all possible civility, informed that there must be some mistake about their pass, referring them back to Grigwee for an explanation.[14]

Routing the movements of foreigners provided a measure of security within Dahomey's environs. Foreign traders were allowed to advance into the interior only after they received clearance from guards on the beach. Although McLeod makes no mention of the name Zoungboji in his description of slave-trade protocol, he does name Grigwee as the location of the village to which he is referring.

Grigwee is an English distoriton of the Fon name Gléxwe, a "farm-field" (the "x" assumes the "h" sound in Fongbe, the indigenous language of Fon peoples), located in the south of Whydah.[15] McLeod referred to the viceroy of this village as Kakaraken. This is a distortion of the Fon name Kakanakou, the name of the supreme chief of the village of Zoungboji that is extant as one of Whydah's important historic sites. I traveled there to interview Dah Akolemin Dossou Agadja Kakanakou, the thirteenth Kakanakou to preside over the political affairs of that village.[16] I wanted to learn more about Zoungboji's role as a garrison for monitoring the movements of foreign traders. With the Fon, as with other African peoples, verbal communication between royal, titled persons and outsiders is seldom direct. With few exceptions, meetings are held on their time, or at the "appropriate" time, which could be one or two hours later than the time that was originally agreed upon. The time and

Supreme Chief Kakanakou's Fon ancestors presided over slave trade protocol in the village of Zoungboji in the Kingdom of Dahomey. Photograph by Natalie S. Robertson, PhD (1994)

order of communications are carried out in accordance with their own social, cultural, and political etiquette. That is the African way, giving credence to the black vernacular expression "African peoples' time." An astute researcher respects cultural protocol, never infringing upon peoples' basic human rights to be self-determined. Thus, I waited humbly for my opportunity to interview Supreme Chief Kakanakou.

In West Africa, conversation never begins without an offering of food or drink to the visitor, who is customarily obliged to accept, or gracefully reject, the offering. This custom is uniformly practiced in the houses of royal figures and in those of lay persons. Pouring water or some other type of drink on the floor or ground is one of the many ways in which African peoples acknowledge their ancestors. In African-America, libations are also poured for the ancestors or, in the vernacular, "for the brothas and sistas who ain't here."[17] But, libations also open the way for conversation among the living. After acknowledging the ancestors, Supreme Chief Kakanakou discussed

Zoungboji's role in Dahomey's political and economic history. He confirmed the fact that King Agadja designated the village as a military garrison for monitoring the movement of foreign traders, installing the first Kakanakou to oversee the political and economic affairs of the village.[18] Indeed, Supreme Chief Kakanakou bears the name of his royal ancestor, descending from a lineage of men whose responsibility it was to manage the politics and economics of Zoungboji.

From McLeod's description, it is clear that Zoungboji was one of three garrisons on the main road that stretched from the beach to Whydah proper. However, the interview with Supreme Chief Kakanakou revealed that Dahomey's slave-trade protocol was more complex than McLeod's description indicates, involving four additional officials who were responsible for tracking the movements of foreigners from the beach to Zoungboji.[19] While Chief Kakanakou reigned supreme, he was assisted by Chief Gankpe, Oundehouwa, Ahokin, and Donou. Foreigners arrived in the village of Zoungboji only after receiving their passes from Oundehouwa, the customs official who was garrisoned on the banks of the river Djebaji that hydrates Gléxwe.[20] Oundehouwa would have been responsible for giving Captain Foster his pass that allowed him to advance towards Zoungboji, after searching his person to make certain that he carried no weapons into Dahomey's interior. Before foreigners advanced to the river Djebaji, however, they had to pay customs duties to the Ahokin, who was stationed at the beach. Although Captain Foster makes no mention of the Ahokin in his account, it is certain that he paid customs duties that constituted an important source of revenue for the Dahomean state.[21]

Foreign traders were required to pay customs duties upon setting foot in Fon territory and upon anchoring in Fon waters, the price being determined by the number of masts that a ship possessed. As captain of the two-masted schooner *Clotilda*, Foster would have been made to pay duties in the form of certain goods that equaled the established price of seven slaves per mast (or 14 slaves, since the *Clotilda* had two masts).[22] Foreigners were still being monitored when the English traveler Richard Burton arrived in Whydah in 1861. Dahomean officials allowed Burton to advance to a village that he called "Zumgboji," describing the village as "a poor place containing a few thatched mat-huts."[23] Upon ascertaining that Burton was on a mission to King Glele's palace in Abomey, Fon officials permitted him to proceed into the interior. They gave him a kola nut and some malguetta pepper, customarily given to Europeans and special guests when entering or leaving Zoungboji.[24] In keeping with that tradition, Supreme Chief Kakanakou gave me a kola nut and some pepper when I was a guest in his house in 1994.

Donou was the chief of army at Zoungboji. The presence of a military reflected the enormous value that it held not only as a garrison for monitoring foreigners, but as a center for processing Africans for the trans-Atlantic trade. When captives arrived at Zoungboji, Chief Gankpe (not to be confused with Prince Gankpe, who ruled Dahomey under the name of Ghezo) placed them in a building referred to as *Zomai* or "the place where fire or light cannot go."[25] Africans were warehoused in this dark building in order to prevent them from detecting their location, thereby thwarting plans to escape. Zoungboji's schemata seems not to have been as elaborate as that of the slave house on Gorée Island, with compartments for men, women, young girls, infants, recalcitrant captives, and those thought to be diseased. Nevertheless, it was equally haunting. Chief Gankpe, the second in command at Zoungboji, descends from a line of chiefs who bore the responsibility of feeding the African captives, attending to their health, and preparing them for sale to foreign slave traders.[26]

Before foreigners were allowed to come ashore to purchase slaves, Dahomean interpreters canoed out to their ships to learn the nature of their visit. The messengers relayed that information to the Dahomean officials on the beach, after which the foreigner was granted, or denied, permission to come ashore. Adhering to that aspect of trade protocol, a Dahomean messenger came out to greet Captain Foster aboard the *Clotilda* that was anchored one and one-half miles from Whydah's beach. "I told him I wished to exchange commodities and therefore would have to see the Prince and officials," wrote Foster.[27] After Captain Foster was granted permission to come ashore, the Dahomean canoemen came to the *Clotilda* to retrieve him. Throughout the history of the slave trade, the responsibility of transporting captains from their vessels to the shore was often left to West African men who used their skills to navigate the rough sea, with a dangerous undertow. "The sea rolling at a fearful height at the time we could not land in our boats but the natives had boats...60 feet long manned by 20 natives darted through the waves like fish," wrote Captain Foster.[28]

The Dahomean rowers placed Captain Foster in a canoe, and they transported him to shore. Ashore, a Dahomean interpreter ordered three men to follow the custom of placing the foreign traders in a hammock, a canopied hammock in Foster's case, and transporting him to the city of Whydah, which, by Foster's reckoning, was "six miles distant."[29] In reality, Whydah central is approximately three kilometers from the beach. "Upon arrival I found splendid accommodations for traders. I spent the night in Merchant's Exchange," wrote Foster.[30] The historiography on Whydah does not record a place by that name. In general, an exchange is a place where goods are traded.

African captives were bound and gagged while awaiting sale at Zoungboji. Photograph by Natalie S. Robertson, PhD (1994)

Once occupied by English traders, Williams Fort continued to serve as a trading post and as a lodge for English-speaking foreigners until 1861.[31] On May 16, Captain Foster breakfasted, after which an individual whom he called Cicerone accompanied him through the city of Whydah. In Italian, the name "cicerone" is used to designate a "tour guide." In Foster's experience, however, Cicerone played a far greater role, serving as an interpreter. Historically, the Dahomeans assigned two interpreters to foreign traders; one checked and balanced the interpretations of the other.[32]

Then and now, the interpreter is essential to the success of trade, facilitating indigenous communications and helping foreigners navigate the cultural protocol of diverse West African peoples. The interpreter is a liaison between foreigners and indigenes. In that capacity, Cicerone escorted Captain Foster to see a high official whom Foster described as "the ebony Prince: a man of 250 lbs *avoirdupois*."[33] The black prince was stout, the extra weight existing as a symbol of affluence that contributed to his political stature. "Presentation consisted of myself and fifty officials all of whom fell on their knees in acknowledgement of His Majesty," wrote Foster. Prostrating, bowing, and kneeling are, indeed, gestures of respect toward elders and titled persons in West Africa. "We then partook of social drink and then I told him my business, that I had nine thousand dollars in gold and merchandise, and wanted to buy a cargo of negroes, for which I agreed to pay one hundred dollars per head: for one hundred and twenty-five," wrote Foster.[34] Slaves that had been advertised in the *Daily Register* (Mobile) for $50 and $60 in 1858 now commanded $100 in 1860. This, however, remained a small investment for a "prime" African who would sell for as much as $2,500 in Alabama and other Gulf states at this time. Captain Foster did not bring enough gold to buy 125 slaves at $100 each. But, he could use his aguardente rum, a valuable trade item, to complete the purchase.

Although Captain Foster did not record the name of this Prince, he is likely to have been the *yovogan*. In the Fon language, *yovo* means "white" and *gan* means "chief." Thus, the yovogan was the "chief in charge of relations with whites."[35] The yovogan ranked high in the Dahomean king's administration. Within the context of Dahomey's slave-trade protocol, the yovogan officially received all foreign traders on the king's behalf, arranged the customary grand welcoming ceremony for foreigners, explained Dahomey's slave-trade policies to them, and warned them of the consequences of breaching the protocol.[36] Under his nationalistic regime, Glele appointed Fon indigenes, usually members of his family, to important positions in his administration. In this case, he gave his nephew, Prince Sodaaton, the youngest son of King Agonglo, the title of yovogan. *Sodaaton* means "all that comes from the sea belongs to the king."[37]

"After detaining me eight days, I thought him purposing my capture," wrote Foster.[38] Captain Foster's fears were well founded, for Dahomean slave traders did not fit the stereotype as passive, disorganized, and ignorant peoples generally applied to blacks by foreigners. In fact, foreigners who held and operated on those stereotypes placed themselves in jeopardy. Slave-trade negotiations were not to be hastily transacted with the Dahomeans who aimed to secure the best deal for the king. Slave-trade negotiations could, and did, erupt, with the slightest provocation, into volatile disputes at any given time, if the Dahomeans suspected fraudulent activity. When dealing with them, many foreign traders feared for their own lives, as reflected in the following excerpt from a letter written by M. Levet who served as director of the French fort in Whydah under the reign of the Dahomean king Tegbessou in 1743:

> The mission seemed delicate to me and nonetheless necessary, because it could influence the thing about which Mr. Bazile [director of a Portuguese fort] was fearful. In fact, if the Dahomeans (fierce people) once began to cut the throats of the whites, this country would become a slaughter house for us, and with the

slightest discontent which these people might pretend to have, they would kill us like sheep.[39]

Foreigners could be jailed, or decapitated, if they breached slave-trade protocol in Whydah.[40] On several occasions, Tegbessou and his successor, King Kpingla, imprisoned, held for ransom, and deported foreign traders and directors of European forts in Whydah if they ignored protocol or if they purchased Africans from neighboring competitors.[41] King Tegbessou's major contribution to the framework of slave-trade protocol was creating the title of yovogan at Whydah, vesting in him the authority to negotiate slave deals on the king's behalf and to enforce slave-trade protocol.[42] The yovogan could be severely sanctioned if he neglected his duties in the capacity of the king's primary negotiator.

The longer a foreign trader remained in Whydah, the chances that he might be accused of a breach increased. A trader's stay in Whydah could be extended if trade negotiations required further consideration, or arbitration, by the king in Abomey. In that case, the Yovogan would initiate another dimension of Dahomey's trade protocol; he would "ask the way (road) to Abomey" be opened via the *Kusugan,* the chief of the road police.[43] The *agoligán* (royal messenger) would carry the matter to the royal palace in Abomey, located approximately 65 miles in the interior.[44] The king entrusts the *agoligán* with his royal recade that symbolizes his authority and his word. If the *agoligán* returns with the royal recade, it signals to the Yovogan that the "road," in fact, has been opened for safe passage to his palace.[45]

By foot, the round-trip journey from Whydah to Abomey was three to four days. Considering the complexity of slave-trade relations, eight days is a relatively short period of time for Captain Foster to be "detained" in Dahomey. "But during this time I thought it not waste, as I was storing up knowledge [of] the many things it takes to make up this world,"[46] wrote Captain Foster, who, in addition to appearing inexperienced as a slave trader, underestimated the business acumen of the Fon officials as well as the elaborate nature of slave-trade protocol in their kingdom. According to custom, the Dahomean officials did not automatically accept Captain Foster's offer. Instead, they deliberated the terms of the offer. Meanwhile, Foster received the requisite tour of Whydah's historic sites, one of which was worthy of the following notation in his account:

> [A]mong the many things that attracted any attention as we refrained to the place of worship which consisted of a large square of ground with a wall ten feet high upon which was covered with snakes—trees in there were loaded with the repulsive things, reveling in their deified relation: Devotees attending had them wound around their necks and waists. [They] had the appearance of our rattlesnake.[47]

Owing to the description of this site, Foster is referring to what is contemporaneously known as the Temple of Pythons. The python is the archetypal symbol of Dangbe, the Fon deity who regulates agricultural and human fertility.[48] Collectively, Fon deities are referred to as *Vodu*.

Outside of Benin, Vodu is derogatorily called "voodoo." It is associated with evil, zombies, and cannibals in the minds of the misinformed. In its indigenous context, however, *Vodu* is defined as a positive and sacred religion that addresses fertility issues in the life cycles of crops and humans. Without fertility, life cycles and ancestral lines are broken. This reality is addressed in Vodu, whose devotees, *Vodunsi,* endeavor to keep procreative and ancestral ciphers intact. In the worldview of many African and African-descended peoples, the flesh perishes but the spirit crosses over into ancestorhood. And, the spirits of our ancestors continue to influence our thoughts and actions. Therefore, *Vodu* is also dedicated, in large measure, to honoring ancestors.[49] The Temple of Pythons remains extant as one of Whydah's great historic sites. I went there to photograph the resident pythons that are maintained for religious ceremonies. Photographing them in a narrow enclosure that measured approximately five feet wide by seven feet long was a daring venture, especially after my encounter with a snake that fell on me while I was sitting under a tree at the Musée Historique de Whydah on the previous day. Nature is ubiquitous, up close, and personal in Africa.

After I photographed the pythons, I walked to the compound of Dagbo Hounon, who was the Supreme Chief of Vodu—the authority on all matters relative to Vodu, its initiation rites, and its devotees or *Vodunsi*. Our meeting provided an opportunity to discuss the intersection between religion and politics in the Kingdom of Dahomey and in contemporary Benin. He told me that every Dahomean king, in order to be a legitimate ruler, had to be *Vodunsi*. Therefore, kings ascended to the throne by divine sanction of the Supreme Being.[50] Understanding Vodu's importance as the foundation for kingship in the Fon nation, I wanted to discuss Eurocentric Christianity's encroachment upon Fon culture. Supreme Chief Hounon confirmed that which I had observed, namely that the primary reason why the Fon peoples are failing to solve indigenous economic, social, and political problems is because they are propitiating foreign gods and propagating foreign doctrines that do not reflect their cultural values or interpret their reality in a way that would help them to fight oppression and domination by external forces. This problem exists in Benin, Nigeria, and wherever Europeans have colonized Africans.

Globally, Eurocentric Christianity has contributed to the erosion of indigenous worldviews and cultures. E. Mveng, a Jesuit priest in Cameroon, recognized, and courageously described, the pandemic in this way:

> Unfortunately the West is less and less Christian: and Christianity, for a long time, has been a product of export for Western civilization, in other words, a perfect tool for domination, oppression, the annihilation of other civilizations. The Christianity preached today, not only in South Africa, but by the West as a power and civilization, is far, very far, from the gospel. The question is therefore posed radically; what can be the place of Third World peoples in such a Christianity? And this question is first of all aimed at the official churches.[51]

This question is also aimed at adherents who prostrate themselves before, and *passionately* surrender their souls to, images of a Caucasian Jesus without considering the ideological and imperialistic functions of that image that does not comport with the Biblical description of him as a wooly haired, bronze-hued individual.

The earliest images and statues of Christ were black-hued and wooly haired, corresponding not only to his nigritic phenotype and hair texture but to those of the East African, Ethiopian, Coptic, Cushitic peoples who laid the religious foundation upon which Judaism and Christianity were constructed.[52] East Africans carried the image of the Black Christ and his mother (referred to as Black Madonnas) across the world, accounting, in part, for the presence of Black Christs in India, the Phillipines, Central America, and behind the walls of the Vatican.[53] Moses was also a person of color. In the book of Exodus, God punishes Moses by turning his hand white, leprous like snow. In Numbers, Miriam, Moses' sister, receives the same punishment, when she scorns Moses for marrying an Ethiopian (Greek for "burnt-faced," brown, or black; alternately called Cushite) woman. There are two important conclusions that can be drawn from theses events: 1) if one is already white, one cannot be turned white; 2) and, one would have to be a person of color originally, in order to be turned white subsequently.

The image of Jesus as a Caucasian has become the most powerful device in the political economy of Eurocentric Christianity that has been used as an instrument of imperialism from the time of Constantine to the present, particularly where black and brown peoples are concerned. If, as the French financier Jean Baptiste Colbert argued in Whydah, "the surest way to convert the Negroes to Christianity is to enslave them,"[54] then the surest way to keep them enslaved was to replace their African deities, icons, and worldviews with European ones. Consequently, their indigenous cultural and spiritual foundations were altered, having disastrous effects on the psychology of black people who came to worship God as a white man and the white man as God. To the extent that cultures draw their identity and strength from their indigenous religions, without them, they are weakened and made pliable participants in their own exploitation and destruction, their worldviews and psychologies altered in favor of their colonizers so much so that they now bleach their own skins, discard their blackness and Africanity, and permit the raping and pollution of their land in honor of their colonizers whose descendants have become their saviors.

Enslavement was, in contemporary terms, faith-based imperialism in which Europeans defined themselves as not only godlike, but they took on the role of God, vesting in themselves the power of life and death over "infidels" or nonbelievers in their Eurocentric Christianity *cum* imperialistic agenda that is still being advanced. Just as Eurocentric Christianity served as the justification for enslaving, exterminating, and colonizing peoples of color worldwide, liberation from its oppressive forces requires a return to the meanings, lessons, and values of indigenous African cultures and religions. However, total liberation cannot be achieved when one's religious and cultural icons do not reflect one's identity or spirituality. Toussaint L'Ouverture's victory over French enslavers was due, in large measure, to his ability to invoke the warrior spirit of his Fon ancestors, who helped him devise a successful war strategy to liberate black people from European domination in Saint Domingue (now Haiti).[55] It is from indigenous African cosmologies and deities that African liberators drew their strength to fight and overthrow their enslavers.

L'Ouverture's victory caused widespread panic among whites in the United States. The fear was not merely that blacks would see L'Ouverture as a hero, but that they would look back to Ausaru, Heru, Ma'at, Dangbe, Shango, Ogun, Nana Buruku, Woot, and other powerful, wise African deities for strength and strategies for unlocking the chains of their oppression. This is, in fact, why enslavers outlawed indigenous African religious practices in slave systems. As a result of L'Ouverture's victory, the United States also strengthened its anti-importation laws.[56] In essence, they were preventing the importation of elements of African indigenous culture, and the warrior spirit, that newly imported Africans were bringing with them. Enslavers and colonizers understood very well that by stripping Africans of their indigenous deities, icons, and artifacts, they were breaking an important cipher of power that exists between the indigenes, their culture, and their ancestors. Thus, enslavement and colonization were processes that involved much more than physical bondage; they also included psychological manipulation.

Vodu continues to survive vis-à-vis Eurocentric Christianity because it is powerful and empowering, allowing adherents to draw on the wisdom of their ancestors who strengthen them spiritually, culturally, and politically. After visiting the Temple of Pythons, Cicerone took Captain Foster to see the King of Dahomey.[57] But, Foster gives no further information about the nature or location of this meeting. Rarely did Dahomean kings enter into direct trade relations with foreign traders. Generally, Dahomean kings remained at the royal palace in Abomey while their administrators transacted slave deals on their behalf at Whydah.[58] Dahomey's slave-trade protocol dictated that Captain Foster meet with officials who acted on the king's behalf. While the yovo-gan was the chief in charge of public relations with whites, the *ChaCha* was responsible for exchanging the slaves for foreign commodities and currency.

The title *ChaCha* was given first to Francisco Felix Da Souza, the Afro-Portuguese slave trader who helped King Ghezo, Glele's father, depose King Adandozan in 1818.[59] According to one of his descendants, Martine Francoise De Souza, who served as my interpreter while I conducted research in Benin, the name *ChaCha* indicated the speed with which Francisco negotiated trade deals.[60] King Ghezo also gave Francisco the name *Ajinaku*, which means "elephant" in the Fon and Yoruba languages, signifying Da Souza's ability to trample his competitors.[61] Francisco's Fon-Portuguese ancestry afforded him a unique position in the trade because he, like other Afro-Brazilians, could serve as a liaison between African and European traders.[62] By the time that Captain Foster arrived in Whydah, however, Prince Sodaaton had been appointed the primary slave dealer by King Glele who retired the title of *ChaCha*.[63]

After being subjected to eight days of protocol, Captain Foster was allowed to purchase slaves in Whydah. "Having agreeably transacted affairs with Prince, we went to the warehouse where they had in confinement four thousand captives in a state of nudity from which they gave me liberty to select one hundred and twenty-five as mine offering to brand them for me, from which I peremptorily forbid," he wrote.[64] Captain Foster knew that brands would serve as incriminating evidence against him and his co-smugglers. More than other symbols, brands burned into the flesh of slaves the reality that they were the "property" of their owners. Within the context of the slave trade, the black body was commodified, assigned value, traded, and taxed for capital gain. Slavery's designation as the "peculiar" institution was bound up with the dual nature of the slaves who were both human beings and commodities with market value. The process by which Africans were reduced to the status of merchandise involved denying and removing the humanity of the commodities, such that Africans became "bozales," "ladinos," "guineas," "black gold," "black ivory," "blackbirds," "niggers," "prime," "sound," "No. 1 field hands," "domestic," "wenches," and "bucks" in the psyches and in the jargon of slave traders.

Conversely, traders acknowledged aspects of the commodities' humanity relative to market value, including, but not limited to, height, weight, health, cultural background, port of origin, possession of certain skill sets, and extent of knowledge base. A metallurgist, mason, carpenter, or tanner commanded higher prices, for example, than Africans who did not possess these skills. After paying $3,500 for a skilled slave in the United States, a minister received an offer to purchase his slave for $4,000.[65] The human elements of the commodities heightened their value within the context of sexual exploitation. White men developed an insatiable, predatory sexual appetite for beautifully hued African girls whom they commodified based upon the size of their breasts and whether or not their virginity was intact, the buyer desiring first access. Pregnant women commanded one price, and the prenatal fetus brought an additional price that differed from the price of an infant. Every part of the black body had a value for the sellers as well as for the buyers, and that value was defined in economic, physical, and psychological terms.

Captain Foster arrived in Whydah in May, after the dry season and after the major slave-raiding season, when Dahomean traders had a large supply of captives available for sale, including Cudjo and the other Africans who were destined for slavery in Alabama. Cudjo recalled the experience of being selected and inspected by Captain Foster at Whydah:

> When we dere three weeks a white man come in de barracoon wid two men of de Dahomey. One man, he a chief of Dahomey and de udder one his word-changer. Dey make every body stand in a ring-'bout ten folkses in each ring. De men by dey self, de women by dey self. Den de white man lookee and lookee. He lookee hard at de skin and de feet and de legs and in de mouth. Den he choose. Everytime he choose a man he choose a woman.[66]

Foster's pattern of selecting one woman for each man suggests that the *Clotilda* cargo was divided almost equally between the two sexes. After purchasing 125 captives, Foster wrote, "I told interpreter if he would send the negroes down to the warehouse on the beach and deliver them on board by 10.am. I would transfer my cargo to him, to which he agreed."[67] Foster's account indicates that there are two warehouses involved his transactions in Whydah. He selected the slaves in an interior warehouse, but he told the interpreter to deliver them to a second warehouse on the beach. Regarding the identity of the interior warehouse, two possibilities exist—the old Portuguese fort in the heart of the city of Whydah, or the village of Zoungboji that is situated approximately one mile north of the beach. Hurston documented that Cudjo and his co-captives were stockaded in a warehouse that the Dahomean king had built for the purpose of storing slaves.[68] Supreme Chief Kakanakou informed me that Zoungboji continued to serve that historical function well into the nineteenth century.[69]

In a separate interview, Cudjo told Hurston that he was warehoused near a river that he was made to ford in order to reach the beach.[70] Cudjo's accounts indicate that this river was in very close proximity to the warehouse. Corroborating Hurston's data, Roche documented that the warehouse in which Cudjo and his co-captives were confined was located on a river bank in an area called "Gréfé."[71] The term Gréfé is a distortion of the Fon name Gléxwe. European slave traders defined Gléxwe as encompassing the whole of Whydah. However, Fon indigenes define it as a coastal community, and they restrict its location to an area between Whydah proper and the beach. The river Djebadji flows through Gléxwe, and Zoungboji rests just beyond the river. After closing the deal in Whydah, and after selecting his 125 captives from the interior warehouse, the Dahomeans placed Captain Foster in a hammock, they carried him across the river, and they proceeded to the beach.[72] Before doing so, however, Foster had instructed the interpreter to send his "negroes" down to a second warehouse that was located on the beach. This second warehouse is more likely to have been a barracoon or a temporary holding pen. Barracoons were built at various points along the West African coast. Like other slave dealers, the Dahomeans never barracooned slaves on the beach for long periods of time, preferring to stockade them inland where they would be out of the reach of pirates.

While he was barracooned on the beach, just prior to being placed in the hold of the *Clotilda*, Cudjo remembered hearing the sound of the turbulent waves crashing against the shoreline:

> I hear the noise of the sea on shore, an' I wanta see what maka dat noise, an' how dat water worka—how it fell on shore an' went back again. I saw some of my people in a little boat [being transported to the *Clotilda*] and I holler to them. Then Captain Foster spied me, an' he say 'Oh hee! Oh hee!' an' pulla me down. An' I was the last to go. Supposy I been lef' behind what become of Kazoola? Or supposy de ship turns over, an' de sharks eat us. Oh Lor'! God is good![73]

Cudjo was captured more than 50 miles from the coast.[74] Ossie Keeby, his shipmate, reckoned that his place of origin was "seven days from the sea."[75] Like other Africans who were captured in interior regions, some of the *Clotilda* Africans had never seen the tumultuous sea imbued with its own force and spirit.

Many Africans had never seen the sea, big ships, or whites, and they were frightened by all three. For quite some time after he was smuggled into Mobile, Cudjo recalled various aspects of his ordeal that began in West Africa. On one occasion, he discussed the fear expressed by the *Clotilda* Africans upon seeing Captain Foster and his crewmen for the first time:

> All of us were taken to the coast and loaded into a big ship by white men, a sight we had never seen before. We were mighty scared, but we thought anything was better than death such as our brothers and sisters suffered so we came peacefully with those strange white men.[76]

Cudjo was traumatized by the carnage he witnessed at the point of capture and by the severed heads of his people in the possession of the Amazons who presented them as war trophies to King Glele. He could not imagine being subjected to anything worse than that, but he was not familiar with permanent, chattel slavery in the Americas. Finding themselves suddenly forced into the midst of whites with whom they had no prior contact, many Africans feared being cannibalized by them.[77] This fear was not an irrational one. Having no other explanation for their captivity, they could only deduce that they had become targets of some diabolical plan. And, they were correct. Although there are no sufficiently documented cases of whites cannibalizing blacks on that side of the Atlantic, enslavement, subjecting humans to torture and death for the benefit of the enslavers, was diabolic nonetheless.

"I went on board at 6 a.m. [May 23] and had my cargo thrown overboard in water tight casks [of aguardente rum] and they sent their surf men who swam the casks ashore safely: early in the morning I went on board and left the first mate on shore to tally them aboard," wrote Captain Foster.[78] Before Cudjo and others were loaded into the *Clotilda,* their clothes were snatched off of them. "Oh Lor,' I so shame! We come in de 'Merica soil naked and de people say we naked savage. Dey say we doan wear no clothes," recalled Cudjo who, when he and his co-captives were being placed in the canoes to be transported to the *Clotilda,* cried out for Ossie Keeby, whom he had befriended in the barracoon.[79] With the help of his first mate, who was left ashore to tally the slaves, and in direct violation of Section 5 of the Piracy Act that prohibited Americans from confining or detaining Africans on board any vessel with the intent of selling them as slaves, Foster began to stow Cudjo and his co-captives into the hold of the *Clotilda.* Slaving a ship, or putting the desired number of Africans in the vessel's hold, took weeks, sometimes months, depending upon the availability of captives for sale and the number of captives being stored for transport. Captains made every attempt to use their storage capacity efficiently, to accommodate as many captives as possible.

Slaving a vessel was dangerous activity. Federal officers patrolled the West African coast in search of slave-laded vessels to claim as prizes. In some cases, federal officers watched captains load their vessels with captives, knowing that only those vessels that had captives in their holds yielded prizes. When the vessels weighed anchor, and proceeded to sail away from the coast, federal cruisers gave chase. Captain Foster wrote, "after securing 75 aboard, we had an alarming surprise when man aloft with glass sang out "sail ho" steamer to leward [sic] ten miles: I looked and behold black and white flags signals of distress interspersed the coast for fifteen miles and two steamers have in sight for purpose of capture."[80] Captain Foster's statement regarding the use of a series of black flags and white flags as signals of distress provides further insight into the sophistication of their slave-trade protocol that involved reconnaissance and early warning systems to alert traders of the presence of cruisers. Perhaps the *Clotilda* was being approached by the USS *Mohican*, a 1,461-ton steam sloop of war fitted out with four 32-pounder long guns. Recently joining the African Squadron on January 19, 1860, she was very energetic and eager to catch slavers. The *Mohican* intercepted the infamous American slaver *Erie* with 897 Africans in her hold in August 1860.

"The crew thinking our capture inevitable, refused duty and wanted to take my boats from the vessel and go on shore but could not have landed with our boats owing to the surf: while getting underway two more boats came along side with thirty-five more negroes making in all one hundred and ten, left fifteen on the beach having to leave in haste," wrote Captain Foster.[81] Owing to their lack of skill at navigating the rough waves in the port of Whydah, the *Clotilda*'s crew would never have made it to shore. The mutiny delayed the *Clotilda*'s departure just enough to add more slaves to the cargo. As he left 15 Africans on the beach, Captain Foster did not collect all of the merchandise for which he had paid $9,000 in gold, several casks of rum, and eight tense days of his life.

The moment that the *Clotilda* set sail with Africans in her hold, she became a valuable prize for the authorities. In the event that she was overhauled, Captain Foster, in the tradition of most smugglers who arrived in West Africa via Havana and the Cape Verde islands, possessed two ship registries.[82] If the *Clotilda* was overhauled by U.S. or British authorities, for example, he could provide "proof" that the vessel was registered in a foreign country over the United States and Great Britain had no maritime jurisdiction. Captain Foster also possessed a false registry that listed Luanda as the place where the *Clotilda* was purchased,[83] a document that would help mask her North American origin. Luanda is 8°50´ S of the equator, below which slave trading remained legal for some time after the United States and several European nations had prohibited slave smuggling at various points north of the equator. "All under headway both steamers changed their course to intercept us: the wind being favorable: in a short time we knew we were outsailing them; then my crew show'd their appreciation for not letting them take my boats to go on shore, in four hours we were out of sight of land and steamers," wrote Captain Foster. Bearing down on the *Clotilda* from the leeward side placed the steamers at a nautical disadvantage. Once windward, the sleek *Clotilda* would not be captured. She got away with Cudjo and the other captives in her hold.

CHAPTER 4

Atlantic Passage

Twelve days after leaving Whydah, on June 5, the *Clotilda* sighted another man-of-war. "We thought we were captured," wrote Captain Foster.[1] But, the man-of-war did not give chase. Instead, the *Clotilda* had to contend with a heavy squall. Foster was within sight of Cape Palmas, Liberia, which shares its western boundary with Sierra Leone, the location of one of the courts of mixed commission established to adjudicate cases involving slavers seized by cruisers. Africans liberated from the holds of condemned slavers, such as the *Erie*, were sent to Liberia, where they joined with blacks that had repatriated from the United States. While some Africans and black Americans were being freed and repatriated in Sierra Leone and Liberia under a variety of circumstances, enslaved Africans were crossing their paths in route to plantations in the Americas and the Caribbean. On its return voyage, the *Clotilda* would access the northern boundary of the South Equatorial Current (SEC) below Cape Palmas, 4° N, 8° W. The SEC would propel the *Clotilda* in a westward direction, towards the northern region of South America and to the Bahamas.

"Next day, struck northeast trade winds and going twelve to fourteen miles per hour," wrote Captain Foster.[2] The *Clotilda* was a fore-and-aft rigged schooner whose foremast had at least one square-rigged topsail anchored to horizontal spars (yards). The *Clotilda's* square rigging allowed her to efficiently harness and exploit the force of the northeast trade wind that drove her at top speeds, in combination with the strength of the SEC, in the direction of

Alabama. North Americans altered the very notion of the Middle Passage when they employed their own ships in the Atlantic slave trade. In cases where American slavers arrived in West Africa via Cape Verde, their travel route formed a triangle, but the third leg of that triangle, representing the return route to North America, no longer fit the description of a "Middle Passage." Conversely, those ships that traveled directly to West Africa without calling at Cape Verde reduced the triangular trade to a 180° angle. The *Clotilda*'s voyage formed two triangles, arriving in the Bight of Benin via Havana and Cape Verde. Therefore, her return voyage cannot, in the historical sense, be called a Middle Passage. The *Clotilda* embarked upon her Atlantic passage with 110 captives in her hold. Various nations attempted to regulate the number of captives transported by a vessel, based on her tonnage. Brazilian vessels were permitted to carry two captives per ton, or 2:1.[3] In 1788, the British Parliament passed a bill allowing for a ratio of 5:3, for every vessel less than 150 tons.[4] It does not appear that the United States established its own standard. Based upon the British standard, however, the 120-ton schooner *Clotilda* could transport 200 Africans. Since she was transporting 110 captives, she was not considered a "tight-packer."

There is evidence that Cudjo and his co-captives underwent a health inspection, routinely performed by ships' surgeons and captains who aimed to purchase "prime," "No. 1" Africans. The *Clotilda* captives were spared the torture of the branding iron. However, Cudjo and his co-captives were completely nude when they entered the *Clotilda's* hold, and Captain Foster followed the tradition of separating them by sex.[5] Pre-embarkation, Africans suffered psychological and physical traumas that were exacerbated by new ones that they experienced in the bowels of slave ships. Men were shackled to prevent them from rising against their captors. But, women were not shackled, exposing them to brutal sexual assaults by captains and crewmen who converted the slave ship into a floating den of the most perverse behavior that would make Satan envious. The screams of rape victims reverberated throughout the hold, rape-induced miscarriages produced blood-soaked fetuses born prematurely into the violent world of the slave trade, their mothers having no instrument to cut the umbilical cord severed by the crude instrument of the ship's surgeon. The definitive work regarding the extent to which men were also raped has not been written. Given the fact that slaver crews consisted of rogues, criminals, and sexual deviants, however, there is no reason to assume that men and children were not victims of those predators who manned slave ships.

Survivors of sexual violence, in addition to contracting venereal diseases, developed psychoses and emotional disturbances that continued to haunt them long after the sexual attacks had occurred. Many descended into deep, often deadly, depressive states. They refused to eat what amounted to no more than the slop, not simply because it offended their palates, but because it came from the hands of persons with unclean spirits and hands that committed sodomy prior to issuing the "food." To keep the captives alive during the Atlantic passage, Captain Foster laded the *Clotilda* with 50 bags of farina (cassava flour) and four barrels of palm oil. Meaher instructed him to mix the farina with water to form a mush that was to be "sprinkled over with palm oil,"[6] to make a gruel that would be pleasing to the palate of the West African captives, who were fed twice per day.

Slavery was a business in the strictest sense of the term. As such, the laws of supply and demand that governed other enterprises also regulated the slave trade. Captains and their employers invested very little in the health of slaves, sometimes purchasing bacteria-contaminated foods to cut costs. If the *Clotilda*'s hold was bacteria-free when Cudjo and his co-captives entered, it did not remain that way. Nausea and diarrhea are two of the body's mechanisms for expelling toxic-level bacteria, in an attempt to prevent death. Frothy, bloody dysentery, a symptom of ulcerated, hemorrhagic, gangrenous stomachs and intestines, became the cause of death for many Africans in the holds of slave ships. Like other captives, the *Clotilda* Africans were forced to excrete their bodily fluids where they lay. Littered with feces and vomit, the damp, dark hold of slave ships constituted the perfect breeding grounds for infectious diseases.[7] The hold was a veritable death chamber in which dangerous pathogens attacked, mutated, and attacked again as new strains.

Disease increased the cries for water. "We so thirst! Dey gib us leetle beeta water twelve hours," said Cudjo.[8] He is referencing the fact that he and his shipmates were given one-half of a pint of water every 12 hours. Such rationing was in keeping with the tradition, and it ensured that the 125 casks of water on board the *Clotilda* would last for the duration of the trans-Atlantic voyage. However, one pint of water, per day, could not fully hydrate the body that was robbed of fluids not only as a result of illness but because of the salt-cured meats that were incorporated into the slop given to the captives.

Contagious diseases converted several slave ships into floating crypts, killing everyone on board, the captain, the crewmen, and the African captives, save the rats that gorged themselves on the remains. Captains had very few means of preventing the spread of deadly infectious diseases and other health problems posed by confinement in unsanitary environments that threatened the lives of the captain and crew, one of those means being the throwing overboard of those captives suspected of being carriers. To the extent that the trans-Atlantic slave trade was a capitalistic venture, many slave cargoes were insured. Therefore, captains and investors could file claims against their insurance policies to recover their losses incurred at sea.

The Atlantic Ocean sings the dirges of millions of Africans who died in route to their final destinations, after their flesh and bones have long washed away. While many died of disease, others committed suicide and infanticide because death, taking one's rightful place among the ancestors, was preferable to a life of enslavement. It is very difficult to imagine killing one's self or one's children as a form of escape. Typically, suicide is not the problem-solving, or escape, mechanism chosen by blacks. But, enslavement and its attendant horrors constituted no ordinary problem for Africans, many of whom descended from titled families. Ibo captives were known to kill themselves, not only as a method for escaping slavery, but because their royal ancestry would not permit them to live in subjugation to others.[9] In the minds of many Africans, ancestorhood was a nobler place for the spirit than the plantation was for the flesh.

Recalling an instance when the captives were brought on the *Clotilda*'s deck for feeding and exercise, Cudjo said, "We looka, an' looka, an' looka. Nothin' but sky and water. Whar we come from, we do not know; whar we go, we do not know."[10] The *Clotilda* was so far into her Atlantic passage that the captives could no longer see the West African coast, the last traumatic memory of which included seeing the carnage and the severed heads of their relatives and friends suspended from the uniforms of the amazons.[11] If that be their last memory, and if their trans-Atlantic experiences serve as portents, then they could only imagine, with horror, the conditions that awaited them at their destinations. The combination of a swift South Equatorial Current and strong northeast winds allowed the *Clotilda* to complete her Atlantic passage in a record six weeks.

"On June 30th made Abaco light and came through the hole in the wall: in coming on the Bahama bank at 8 P.M. were running onto a sunken ship with stansions in sight: the lookout sang out "hard a starboard" and we passed the ship within ten feet," wrote Captain Foster.[12] Abaco comprises a chain of islands in the Atlantic Ocean. At the southern tip of Great Abaco Island, a lighthouse guides ships in from the Atlantic into the Northeast Providence Channel and through the Hole-in-the-Wall, leading to the Northwest Providence Channel, past Nassau, and into the Gulf of Mexico. Frequent shipwrecks in that area generated an occupation known as "wracking" or "wrecking," in which the inhabitants of Abaco made a living from salvaging the parts of wrecked vessels. Ships coming through the Hole-in-the-Wall, in route to the Gulf of Mexico, faced a secondary threat from the pirates of Nassau like Sam Bellamy. A black pirate, Bellamy was one of the most flamboyant and daring personalities in the history of Caribbean piracy, capturing and transforming the British slaver *Whydah* into his personal pirate ship manned by a black crew.

Because of piracy, barrier reefs, and treacherous weather, the voyages of several ships terminated in the Caribbean. The *Clotilda* tacked "hard" or aggressively on her starboard side to avoid having her hull damaged by the stansions of a sunken vessel lying within ten feet. "Next day passed 'Tortugas' and two men of war in sight but took no notice of us as we disguised our vessel by taking down squaresail, yards, and fore topmast; appearing as a common coaster; and sailed for Mobile. Coming through Pitaboy [Petite Bois] channel into lake Pontchartrain and anchored off 'Point of Pines' Grand Bay Miss: July 9th," wrote Captain Foster.[13] The capability of lowering the mast was a special design feature of schooners and other small vessels built for the slave trade,[14] instantly transforming them into common or local coasters. Under this disguise, no one would suspect the *Clotilda* as being an oceangoing slaver, and no one would suspect her of having recently completed a trans-Atlantic voyage if she coasted into Mobile from the direction of Lake Pontchartrain. Captain Foster was keenly aware of this ruse.

"Capt. Tim Meaher and party were to have met me there [Point of Pines] for the purpose of landing negroes, and pay the crew off: and I had made arrangements with the mates and crew to take the vessel to Tampico and change her name and get clearance for New Orleans—the parties failing to meet me in time compelled me to come up to Mobile," wrote Foster.[15] In the Atlantic slave trade, Tampico, Mexico, served as a smugglers' den where captains could change the name of their vessels and obtain false clearance papers to mask their vessels' genealogy and nefarious activities. Tim Meaher's failure to meet Foster for the purpose of landing Cudjo and his shipmates necessitated a change in plans. Instead of sending the *Clotilda* to Tampico, Foster was forced to go ashore to Mobile to find a tug to pull the *Clotilda* up the Spanish River. Plans for landing the Africans were complicated further by his mates and crew members, who did not want him to leave the *Clotilda* to go ashore. "When anchored off 'P. of P.' Miss. The mates and crew did not want me to leave the vessel until they were paid for voyage. And said they would kill me if I attempted to take the negroes ashore without their money," wrote Foster.[16]

The crew's threat to kill Captain Foster was a dangerous development, one that he may not have foreseen. However, hiring and working with slaver crews comprised, often, of mere strangers with questionable, even criminal, backgrounds always added an element of danger to slaving voyages. Crew members, however, were not ignorant of the value of their labor relative to the illegality of, and the threats to life posed by, smuggling voyages. As captains of slavers were known to force crewmen into service at gunpoint, crewmen were known to return the gesture when demanding fair wages. The fact that Captain Foster needed to go ashore to get enough money to pay the crew members did not bode well for him, especially since he had promised to double their wages at Praia, Cape Verde. The crew allowed Foster to go ashore, where he paid $25 for a horse and buggy to take him to Mobile, where he dispatched a messenger to Tim Meaher's residence on Telegraph Road to inform him that "the niggers have come!"[17]

This communication set into motion the final phase of this smuggling expedition that included moving the African captives from the Gulf into the Alabama interior. "I hired a tug [in Mobile], went to the vessel, to tow her up to Mobile into Spanish River and crew refused to let me have her because I didn't have time to get the money to pay them," wrote Foster.[18] The crew held the *Clotilda* and her African captives for ransom, representing another dangerous development. The longer the *Clotilda* remained anchored in Point of Pines, the chances of her being detected by customs authorities increased. If Foster was not able to secure her human cargo, the smuggling venture, and the bet that launched it, would be lost. Foster's crew left him with only one option. "I came back to Mobile and took on board the tug five men and $8,000 dollars landed at vessel 9 P.M. went aboard and settled with them according to my first agreement in Mobile. We put the mates and crew on Steamer and sent them to Montgomery on their way to the northern States," wrote Foster.[19] The steamer *Texas* transported them to Montgomery where they obtained passage on a northbound train, using tickets that had been supplied by Meaher.[20] Although they had not been informed of the true nature of the *Clotilda*'s voyage until she was at sea, the crewmen would be adjudged pirates under the provisions of the Piracy Act. They were eager to put some distance between themselves and the place where the smuggling scheme was hatched. By sending them north, Meaher removed the threat of having them serve as informants against him and his conspirators.

After transferring the mates and crew members to the *Texas*, Captain Foster used James Hollingsworth's tug, *Billy Jones*, to tow the *Clotilda* into Mobile Bay.[21] From there, the tug pulled the *Clotilda* up Spanish River, to Mobile River, and to Twelve Mile Island.[22] Twelve Mile Island is an important navigational landmark surrounded by the Mobile River. Tim Meaher, his brother Byrnes, and James Dennison boarded the steamboat *Czar*, and they sailed up the Mobile River to await the *Clotilda*'s arrival at Twelve Mile Island. Dennison, Byrnes's slave, had an intimate knowledge of the local rivers because he was an experienced steamboat pilot who helped the Meahers navigate the local rivers and their tributaries, Mrs. Mable Dennison said of her grandfather.[23] Southern Alabama is well drained by numerous rivers, creeks, and bayous that would facilitate smuggling operations in the interior. As the schooner *Clotilda* possessed a centerboard that helped her to maintain stability in deep sea, that centerboard could also be raised to allow her to navigate shallow bayous and estuaries such as those in the Alabama interior.

When the *Clotilda* arrived at Twelve Mile Island, the smugglers pulled Cudjo and his co-captives from her fetid, feces-stained hold. Subsequently, Captain Foster navigated the *Clotilda* into Big Bayou Conner, on the northwest corner of Twelve Mile Island. "I then burned my Schr to the waters edge and sunk her. I transferred my Slaves to a river Steamboat and sent them up into the canebrake to hide them until further disposal," wrote Foster, who burned the *Clotilda* to destroy the feces and other evidence that she was a slaver.[24] The steamboat *Czar*, owned by Byrnes Meaher, transported Cudjo and others to John M. Dabney's Mount Vernon plantation, where they were unloaded and hidden in a canebrake, at the 49-mile mark on the Mobile River, in Mobile County.[25] Dabney was a merchant of foods and dry goods. Among his prominent patrons were Harry Theophilus Toulmin, James Lyon, Colonel Thomas Buford, Dr. Josiah C. Nott, Dr. Aaron Lopez, and Dr. Solomon Mordecai.[26] In addition to owning a successful store, Dabney owned 47 black men, women, and children, between the ages of one and 70.[27] After depositing the captives on Dabney's plantation, Tim, Byrnes, and Dennison sailed aboard the *Czar* to the Tombigbee-Alabama confluence to await the arrival of the steamer *Roger B. Taney* in route to Wetumpka. Tim Meaher boarded the *Roger B. Taney* to have dinner that had been delayed for him, per his instructions.[28]

Meanwhile, the Mobile Custom House authorities learned that Captain Foster had entered the bay without paying customs duties and without providing, and confirming, his ship manifest. Mobile revenue collectors manned the *Eclipse*, and they launched a search for the slaver *Clotilda*. In his fourth State of the Union Address, delivered December 3, 1860, President Buchanan made the following statement about the illegal slave trade:

> It is with great satisfaction I communicate the fact that since the date of my last annual message [December 19, 1859] not a single slave has been imported into the United States in violation of the laws prohibiting the African slave trade. This statement is founded upon a thorough examination and investigation of the subject. Indeed, the spirit which prevailed some time since among a portion of our fellow-citizen in favor of this trade seems to have entirely subsided.[29]

The thorough examination and investigation of which Buchanan boasted overlooked the intelligence of the Interior Department, whose officials reported the *Clotilda*'s arrival in Alabama waters as early as July 23, 1860.

On August 7, A.J. Requier, the U.S. district attorney, informed William Giles Jones, judge for the Circuit Court of the United States for the Fifth Judicial

Circuit, and Southern District of Alabama, that Captain Foster failed to report the arrival of the *Clotilda* to the Collector of Customs at Mobile. On October 28, 1860, Cade M. Godbold, U.S. marshal for the Southern District of Alabama, hand-delivered two summonses to Foster to appear in court to answer charges relative to the arrival of the *Clotilda* in the port of Mobile. On the second Monday of December, Foster appeared in court to answer the charge that he failed to report her arrival in violation of customs laws, as explained in the following excerpt from a summary of the charge:

> William Foster, master or commander of the Schooner Clotilda, heretofore towit: on the _____day of____1860 arrived from a foreign port or place with the said schooner in his charge or under his command, within the harbor or port of Mobile, it being a port in the United States established by law in the district afore-said and within the jurisdiction of this court. That the said master wholly failed to report the arrival of the said schooner Clotilda to the Collector of the said port within the time prescribed by law in such case made and provided. That the said master wholly failed to make the further report in writing to the collector of said district, prescribed by the 30th section of an act entitled "An Act to regulate the collection of duties on imports and tonnage." Approved 2nd March 1799, which report should contain all the particulars required to be inserted in a manifest made under oath or solemn affirmation of the said Master as to the truth of the said report or manifest as the same ought to be in conformity to the Act aforesaid. But all these duties of him required by law, the said William Foster has wholly failed to do and perform.[30]

For violating the 30th section of the 1799 Act regulating the collection of duties on imports and tonnage, Captain Foster would be required to pay a $1,000 fine. Shortly after receiving his first summons, Captain Foster married Adalaide Vanderslice, daughter of Jacob and Mary Vanderslice, on September 6, 1860. In an interview with a reporter from the *Herald*, she said that she and Foster spent their honeymoon in Exchange Hotel in Montgomery, attempting, to no avail, to avoid the attention that he was receiving regarding his daring feat as the commander of what was being touted as the last slave ship to America.[31]

Violating customs laws was necessary to avoid having the scheme foiled and to move Cudjo and his co-captives to the plantations of James Dabney and Byrnes Meaher, where they could be hidden from customs officials who launched a search for them. However, District Attorney Requier obtained information that some of the *Clotilda* Africans had been hidden on Dabney's plantation. In court, Requier filed the following information:

> [A]gainst Jno M. Dabney that One Hundred and three negroes were imported or brought to the United States from a foreign kingdom place or country with intent to hold sell or disposed of such negroes as slaves, or to be held to Service or Labor. And that the said John M. Dabney has a large number of said negroes towit: ten

men and ten women ten boys and ten girls contrary to the provisions of the acts in such case made and provided for. . .[32]

The above language comports with that of the 1794 and 1807 acts prohibiting new importations of Africans from foreign places for the purposes of making them slaves. Although Dabney did not import the *Clotilda* captives, he is said to be holding them as slaves. Possession of illegally imported slaves is contrary to the Acts. Based upon the information filed by Requier, on July 27, 1860, Judge Jones issued a writ of seizure ordering U.S. Marshal Godbold to seize and take into his possession the "Said negroes and keep the said subject to the further orders of the Said District Court."[33]

On that same day, U.S. Marshal Godbold lodged information with Requier that 103 negroes, of unknown names and descriptions, were imported into the United States from a foreign country with intent to hold, sell, or dispose of as slaves. The information further alleged that, "Burns [Byrnes] Meaher, of the county of Clarke, state of Alabama, to wit, in the district aforesaid, & within the jurisdiction of this court, holds the negroes aforesaid to wit, twenty-five men, & twenty-five women, twenty-five boys, & twenty-five girls, contrary to the provisions of the acts in such case made & provided."[34] Acting on this information, Judge Jones issued a writ for seizure of the captives being held by Byrnes Meaher. Both he and Dabney were also ordered to appear in court at the same time as Captain Foster's first hearing.

On the fourth Monday of December, 1860, Captain Foster appeared in court a second time to hear a complaint brought by the United States of America, who charged that he breached customs laws when he failed to pay customs duties and when he failed to produce two lists or manifests—one for the passengers, and one for the crew of the schooner *Clotilda*. The court was seeking a separate fine in the amount of $400, something Captain Foster could have avoided paying had he fulfilled the maritime obligations outlined in this excerpt of the court's summary statement:

> Commander William Foster hath delivered to the Collector of the Customs for the district of Mobile, in the state of Alabama, a verified list containing, as far as he can ascertain then, the names, places of birth, residence and description of the persons who compose the company of the said Schooner called the Clotilda when lying in the said District, of which he was then Master or Commander, of which list the said Collector delivered to the said Master a certified copy, it was provided that if the said William Foster shall exhibit the aforesaid certified copy of the list to the first boarding officer at the first port in the United States at which he shall arrive on his return thereto, and then and there also produce the sum named therein to the said boarding officer, except any of the persons contained in the said list, who may be discharged in a foreign country with the consent of the Consul, Vice Consul, Commercial Agent, or Vice Commercial Agent there

residing, signified in writing under his hand and official seal, to be produced to the Collector of the District within which he may arrive, as aforesaid, with the other persons composing the crew as aforesaid, or who may have died, or absconded, or who may have been forcibly impressed into other service, of which satisfactory proof shall be then also exhibited to the said last mentioned Collector, then and in such case the said bond or writing obligatory should be void and of no effect, otherwise it should abide and remain in full force and virtue. And the said plaintiffs aver that the said William Foster did not fulfill all and singular the conditions above.[35]

Captain Foster did not pay customs duties or produce the *Clotilda*'s manifest because he was transporting an illegal cargo of African captives. The Collector of Customs never had an opportunity to board the inbound *Clotilda* that slipped past the customs house, it is thought, during the night to avoid detection. Just as he failed to comply with customs laws upon arrival in the port of Mobile, it is probable that Captain Foster did not obtain the legal clearances required of all vessels leaving the port of Mobile, knowing that he was bound for a smuggling voyage as revealed by the *Clotilda's* outfit and apparatus.

Of course, slave traders were keenly aware of the fact that paying a fine for failing to produce manifests upon arrival was a less serious violation than being adjudged a pirate. By 1860, however, 40 years after the Piracy Act was implemented, no one had hanged. Hence, the law alone did not act as a deterrent. What was more threatening to white men was the prospect of being the first to hang for blackbirding, a sport they felt entitled to be engaged in at their discretion. One curious aspect of the summonses issued to Captain Foster, John Dabney, and Byrnes Meaher is that they were first witnessed and signed by the judge as early as April, indicating that the court had prior knowledge that the *Clotilda* had gone for a cargo of Africans.[36] The United States summoned several persons to appear as witnesses at Foster's second hearing, including Richard Eames, Edwin Eames (not found), Anatol Rabby (of Bayou La Batre, Mobile County), Joseph Laurendine (Bayou La Batre), D.J. Bryant, Emmanuel Bryant (of Clarke County), and Richard Rivers (of Clarke County).[37] The 1860 Federal Census Slave Schedule for Clarke County lists Rivers as an owner of 36 slaves.[38] The other witnesses might have been prospective buyers, with Tim Meaher, according to one reporter's written account of an interview with him, "unfolding his scheme confidentially to several prominent slaveholders of that day, they each agreed to take a certain number of slaves, the projector reserving some thirty for himself. Thus the cargo of human freight was apportioned for future delivery."[39]

T.G. Morgan also received a summons to appear as a witness in Foster's second hearing. The summons specifically ordered Morgan to "bring with him a certain note, addressed to him on or about the 5th of April, 1860, by Wm Foster."[40] U.S. Marshal Godbold searched for Morgan to serve him with the summons, but he did not find him. Therefore, the note's contents are not known. Its date, however, is significant, since it reveals that Foster penned the note after he had embarked upon the smuggling venture. If the note contained information about the crime, and if this information became public, that might explain why Judge Jones began to prepare and sign the summons and subpoena as early as April 1860. Had the court obtained that letter, and had it disclosed the intent of the *Clotilda*'s voyage, it would have strengthened the federal government's case against the smugglers. Such a letter could also have proven valuable to Morgan, if he wanted to inform on Foster, the Meahers, and their conspirators, according to an 1859 Act providing that informants would be compensated for information that led to the seizure of illegal cargoes, $250 per captive. The *Clotilda* landed 110 captives, so Morgan could have received $27,500. As an informant, Morgan could also expose the slave buyers who would be prosecuted as *purchasers* under Section 6 of the 1807 Slave Trade Act and be forced to pay $800 for each slave in their possession. Nevertheless, Tim Meaher's public wager that he could smuggle slaves into the United States and escape conviction simultaneously provided the opportunity for any one who was privy to that conversation to inform on him and his co-smugglers. Because of the open wager, the *Clotilda* smuggling scheme was not a secret.

In Foster's second hearing, *United States v. William Foster & Richard Sheridan*, and on the recommendation of Requier, Judge Jones ordered that the second case against Foster be continued on January 7, 1861. Judge Jones ordered that the case be continued because certain witnesses failed to appear on the part of the plaintiff as summoned, including George S. Blakeley, Stewart Cayce, William L.D. Humphries, Edwin Dougherty, James S. Dennison, Burns [Byrnes] Meaher, and Timothy Meaher.[41] Because these witnesses failed to appear, Judge Jones also ordered that forfeitures be taken against them. Tim Meaher was arrested, but he was allowed to post bail.[42] Meanwhile, he hired Attorney John Archibald Campbell to represent him at his preliminary hearing. From May 1861 to April 1862, Campbell practiced commercial law in Alabama, where he represented bankers, mercantilists, and planters.[43] He served previously as an associate justice of the U.S. Supreme Court from 1853 to April 1861, hearing cases involving slavery and states' rights.[44] He presided over the Dred Scott case that was doomed at the U.S. Supreme Court level, due to the proslavery bias of Campbell, Chief Justice Taney, and their slaveowning, Democratic colleagues. As a slaveowner, Campbell defined black people as property, and property ownership, he argued, was his right under the U.S. Constitution.[45] Campbell also "held" slaves as a trustee for his sister in a married woman's separate property trust.[46]

Judge Jones presided over all of the cases involving the *Clotilda* smuggling expedition. During his tenure as judge, Jones heard several cases involving the illegal importation, and the holding, of Africans, contrary to federal laws. In *U.S. vs. Horatio N. Gould*, adjudicated in federal court during the Spring Term 1860, the U.S. district attorney argued that the defendant "without any participation in illegal importation, did, within this District, hold, sell, or otherwise dispose of, as a slave, a negro who had been previously unlawfully imported by some other person."[47] Although this case involved the unlawful detention of one individual by another, Jones raised the issue of states' rights to regulate importations by citing the Alien Law of 1798.

This law extended to the president conditional power to deport aliens. In that context, the term "alien" refers to individuals who committed seditious, treasonous acts against the federal government. Based upon that definition, "aliens" could be removed from the United States by presidential decree. That definition did not apply to slaves as property. In Jones's opinion, however, "the right to fix the status of a resident in a State, belonged to the State, and not to the General Government."[48] Ultimately, Jones misinterpreted and misapplied the Alien Law in *U.S. vs. Horatio N. Gould*. He should have cited and upheld Section 6 of the 1807 Slave Trade Act that prohibited American citizens from purchasing or holding Africans who had been illegally imported. But Jones failed to uphold that law, something that he swore to do when he became judge for the Southern District of Alabama.[49]

At his preliminary hearing, Tim Meaher provided an alibi to Judge Jones, claiming that he could not have personally smuggled slaves into Mobile because he was having dinner aboard the steamer *Roger B. Taney* when the said crime was committed. Therefore, he argued, he could not have been in two places at one time.[50] This alibi was strengthened by the fact that U.S. Marshal Godbold noted on the writs of seizure relative to the slaves held by John Dabney and Byrnes Meaher that "the within named negroes not found in my district 20th Dec 1860."[51] Tim Meaher used a number of ruses to mask his complicity and to avoid conviction. However, the evidence leaves no doubt that he was involved in the crime. The *Clotilda*'s manifest reveals that Meaher gave Captain Foster specific instructions regarding the care of the captives aboard the *Clotilda*.[52] Foster's account indicates that Tim Meaher was scheduled to meet Foster when the *Clotilda* arrived on the Gulf Coast. Tim and his co-smugglers arranged and supervised the illegal transferring of African captives from the *Clotilda* to the *Czar* in Alabama. Not only was detaining Africans on board American ships and transporting them to the

United States a crime, but delivering them on shore, and transferring them from one vessel to another within the U.S. territory, were violations of the 1807 Anti–Slave Trade Act and Section 5 of the Piracy Act.

Tim Meaher recounted the entire smuggling scheme for a *Globe-Democrat* correspondent who interviewed Meaher on the porch of his residence on Telegraph Road, describing him in the following way:

> He is now 77 years of age, and is living in retirement at his home. He is a sufferer from partial paralysis, but his bodily infirmities have in no way affected his mental faculties, and he converses with an ease and volubility that is remarkable for one of his years. He never seems to tire of relating reminiscences of his early career, and receives his visitors with a cordial Southern welcome.[53]

Regarding how the smugglers managed to elude Mobile revenue collectors who did not find the *Clotilda*, Tim Meaher informed the reporter that he slipped $50 in gold into the hands of a trusted employee, saying, "the *Eclipse* is going after the negroes this evening. Take this and fix the crew with liquor."[54] Plying revenue officers with liquor was a common tactic employed by Meaher, Lamar, and other slave smugglers who understood that the inebriated officers could not complete their search, and they would simply "look the other way." That would have been easily accomplished by the collector of customs, Thaddeous Sanford, who, as a slaveowner, sympathetic to slave smugglers, was vulnerable to being bribed by them.[55]

In addition to obstructing justice, it has been argued that Tim Meaher bribed the judge who heard the *Clotilda* case.[56] However, it may not have been necessary to bribe Judge Jones, who was a proslavery Democrat, born into the planter class in Powhatan, Virginia, in 1808. In 1836, Jones relocated to Greene County, Alabama, when tobacco and rice planters were flocking to the Gulf states to reap huge profits from cotton production.[57] His last will and testament reveals the extent of his slaveownership. To his sons Wallace and William M. Jones, he left his "negro slaves" in Virginia, along with all the monies obtained from hiring out those slaves.[58] Jones acquired several slaves (Ellen, Aggy, Holly, and Phil) through his marriage to Eliza Ann Hobson, to whom he relinquished full ownership of those slaves along with "their future increase."[59] However, the extent to which black men, women, and children were commodified as property is revealed in the following excerpt from Jones's will:

> It is my will that my negro man London, and my negro man Edwin be each appraised separately by two intelligent disinterested gentlemen to be called on by my Executor and Executrix for that purpose. If the two so called on shall differ in the amount at which they appraise said negroes respectively then the medium [median] between the two to be considered the appraisement and they are to certify such appraisements under their hands.[60]

It was his will that his wife keep one-fifth of the appraised amount, the balance to be divided amongst his children. It was also stipulated that if his wife did not take the negroes on those terms, then he wished them to be sold at private sale. Finally, to his daughter, Mary Elizabeth Jones, he gave, by deed of gift, "a mulatto girl named Julia."[61]

Three years before President Buchanan appointed him judge for the Southern District of Alabama, Jones, acting as trustee for Philip A. Aylet, purchased land and "negroes," including Wilkins, George, Vina, his wife Emily, and her two children, George and Fanny.[62] In 1858, Jones served as the attorney for Benjamin Ballard during the sale of three slaves (William Dickson, about 20 years old; a girl named Mary Catherine Lucas, a negress about 18 years old; and a girl named Sara Jane Lee, a mulatto about 10 years old) to Charly and Caroline M. Bright.[63] Prominent Mobilians seemed to make a regular business of having a power of attorney represent their interests in transactions involving slaves, the transaction being legally binding and the slaves being "real property." In 1843, Henry Burgett conveyed a slave named "Eliza age about eight years black complexion—To have and to hold the slave with her future increase," to Theophilus L. Toulmin, on the condition that Toulmin permit Sarah B. Lyon, daughter of James G. Lyon, to use and hire the slave when she desires. The document further stipulates that Toulmin may, at the request of Sarah, sell the slave and her increase on the condition that Lyon collects the proceeds from the sale.[64]

As a slaveowner, Jones was biased in favor of the institution of slavery, interfering in his ability to uphold antismuggling laws and to render impartial verdicts. Under these circumstances, justice for enslaved persons was denied in cases presided over by judges who were slaveowners. After 1808, slave smugglers avoided conviction, and the death penalty, with the support of judges like Jones who supported, and protected, states' rights to regulate slavery and who manipulated federal, state, and local laws in order to serve their own proslavery agendas. Tim Meaher may have had a personal relationship with the Jones family, naming one of his steamboats the *William Jones, Jr.*[65] The court cases of Byrnes Meaher and John Dabney's cases were dismissed,[66] lacking the evidence in the form of the slaves who were not found by Godbold. Lags of time between the *Clotilda*'s arrival in the port of Mobile and the issuance of writs of seizure provided the smugglers with ample opportunity to conceal the evidence of their crime. Without the *Clotilda* or her captives, gaining a conviction was extremely difficult in Southern courts that were known to acquit smugglers even when *prima facie* evidence and informants were stacked against them.

Foster's case was held over for continuation on January 7, 1861. However, with the January term (1861) of the Circuit Court of the United States

(Southern District of Alabama) falling on the threshold of Alabama's secession from the Union, Foster's case was never closed. The *Clotilda* was no stranger to Alabama courts. One year before she smuggled Cudjo and his co-captives into Alabama, she struck a skiff in Mobile Bay, causing the drowning death of a slave named Alfred who was sitting inside of it.[67] In the City Court of Mobile, Alfred's master, W.D.F. Holly, successfully sued William Foster for damages in the amount of $1,500, the cost of the drowned "property." On appeal, however, the Supreme Court of Alabama ruled in Foster's favor, deciding that Holly was negligent for anchoring his skiff to a bar and, as such, preventing Alfred from getting out of the path of the *Clotilda* after he had been given ample warning of her approach.

The Meahers and their conspirators were never convicted as perpetrators of the *Clotilda* smuggling crime. On the eve of secession, Judge Jones would not pursue a case against a fellow slaveowner. One year after he was sworn in as a U.S. judge, and immediately following Alabama's secession from the Union, Jones submitted his handwritten resignation to President Buchanan, stating that his judgeship was "inconsistent" with his "duties as a citizen."[68] Subsequently, Jones became district judge for the Confederacy. John Archibald Campbell, Tim Meaher's attorney, became the Confederates' assistant secretary of war for the draft. Campbell is also remembered for his imprisonment by Union troops for conspiring to have Abraham Lincoln assassinated.[69] A.J. Requier became the Confederacy's "poet laureate."

John Dabney became justice of the peace for Mobile County, an office in which he swore to "support the Constitution of the United States and of the State of Alabama and to discharge his duties according to Law."[70] Captain Foster, James Meaher, Timothy Meaher, and Cade M. Godbold swore allegiance to the Confederacy.[71] Timothy Meaher further demonstrated his allegiance to the Confederacy by becoming a blockade runner. Mobile became the intrepid center of blockade running in the Gulf. On December 30, 1863, under the cloak of night, the steamer *Gray Jacket*, built and commanded by Meaher, breached the blockade at Mobile. On the following day, immobilized and damaged by a storm, the *Gray Jacket* was fired upon by gunners of the USS *Kennebec*, a 691-ton gunboat of the West Gulf Blockading Squadron. Upon boarding the *Gray Jacket*, Lieutenant Commander William P. McCann discovered that she was laded with 513 bales of cotton, tobacco, turpentine, and rosin (25 barrels).[72] A prize crew escorted the libeled *Gray Jacket* to the District Court of the United States for the Eastern District of Louisiana for adjudication.

In the initial deposition, Meaher said, "I am a citizen of the State of Alabama to which I owe my allegiance."[73] He further stated that he was the builder and owner of the *Gray Jacket* that was in route to Havana, her final destination, when she was overhauled by the U.S. authorities. Despite the fact that she was flying the American flag, a cover for her Confederate operations, the U.S. authorities confiscated the *Gray Jacket* as an enemy vessel and as a prize. In response to the federal government's accusations and actions against his property, in February 1864, Meaher filed a "claim and answer to the libel."[74] In it, he said that he aimed to find a safe haven in Havana, after the outbreak of the rebellion to which he gave no aid. Therefore, in his opinion, the U.S. authorities had no right to capture the *Gray Jacket* and that under the presidential proclamation of 1863, he, along with others who had participated in the rebellion, was entitled to full pardon and remission of his confiscated property. Only those ex-Confederate sympathizers and aides who had taken an oath of allegiance to the United States could receive these entitlements. Understanding this, and in his defense, Meaher rushed to take the oath on March 18, 1864.[75]

However, *prima facie* evidence showed that Meaher was no ex-Confederate sympathizer. On board the *Gray Jacket,* the officers seized a written agreement between "Messrs. Meaher & Bro., owners of the st'r Gray Jacket, and Henry Meyers, Major and Ch'f Ord. Officer, acting for the gover't of the C.S.," written at Mobile and dated "Oct. 22, '63."[76] In it, Meaher agreed to deliver a cargo of cotton, one-half of which belonged to the Confederate government, to Havana. On the return voyage, the government was to receive one-half of the *Gray Jacket*'s storage capacity. Once again, Havana, Cuba, played a significant role as a haven for smugglers, now called blockade runners, who used the port as a neutral zone where they could devise their strategies for penetrating the blockade; off-load bales of cotton (the principal currency of the Confederacy) for transshipment to England or New England; and, take aboard food, clothing, munitions, and stores critical to the Confederate cause. What the document reveals, however, is that Meaher was aiding the Confederacy, and that he, rather than remaining in Havana as a safe haven from the hostile rebellion, aimed to return to Mobile.

To mask the discrepancies between this document and his statements, Meaher filed a new affidavit on May 25, 1864. In it, he said that he opposed secession, doing all that he could to prevent it; that he was traveling to Havana to sell his cotton made on his own plantation.[77] He further stated that he had made no contract with the Confederates, who forced him to carry one-half of the cargo for the Confederate government, but he intended to defraud the Confederacy by regaining complete ownership of his entire cargo beyond the blockade.[78] In a final act of desperation, Meaher claimed that he was returning to Maine, his birthplace, via Havana, to take up permanent residency, and that he had planned to carry his wife and children, but doing so would reveal his intentions to make completely off with the Confederate government's half of the cargo.[79] Regarding Meaher's petition to the U.S. Supreme Court to hear further proof in the matter relative to confiscation and remission of the condemned *Gray Jacket* and her cargo, the court issued the following ruling:

> This is not a proper case for an order of further proof. The order is always made with extreme caution, and only where the ends of justice clearly require it. The claimant forfeited all right to ask it by the guilty concealment in his first affidavit, and in his subsequent affidavit and claim. The allowance would hold out the strongest temptation to subordination of perjury. There is nothing to warrant such an exercise of our discretion. We are entirely satisfied with the testimony in the case, and entertain no doubt of the correctness of the conclusions we draw from it. If the allegations of the claimant are true, he postponed his effort to escape too long to derive any benefit from it. The law does not tolerate such delay. The motion is overruled.[80]

The U.S. Supreme Court questioned why he did not seek refuge among the U.S. naval officers, if, as he claimed, he breached the blockade to escape the Confederacy. It was entirely unreasonable to think that by seeking permanent residency in his birth state of Maine, via Havana, he would abandon his plantation and other businesses in Mobile.

The U.S. government accused Meaher of *interlining* his deposition and affidavits with statements to mask his complicity, contradicting himself on several occasions. As a seasoned smuggler, Meaher was quite the chameleon, changing his allegiances, alliances, stories, and schemes to fit the legal, political, and economic exigencies of the situation. In the original deposition, Meaher claimed that he, "by a life of industry and economy, and the prosecution of legitimate business, acquired a large amount of property."[81] However, the *Clotilda* case revealed that not all of his business was legitimate. Like slave smuggling, blockade running was a lucrative enterprise that allowed him to recoup the money that he lost on the *Clotilda* smuggling venture that, including court and attorney's fees, cost him approximately $100,000.[82] But, that was a small price to pay for having the opportunity to exercise his "right" to smuggle slaves, in defiance of federal laws, and to demonstrate his ability to use his wealth and political connections to persons in key positions of power to escape conviction. He won his bet.

CHAPTER 5

In the Jaws of the Lion

For the second time, Timothy Meaher and Captain Foster escaped conviction and execution for smuggling slaves and for fitting out ships for that purpose. The *Clotilda* Africans remained hidden on Dabney's plantation before being relocated to Byrnes Meaher's plantation located at the 58- and 59-mile marks on the Tombigbee River in Clarke County, where Byrnes Meaher claimed his portion of the cargo, including the African called Kanko.[1] James Meaher also retained some of the captives for himself.[2] Published just prior to the arrival of the *Clotilda*, the 1860 Federal Census Slave Schedule identifies James Meaher as a "slave owner," with 22 black and mulatto men, women, and children in his possession as property, ranging from 10 to 55 years of age.[3] That number increased with the addition of his portion of the *Clotilda* cargo. Captain Foster was also given a portion of the cargo, amounting to 10 Africans.[4]

Tim Meaher received the largest portion of the *Clotilda* cargo.[5] Among those captives that he deposited on his land in Magazine Point-Plateau area were Cudjo Kossula, Albine, Polee, Abackey, Kazuma, Jabba, Chamba, Ossie Keeby, Ardassa, Monabee, and Gumpa. Other captives were sold to prospective buyers, some known—several unknown. Char-Lee, described as one of Cudjo's brothers, was sold to Colonel Thomas Buford of Mobile.[6] Cudjo also had a second brother who was sold to a man who lived near Selma, Alabama.[7]

To argue that Africans were bought and sold is to overlook the complexity, and the extent, of their commodification. Their value was determined, in part, by their point of export. The fact that the *Clotilda* Africans were exported via Whydah, for example, made them extremely attractive to foreign buyers, enhancing their marketability. As a slave port, Whydah was "esteemed to be the finest Country in Africa, greatly preferred to any other."[8] Whydah was the port of choice for slave buyers, due to the "quality" or "skill-knowledge base" of Africans who could be purchased there, as one slave buyer explained:

> The Gold Goast, Popo, and Whidah Negroes are born in a part of Africa which is very barren...On that account, when able to take hoe in hand, they are obliged to go and cultivate the land for their subsistence. They also live hardily; so that when they are carried to our plantations (as they have been used to hard labour from their infance) they become strong robust people...[9]

The buyer attests to the Africans' ability to convert what appears to be barren (uncultivated) land into productive fields. Africans possessed the ability to cultivate the soil using handheld hoes, without the benefit of beasts. Foreign buyers were quick to realize the economic potential that this indigenous agricultural expertise held for their own plantation schemes across the Atlantic.

Cultural identity, as an indication of skill, also influenced slaves' market value and buyers' preferences.[10] Whydah was the exit point for large numbers of Yoruba captives who were in great demand by American and European buyers who considered them to be "industrious."[11] In this context, the term *industrious* refers to the fact that Yoruba captives possessed agricultural, artistic, and technical skills that were essential to the success of plantation and industrial economies. Hence, Africans gave to the building of the Americas much more than just labor; they contributed skills and ideas that were exploited for capital gain. The African was a multidimensional, transmarketable commodity within the enterprise of slavery. This is especially true of Yoruba captives. And, it is for this reason that the African diaspora consists, in large measure, of Yoruba-descended peoples.

The *Clotilda* Africans shared Whydah as their West African point of departure. But, point of departure rarely signified place of capture. The *Clotilda* cargo was comprised of Africans with heterogeneous geographical and cultural origins, consistent with the composition of most slave cargoes. Neither Roche nor Hurston delineated the *Clotilda* Africans' origins with specificity. Therefore, this study uses primary field and archival data, indigenous histories as collected via interviews; geographic surveys and spatial analyses; place-names, idioms, and other ethnographic source material to trace their origins back to specific people and places in Benin and Nigeria. Analyzing this data within the contexts of political and military events in Benin and Nigeria during the second half of the nineteenth century has elucidated the *Clotilda* Africans' origins. Consequently, this search for origins has been the major part of a 15-year research odyssey whose momentum has been sustained metaphysically by the spirits of those ancestors about whom the manuscript has been written.

This search for origins begins with Cudjo Kazoola, the most vocal member of the *Clotilda* group, who talked extensively about his homeland and the events that led to his capture by Dahomean slave raiders. By sharing information with almost anyone who wanted to interview him, he hoped to be discovered and returned to West Africa. When Hurston interviewed Cudjo in 1927, she transcribed that he originated in Togo.[12] She later wrote that he hailed from Nigeria.[13] However, the names Nigeria and Togo are contemporary ones that did not exist at the time of Cudjo's capture. The geopolitical boundaries that currently separate African countries were not extant prior to the Berlin Conference of 1884. Assigning a Togolese origin to Cudjo, furthermore, does not comport with Dahomey's slave-raiding activities in the second half of the nineteenth century.

At the time of Cudjo's capture, Dahomean warriors were slave raiding in an eastwardly, and northeastwardly, direction, beyond the river Weme and into southwestern Nigeria, where Yoruba groups reside. It is not surprising, therefore, that the *Clotilda* cargo contained a large pocket of Yoruba-speaking peoples, including Cudjo himself. Indeed, Yoruba peoples comprised the largest group of Africans to be sold into the trans-Atlantic slave trade by Dahomeans between 1851 and 1860.[14] Cudjo never referred to his homeland as Nigeria. Instead, he drew a map in which he indicates that his place of origin rested northeast of Abomey, the royal seat of the Dahomean Empire.[15] His use of Abomey as a landmark is meaningful, for Abomey, as the name of Dahomey's royal seat, is much older than the contemporary name *Nigeria* that would have been unfamiliar to Cudjo in the nineteenth century. Residents of the Yoruba frontier zone, a natural, forested boundary that separates modern-day Benin from southwestern Nigeria, and those residing east of that zone, knew and feared Abomey as the home of powerful Fon warriors. Thus, it is easy to understand why Cudjo might define his homeland in relation to Abomey, controlled by the Fon slave raiders who captured him.

Prior to Roche and Hurston, S.H.M. Byers traveled to AfricaTown to see the survivors of the *Clotilda* smuggling venture. During an interview, Cudjo told Byers that he and his wife, whose name Byers recorded as Albiné (later written as Abila) originated in a place that Byers recorded as "Whinney."[16] Pierre Verger asserts that, "the passage of a word from the one language to the other very generally involves the elision of the first vowel."[17] This applies particularly to African words that are modified when they are translated into English. One's indigenous language and culture govern what one hears or does not hear in foreign languages. When English speakers attempt to translate African words, invariably, certain letters and syllables are dropped while the basic morphology generally remains the same. For example, the African word *Owinni* became Whinney, when Byers translated it. Owinni is currently located five kilometers outside of the Yoruba town of New Oyo (Oyo State, Nigeria). It rests on the Ogbomoso road, a prominent trade route that connects Ogbomoso to Oyo. As a part of the New Oyo Empire, Owinni served as a place of refuge (military outpost) for the *Alafin* (Oba, or king), who fled the *Afin* (Royal Palace) when it was under siege.[18]

Cudjo's and Albiné's connection to Owinni must be understood within the contexts of the economic and political events in, and around, the New Oyo Empire in the second half of the nineteenth century; Dahomey's slave-raiding activities at that time; and the reasons underpinning Dahomey's raid on Cudjo's village. Dahomey had been the vassal of Old Oyo until 1827, when the Dahomean army, under the command of King Ghezo, defeated an Oyo brigade sent to collect delinquent tribute from Dahomey. Ghezo combined the Oyo captives' blood with mud that he used to construct a palace at Cana, the place where Oyo envoys collected the annual tribute.[19] These events signaled the end of Oyo's reign over Dahomey and the beginning of Dahomey's imperialistic expansion eastward into Yorubaland.

King Ghezo seized the opportunity to trample his Yoruba enemies, retaliating against Oyo-controlled territories and those controlled by Yoruba groups allied with Oyo. He sacked numerous Yoruba towns situated along the Weme river corridor. Sabe was especially troublesome for Dahomey, since a Sabe contingency buttressed the Oyo brigade that fought against Dahomey in 1827.[20] In the 1830s and 1840s, Ghezo destroyed 143 Sabe-controlled villages.[21] Sabe, and the frontier-Yoruba Kingdom of Ketu, served as gateways into Yorubaland that represented a commercial complex of lucrative trade routes, market hubs, and fertile, productive farms. Resting on the Benin-Nigeria border and on the periphery of Dahomey's geopolitical sphere of influence, Ketu challenged Dahomey's advancement towards the east. But, Ketu was an obstacle that Dahomey could not easily control or remove, situated on a plateau of laterite rock and fortified by double clay walls that were 12 feet high and that encompassed approximately 85 hectares.[22] These walls were surrounded by ditches that were 20 feet wide and nine feet deep, a tertiary barrier constructed to trap approaching infantry and cavalry forces. Access to Ketu's interior was via a pair of gates, the outer one being known as the Idena Gate or "sentry" gate.[23]

Ketu's fortification repelled attacks by the Dahomeans, who resorted to attacking smaller, less-fortified Ketu-controlled towns. After staging a raid in the vicinity of Imeko in 1858, King Ghezo was fatally shot as he passed through Epo in route to Abomey.[24] When he ascended to the throne, King Glele avenged his father's death by ravaging Idahin, Issélu, Irocogny, Okpomèta, and several other Ketu-controlled towns.[25] Imeko was linked via a lucrative north-south trade route to the Yoruba-controlled market center of Abeokuta, and Dahomey battled Abeokuta for control of this north-south trade route that led to coastal markets where European and American traders exchanged goods for slaves. The fact that Abeokuta was well fortified did not deter Dahomean forces. In fact, Dahomey relished the challenge of destroying their enemies, particularly if they were defined as a threat to its sovereignty or economic stability. The inability to destroy or vassalize Ketu and Abeokuta only forced the Dahomeans to take circuitous routes in order to attack weaker, neighboring groups in their environs, as they advanced deeper into Yorubaland.

Wars were multipurposeful affairs, providing opportunities to pilfer coffers; to vassalize new territories from which a tribute could be exacted annually; to gain control over lucrative market centers and trade routes; and to capture Africans who would be reduced to slaves. Yoruba territories were very fertile ones that produced an abundance of food,[26] important for personal consumption and for commercial markets. During the 1850s and 1860s, Glele continued the incursions that his father had made on Yoruba territories in the vicinity of Abeokuta that rests on the east side of the Ogun river corridor. On the west side of the Ogun river, there were no obstacles that would have prevented him from advancing north in the direction of New Oyo and Owinni. Before the end of his reign, Glele would advance as far as the Upper Ogun region that was devastated by Dahomean warriors.[27] If Oyo indigenes are who Glele sought as captives, he would attack them in their major provinces. Those provinces lay east of the Ogun River (Ekun Osi) and west of the Ogun River (Ekun Otun),[28] the Ogun River being an important hydrological landmark within the context of slave-raiding activities of the Dahomean and Oyo empires.

At Owinni, east of the Ogun River, Cudjo would have been within the striking range of Dahomean slave raiders who launched the attack on his farmstead, certain aspects of which help to delineate further his geographical and cultural origins. The King of Dahomey demanded that the chief of Cudjo's farmstead send him half of his crops, consisting of beans, corn, and yams.[29] These are the principle crops that are grown in the forest and savannah regions of southwestern Nigeria, particularly Oyo. Cudjo elaborated on the yam-cultivation process that begins by placing the eye of the seed in a mound of dirt:

> We go way, we come back, push, dig de dirt—great beeg yam like keg, nail keg.
> We cut off vine with little piece of yam and cover it up again. Another beeg
> yam. Whole family couldn't eat at one time. For seven years don't need no new
> seed, it keep making yams.[30]

While various people cultivate yams throughout West Africa, yam cultivation
is the specialty of Yoruba peoples, for whom the yam is the most important
staple crop. The particular variety of yam that Cudjo described is the seed-
yam that may be planted whole, or it may be cut into smaller pieces that will
yield additional yams.[31] Therefore, as Cudjo indicated, new seeds are not
necessary for producing more yams for seven years.

This seven-year period is associated with the process of fallowing. In the
three-year rotational system employed by Yoruba cultivators, yams are alternately planted with corn, beans, and other crops. At the end of the three-year
cycle, the land is left fallow. Although it is plowed, the soil is left unseeded
from five to seven years.[32] Indeed, Yorubaland, of which Owinni is a part, is
located in West Africa's yam belt, and Oyo is the principal area where the plant
thrives in secondary bush (savannah) or in forest zones.[33] Oil palms also grow
well in this location. Ogunremi describes the production of palm oil as a
"major occupation by both men and women" who worked to supply domestic
and European markets where palm products were in great demand.[34] Cudjo
said that the production of palm oil was "the greatest industry" in which his
people engaged.[35]

Nigeria was a major producer of palm products, an occupation that
required a large labor force, thereby increasing slave raids as a means of
satisfying the labor demands.[36] Agricultural practices, plant material, and
topography are valid indices that can point to an individual's geographical
and cultural origins. Within the context of West African political economies,
food had tremendous value for both cultivators and traders. Its importance
is reflected in the fact that it is regularly included in tributary payments
demanded from vassal territories. Delinquent tributary payments served as
pretexts for raiding villages and farms from which food and other commodities were extracted. What is significant about the nature of the tribute that
the Dahomean king demanded from Cudjo's farmstead, insofar as it is a
geographical reference in this search for origins, is that it also included
cattle.[37] The region that is currently referred to as Oyo State has been, and
continues to be, the nucleus of cattle production in southwestern Nigeria.[38]
Owinni rests on the road that connects the major cattle-market towns in Oyo
State, including Oyo, Ogbomoso, and Ilorin. The sight of cattle being herded
along this road, as well as along the road that connects Oyo and Ibadan, is a
common one.

Generally, Yoruba peoples establish symbiotic relationships with Fulani herdsmen who raise the Yorubas' cattle, a specialized endeavor. Cudjo's people did not drink cow's milk, and that is typical of Yoruba peoples. They do consume beef, however. The manure is used to fertilize Yoruba farms. No part of an animal is wasted in West Africa. The hides and tails are fashioned into other useful products. Cudjo's people used hides to make sandals.[39] Wherever cows are slaughtered, skilled tanners transform the hides into beautiful leather bags and shoes. Today, a shoe-making industry flourishes at Ogbomoso. Hides are also used to cover drums. In Oyo, in particular, and in Yorubaland, in general, drumming is a highly respected occupation. As a Yoruba indigene, Cudjo would have been very familiar with drumming. In fact, he told Hurston that his people made drums in three shapes, including the "small tom-tom, the large state drum, and the long drum covered at both ends."[40] These drums, according to their description and number, resemble Bata drums that are associated with Shango, the fourth Alafin of Oyo and the deity of thunder, lightning, and fire.

Raids on Oyo and neighboring towns yielded food and highly skilled cultivators, artisans, and metallurgists with commodifiable, transferable skills that contributed to the success of plantations. The chief of Cudjo's farmstead refused to give into the demands of the Dahomeans, precipitating the raid on that farmstead. Certain dimensions of the raid are characteristic of Dahomey's slave-raiding strategies. The Dahomean infantry preferred to conduct raids during the dry season, from November to April, when the roads were not flooded, thereby facilitating passage. According to Professor Sylvain Anignikin, they launched attacks at dawn, when villagers and farmers least expected such an event.[41] Their maneuvers included espionage and reconnaissance. King Agaja established an organization called *Agbadji-gbeto*, a military intelligence service that collected data regarding the conditions and events in neighboring states.[42] Each Dahomean king refined the empire's slave-raiding strategy. Hwegbaja implemented the tactic of night raids, for example.[43]

From Abomey, the Dahomeans marched in a northeastwardly direction, passing through the forest, to reach Cudjo's farmstead. Many farm-villages were adjacent to forests, since it is from forests that savanna lands are derived or cleared for farming. Neighboring forests provided hunting grounds for local residents. Perimeter forests, like plateaus and gneissic outcroppings, also served as natural barriers against cavalry forces that could not negotiate the trees and thickets. To protect themselves against raids, various groups sought refuge in the forests. Dahomean infantry forces, on the other hand, were aided by the forests that helped to conceal their maneuvers. Therefore, attacking farmsteads and villages via the forest became an integral part of Dahomey's slave-raiding strategy, allowing them to avoid major towns and roads where they might be easily detected.[44] By seeking refuge in and around the forests, therefore, refugees escaped being trampled by *ajinaku* (the elephant) or *Balogun* (Yoruba warlord) of Oyo cavalry forces that could not penetrate the forests, only to be crushed by the jaws of Glele, dubbed the "ferocious Lion of the Forest" and the "terror in the bush."[45] Owinni is located in the savannah plains, at the edge of the forest zone. The preeminent Yoruba scholar Isaac A. Akinjogbin suggested that the Dahomean infantry approached Owinni from the west, via the Ogun river forest.[46]

The Dahomean infantry was comprised of male and female warriors known as amazons. In the nineteenth century, King Ghezo increased the number of females in the army.[47] The corps of amazons continued to expand and strengthen under Glele's leadership. To prepare for the rigors of war, females underwent intensive physical, psychological, and military training. They were fiercely competitive and protective of the Dahomean king (the lion) and his lair (the Dahomean Empire), as indicated by the following expression:

> Lionesses are more fearsome than lions.
> Because she has her cubs to defend.
> And we, the Amazons, have you to defend.
> The King, our King, and our God, King.[48]

Female soldiers were committed to war that generated revenue for the Dahomean State. By capturing enemies who could be sacrificed to the ancestors, forced to serve the king, or sold into the trans-Atlantic slave trade, they contributed significantly to the empire's political economy.

Leading the raids on farms and villages, startling unsuspecting inhabitants, the female warriors opened the way for subsequent attacks by the rear guard of male warriors.[49] That must have been a frightening sight to those who were not expecting an attack, least of all, by powerful women. At the first crow of the cock, the Dahomeans used flaming arrows to torch the palm-frond roofs of the clay houses on Cudjo's farmstead.[50] Fon warriors frequently used this tactic to force inhabitants out into the open where they could be snatched. Cudjo could hear the commotion of the Fon warriors attacking his people, soon after he had awakened from his sleep.[51] He recalled his people's terrifying encounter with the fierce female soldiers who were armed with machetes and French guns:

> Everybody dey run to de gates so dey kin hide deyself in de bush, you unnerstan me. Some never reachee de gate. De women soldier ketchee de young ones and tie dem by de wrist. No man kin be so strong lak de woman soldiers from de Dahomey. So day cut off de head [of those who tried to resist capture]. Some day snatch

de jaw-bone while de people ain dead. Oh Lor' Lor' Lor! De poor folkses wid dey bottom jaw tore off de face![52]

Cudjo tried desperately, but unsucessully, to escape the Dahomean slave raiders who blocked the gates leading out of his farmstead.[53] The Dahomean warriors captured Cudjo, but they slaughtered resistors who threatened their lives as well as undesirable older persons who did not fall within the age range of the target group. Witnessing unimaginable horror, such as jawbones being snatched out of the faces of living persons, and being separated from family, were the kinds of psychological traumas that haunted Africans long after they had left their places of capture.

Since the slave trade was a business in which Africans were commodified, the young male, between 19 and 25 years of age, represented the "prime negro" who fetched the highest price. Cudjo fell into that age range, and he was of sound health, qualities that increased his marketability.[54] He was young

Female warriors, known as Amazons, led Dahomey's slave raids including the raid on Cudjo's farmstead. Photograph by Natalie S. Robertson, PhD (1994).

and strong, with great potential for a long life of labor in the Americas. An unmistakable parallel can be drawn between the characteristics of the "prime negro" who was most desirable by slave traders and the young black male who is the prime target of U.S. prison-industrial complexes.[55] Prisons replaced slave systems as mechanisms for solving labor problems; hoards of black people were arrested, warehoused, and supplied to labor-starved planters and industrialists. Maryland courts had what were referred to as "Negro Dockets," cases involving black adults and children who had been arrested, often on "suspicion" of being runaways, and sold or apprenticed to "good masters."[56] Hence, the commodification of blacks begins with slavery that lays the foundation for their continued commodification as prisoners. Both systems have devastated black communities on both sides of the Atlantic.

According to Cudjo, the Dahomean king who made the original demand on the king of Cudjo's village, and who vowed to sack his farmstead for noncompliance, died before he could launch the raid that was carried out by his son.[57] These events coincide with the death of King Ghezo in 1858 and the ascendancy of his son, King Glele, in that same year. According to Cudjo, the king of Dahomey sent his warriors to deliver a warning to the king of Cudjo's farmstead, saying, "Kini, Kini, Kini, Lion of Lion...an animal done cut its teeth, evil done enter into the bush."[58] At this time in Dahomey's political history, any reference to a lion is a reference to King Glele. Cudjo observed that the Dahomean kings' preoccupation with slave raiding left them little time for raising food that they demanded from other farms, particularly those of their Yoruba enemies.[59]

By refusing to give into Dahomey's demands a second time, the king of Cudjo's farmstead insulted the Dahomean state.[60] To some extent, noncompliance with what was originally Ghezo's demand was viewed by Glele as a mockery of Ghezo's death. Maurice Ahanhanzo Glele, a direct descendant of King Glele, confirms that the Yoruba mocked both King Ghezo and Glele at the time of Ghezo's death.[61] If there were any groups that rejoiced at the death of Ghezo, it was Yoruba peoples who were the targets of successive attacks by the Dahomeans for most of the nineteenth century. Enraged by the fact that his father was killed by Yoruba indigenes at Epo, King Glele needed neither pretext nor provocation to punish Yoruba peoples. When the king of Cudjo's farmstead refused Dahomey's second demand, he sealed his own fate. During the raid on the farmstead, the king tried to escape by running out of one of the gates.[62] At that time, he was captured by Dahomean warriors. They took him to Glele, who was waiting in the bush to interrogate him, and, according to Cudjo, Glele told his interpreters, "Astee dis man why he put his weakness agin' [against] de lion of Dahomey."[63] The king responded by calling

King Glele's nocturnal slave-raiding strategy a cowardly act, not befitting of a man.[64] King Glele ordered the man to prepare to go to Dahomey to receive his punishment, but he refused, and Glele signaled one of his warriors to decapitate him.[65]

My idea that Cudjo's farmstead was located in Owinni would remain speculative without primary data from Oyo, in general, and from Owinni, in particular. If the story was going to advance beyond this stage, and if I was going to elucidate Cudjo's origins, I had to increase my knowledge of Owinni's geography, agricultural practices, political economy, and military history. With support from the National Endowment for the Humanities, I packed my mosquito net, and I traveled to southwestern Nigeria. My research design delineated specific ethnographic baselines for cross-checking the connections between the information that Cudjo had imparted about his origins and the sources of information (intangible and material) that I found in Oyo. Travel to, and residency in, southwestern Nigeria allowed me to access pertinent source material that is housed in the Kenneth Dike Library as well as the Ibadan branch of the National Archives of Nigeria, both of which are located on the campus of the University of Ibadan. My great ambition was to solicit the indigenous perspectives of scholars, titled persons, and others who are of Yoruba descent, in order to maintain one of the important intellectual goals of the book relative to incorporating the opinions of African and African-descended peoples and in order to shed further light on the *Clotilda* Africans' specific West African geographical and cultural connections.

Arriving in Lagos, I was met by Mr. Ferdinand Addo, who provided me with overnight accommodations, an associate of my dear colleague, Dr. Charles Amissah, at Hampton University. The next morning, I went to the Holiday Inn to meet my car that never came. But, Oluwon, the hotel's protocol officer, transported me to the University of Ibadan where I met Dr. Olutayo Adesina, head of the Department of History, and his wife, Kemi. They gave me accommodations in their house, and they helped to facilitate my travels in, and outside of, Ibadan. The largest city in West Africa, Ibadan was congested and bustling with people engaged in all manner of business. Once I settled into my quarters, I made arrangements to travel to Oyo where I would conduct field research. I proceeded there by way of the Oyo road that was in a treacherous state, typical of many West African roads after they have been washed out during the rainy season. Littered with potholes, and having no definable shoulder, the road, and its conditions, had caused several fuel tankers to jackknife and burn. On several occasions, I wanted to stop to photograph the longhorn cattle being herded by Fulani men, but I was deterred, somewhat, by reports of road bandits who robbed indigenes and foreigners.

In keeping with Yoruba tradition, royal drummers greet the author upon arrival at the Afin (royal palace) of Oyo. Photograph by Natalie S. Robertson, PhD (2003).

Considering all of these road hazards, I was lucky to have a good driver who made every effort to ensure safe passage.

One hour or so after we left Ibadan, we arrived in the city of Oyo. We went to the *Afin*, the historic palace of the *Alafin*. Once inside, we proceeded to a secondary gate, where we parked and exited the van. Immediately, I was met by royal drummers playing *Dundun* or talking drums that spoke to me saying, *"Ekaabo,"* which means "welcome" in the Yoruba language. However, traditional African drumming is a sophisticated form of communication, as slaveowners learned in the Americas. As a security measure, the drum cadences alert the Alafin and his officials of not only the presence of a visitor, but the identity of the visitor.[66] I reciprocated by dancing to drumbeats. This opened the way for communication between me and palace officials who came to learn the nature of my business. I told them that I wanted to consult the palace historians regarding slave-raiding activities in Oyo. While they took my request inside, I waited outside for a response.

The curious looks that I received there, and in other places, suggested that some of the indigenes are not accustomed to seeing black Americans operating in the capacity of researchers, an image that counters stereotypical images of blacks as criminals, thugs, and drug addicts that are pervasive in British and North American media. Images are powerfully persuasive, hence the need for Africans to see more black Americans not only as scholars but as consumers of African culture. My identity as an American researcher was, on some levels, complicated by my femaleness in Yorubaland, where a double patriarchy exists. One patriarchy is indigenous; the other is an imported variety from Britain. My femaleness was met with some resistance by males operating in official capacities. In some instances, it was better for my research assistant, Olayinka Adekola, to speak on my behalf, not only as a way of introducing me but as a matter of gender protocol. No doubt, my identity limited my access to certain types of information. But, that was to be both expected and understood in the foreign contexts in which I was working. In most cases, I was well received and respected for the work that I was doing. More importantly, I had come to Yorubaland to hear and learn from the indigenous voice that figures so prominently in this reconstruction of the *Clotilda* case.

Africa is a repository for the most ancient, sophisticated body of knowledge the world will ever know, the true depths of which it will never know. There are various degrees of knowledge in Africa, but they generally fall into two categories: 1) esoteric knowledge (with multiple levels); and 2) knowledge that is shared with the outsider. Access to the first category of knowledge is restricted, and access to the second category depends upon several variables that are both controllable and uncontrollable. An experienced researcher knows, and respects, the fact that there are people, places, and information that will always remain inaccessible. In African societies, esotericism is the essence of power. Insofar as I was not reared in Yoruba cultural contexts, however, I needed to consult the indigenes. The messengers returned to inform me that I had been granted permission to come inside the palace. Once inside, I was asked to remove my shoes. I complied, understanding that this was sacred ground. I was escorted into a narrow passageway where several elders sat, known officially as the *ilari*. They are who the sage visionary Ayi Kwei Armah has called the *Traditionalists*,[67] the keepers of indigenous knowledge, history, and culture.

Consulting the *ilari* and other titled officials of the *Afin* was necessary because truth is not common knowledge. Truth is sought by the brave among us because, in order to arrive at it, one must be willing to tread deep political waters that have dangerous undertows. Survival is one part of the journey. A willingness to change one's perspective, based upon newly discovered truths, represents real intellectual, psychological, and emotional growth. Tradition was what I sought on the inside of the palace, since, on the outside of it, in certain places, the deterioration of culture seems to have reached a crisis level. In fact, many Yoruba peoples, reared on Eurocentric interpretations of African cultures, have come to regard aspects of their own culture as evil. Some Yoruba Christians, for example, would be repulsed by the mere mentioning of Shango, their indigenous god of thunder, lightning, and fire, while statues of Shango are being sold at high prices in the major museums and auction houses of the world as "primitive art."

The material culture that Africans discard, others collect and market. Shango, Oduduwa, Ifa, Ogun, and other African gods required indigenes to be custodians of their cultural heritages and to protect them from destruction. Loss of African culture is understandable outside of Africa, especially in cases where African Americans have been separated from the continent by space and time. But, it is disturbing to see continental Africans, who have full knowledge of their cultural origins, reject their African heritages. I had come to Africa in search of information that would help elucidate the origins of the *Clotilda* Africans. With increased Europeanization of African cultures, however, tracing origins will become more difficult to achieve, particularly if Africans do not mobilize to preserve their own histories and material culture.

In addition to being the keepers of traditional culture, titled and subordinate ilari have served as the Alafin's messengers and agents in religious, political, and economic matters.[68] As royal messengers, ilari meet with strangers, ascertain the nature of their visit, and determine if the business warrants the attention of the Alafin. While my interpreter introduced me to the ilari and others who gathered to learn the nature of my business, I was offered

Obaloluwa (left), Ikudefun (center), and Obakayeja (right) are ilari (royal messengers) at the Afin in Oyo. Photograph by Natalie S. Robertson, PhD (2003).

some water as a welcoming gesture. Kemi Adesina, a University of Ibadan student who served as my interpreter during my first visit to the Afin, told the ilari that I had come to collect some data regarding the history of Owinni within the context of Oyo-Dahomey relations. She told them, more specifically, that I was tracing the geographical and cultural origins of some Yoruba-speaking captives who were smuggled into the United States in 1860.

Ikudefùn was the first titled ilari to contribute some information regarding the history of Owinni. He said that Owinni is a royal farmstead that belongs to the Alafin.[69] Land and farm ownership symbolized the wealth and prestige of the king. One of the intellectual goals of this research entailed deciphering the meanings of Cudjo's names. Onomastic analyses require the assistance of indigenous peoples who understand the cultural nuances of complex Yoruba dialects. Ikudefùn told me that if Cudjo lived at Owinni, he would have been a child of the ilari.[70] As such, Ikudefùn stated further, Cudjo would have had three names. Indeed, Cudjo had three names that the ilari insisted upon hearing in their most corrupt forms, without any adulterations on my part. In that way, they could determine if their morphology corresponded to Yoruba names.

In Alabama, the name Cudjo was also spelled "Kujjo" and "Kogo." The ilari told me that this name would be more accurately pronounced Olakojo or Olukojo, within Oyo-Yoruba dialect and culture. This, they said, was his *abiso* name. In Yoruba culture, abiso names describe the specific circumstances surrounding the bearer's birth.[71] Olakojo, for example, means "the gathering or amassing of wealth," or one who is connected to "wealth, royalty, honor." Olukojo means one who is "close to God or of God." "Ola" and "Olu" are prefixes that were attached to royal names and lineages.[72] As a child of the ilari, and as a resident of a royal farmstead, Cudjo would have been connected to royalty and wealth. For this reason, according to Alhaji R.O. Oladipo, the Alafin's principal private secretary, all of the residents of Owinni would have had "ola" attached to their names.[73] Cudjo's mother gave him a second name that Roche and Hurston recorded as "Kazoola" and "Kossula," respectively. This name, suggested the ilari, is a distortion of the Yoruba name *Esuola* (the letter "e" carries the sound of "ā"), a very old surname that is no longer extant. However, Nobel laureate Wole Soyinka offered *Kasunmola* as a second possibility, one that follows more closely the morphologies of "Kazoola" and "Kossula."[74]

After interviewing titled ilari in the Afin, Prince Ganiyu Ojo led me approximately five kilometers outside of Oyo town to Owinni, where the data suggests that Cudjo was captured. We arrived at the residence of the current Magaji of Owinni, Jimoh Atanda Obagbayi, who allowed us walk a trail that led to the site where Alafin Lamidi Olayiwola Adeyemi III had planned to build a new rest house. Prince Ojo also said that the Alafin used this residence as a retreat during the dry season.[75] To some extent, this information supports J.A. Atanda's claim that Owinni served historically as a place of refuge for the Alafin, since the dry season is when Dahomean infantry launched their attacks. During the dry season, the clay roads are passable, and crops are available for harvesting. Crops are paid as components of tribute, on an annual basis, and they are extorted on a short-term basis as hungry slave raiders travel near productive farmsteads. If the demand for crops is not met, the Dahomeans confiscated the crops. As a punishment for noncompliance, the rulers and residents of farmsteads were killed or captured for disposal at the slave raiders' discretion.[76] Within the context of New Oyo's political economy, Alafin Atiba reserved Owinni as a site for one of his royal farmsteads.[77]

Located outside of the city of Oyo, near the towns of Akinmorin, Aawon, Aawe, and Ilora, Owinni was derived from forest, slashed and burned to facilitate farming.[78] Along the trail, we encountered Mudashiru Adigun Babalola, Magaji Obagbayi's son, who was cultivating yams using only a hoe. Other crops are cultivated at Owinni, including cassava, corn, okra, bananas, tangerines, pineapples, melons, peppers, and oil palms. In fact, oil palms were cultivated on a massive scale in New Oyo.[79] Due to frequent, and violent, incursions on Yoruba territories by Dahomean warriors, New Oyo was encased in a protective dual wall system with gates ("bode") situated at strategic points. In Alabama, Cudjo built an eight-gate enclosure around his house as a memorial to his African town of origin.[80] New Oyo's outer wall contained nine gates. However, one gate, Bode Aawe (also called Bode Bashorun), remained restricted for the exclusive use of the Bashorun of New Oyo.[81]

The Bashorun wielded tremendous power, having authority over all provincial kings and having the ability to influence both the enthronement and dethronement of the Alafin.[82] Such power entitled him to his own compound accessed via his private gate in the city wall. The insightful prince and Yoruba scholar S.O. Babayemi explained the identities and functions of New Oyo's gates in this way:

> Of the nine gates that entered the present Oyo in the nineteenth century, only one, Bode Aawe, was controlled by the Basorun. The ilari were stationed at each of the other gates as toll collectors. They built houses beside the gates where they lived and cultivated the land around the gates. They collected tolls from farmers and traders who entered the town and all the revenues collected at each of these gates reimbursed the palace treasury. The descendants of these gatekeepers still cultivate the land around the gates.[83]

Sikiru Adeoye demonstrates the use of the large hoe in the cultivation of yams at Owinni, Oyo's royal farmstead. Photograph by Natalie S. Robertson, PhD (2003).

As a resident of Owinni, Cudjo would have known that New Oyo's wall system had eight gates for the ilari and one gate for the Basorun. Because Bode Aawe was the exclusive domain of the Basorun, access to that gate, and the concept thereof, would have remained restricted philosophically even in Alabama. As a Yoruba man who carried his indigenous values with him across the Atlantic, Cudjo would have respected the restriction by omitting that gate from the enclosure that he built around his house in AfricaTown.

Being located five kilometers from the Afin means that the royal farm of Owinni had its own wall-gate system. Economically, gates are necessary for regulating the collection of tolls that enrich the royal coffers.[84] In Owinni and its vicinity, ilari collected tolls at Bode Oyatutu, Bode Fatala, and Bode Gogo. Toll gates were also placed strategically at crossings along rivers that surrounded Owinni and other royal farms.[85] Gates regulated tolls at the Awon River crossing on the western bank of Owinni. Further west, tolls were collected at two crossings along the Ogun River, Ogun Fashina and Ogun Alabi. Hence, residents of Owinni were surrounded by gates in every direction, meant to regulate trade and provide security for the royal farms. The rivers Aawon and Ogun, on Owinni's left side, are situated in the forest. Alafin

Atiba further enhanced New Oyo's security system by placing sentinels in the forest. The *tanimola* (sentinel), for example, was garrisoned to conduct reconnaissance and to detect the advancement of *oni sunmomi* (invaders).[86]

The tanimola was responsible for monitoring the approach of enemies advancing from the west. Not only were Dahomean warriors known to pass Owinni in route from Oyo to Ilorin, but Dahomean warriors frequently raided Yoruba farms.[87] New Oyo's farms expanded to the Upper Ogun Forest Reserve.[88] At Owinni, Prince Ojo showed me the remains of a cavernous ditch that extends to Upper Ogun, meant to trap Dahomean forces, thereby preventing them from invading New Oyo's territories from the west.[89] Apparently, sentinels, ditches, walls, and gates did not always prevent attacks by Dahomeans, who approached their target zones by stealth. They camped in the vicinity of rivers and farms, in order to spy on farmers before launching an attack.[90] Akinjogbin suggested that the Dahomean infantry approached Owinni from the west, via the Ogun River forest. Indeed, the river crossing Ogun Alabi, situated parallel to the Iseyin Road, would have provided them direct access to Owinni.

Cudjo's claim that his king was captured when he ran out of the gates has significance relative to both the spatial layout of royal farmsteads and to the functions of ilari stationed there. As gatekeepers, the ilaris' houses would have been located near the gates, their domain. It would have been their responsibilities to investigate any breach of security, and to protect the Alafin's farmsteads that are extensions of the New Oyo Empire. In the spirit of his ancestors, Cudjo installed the eight-gate enclosure around his house in Alabama as a memorial to New Oyo, to which his farmstead owed its allegiance. Moreover, the name Kasunmola, which Soyinka suggested as the formal Yoruba spelling of Cudjo's second name Kossula/Kazoola, is comprised of the words "ka sunmo odi imola." Collectivetly, they mean "let us be near the odi imola or fence of wealth, fence of knowledge."

Allegiance is an integral component of Yoruba political thought and practice. Cudjo's king refused to give up the crops, for the reason that they were the property of the Alafin and the people.[91] This response has nationalistic and nativistic implications: his first obligation was to feed the people of his community and his nation (or empire). The data suggests strongly that Cudjo's king was someone in the form of a Magaji whom Johnson defines as a "provincial king."[92] In 1860, the year in which Cudjo was captured, Magaji Obagbori supervised cultivation at Owinni. To some extent, the management of the royal farms is the collaborative responsibility of the Magajis and ilari. Obagbori is a title that means "the King, the overcomer."[93] The titled officials are thought to overcome all obstacles to the success of their reign and that of the Alafin, whose royal property they were entrusted to protect. Cudjo's king refused to go to Dahomey with King Glele because doing so meant that he would be abandoning, as he was purported to have said, "the land that my father and his fathers rule before I was born."[94] Indeed, the Magaji, as the eldest son, inherits a large estate.[95] As such, he was obligated to protect that estate, an ancestral duty that he cannot neglect. The large size of the estate was reflected in the fact that King Glele demanded half of the crops, vowing to attack if the demand was not met. This is a situation that King Glele would not have preoccupied himself with if the reward was insignificant.

King Glele's demand would have been viewed automatically as an insult to Yoruba sovereignty. And, it was the expressed duty of Magajis "to repel insults and indignities" that befell the Oyo Empire.[96] Moreover, the Oyo would not cower before its former vassal, Dahomey. By 1860, Dahomey had grown too powerful for Oyo to contain. Consequently, many Oyo farms, villages, and towns were ravaged by the Dahomeans. Since Oyo officials were allegiant to the Alafin, attacking them was synonymous with assaulting the Alafin himself, insofar as Dahomey was concerned. The king of Cudjo's farmstead, for example, would have been representative of the Alafin Adelu, not Adelu himself. Oyo's history does not record the capture of Alafin Adelu, during the time of the raid on Cudjo's farmstead. Typically, the Alafin had bodyguards and escape options available to him that many of his titled officials did not. Consequently, Oyo royals found themselves caught in the jaws of the lion.

For the protection of the king, the empire, and the people, titled persons were expected to sacrifice their own lives. In her first interview with Cudjo, Hurston recorded "Adbaku" and "Ibaku" as the name of the king of Cudjo's farmstead.[97] This is a distortion of the Yoruba words *ab oba ku*, identifying the ruler of Cudjo's farmstead as "one who is expected to die with the oba or king."[98] In Oyo, persons bearing this title enjoy high status within the administration of the Alafin. Cudjo, by calling the ruler of his farmstead a "king," was referencing the fact that Magajis, ilari, and other titled persons are the representatives and the embodiment of the king, as is reflected in their names.[99]

Cudjo's third name, the same one borne by his father, was recorded as Olo-loo-ay.[100] Ikudefùn told me that this name is a distortion of the Yoruba name Obalolu, or more completely, Obaloluwa. This was confirmed by Obakayeja, the oldest titled *ilari*. Indigenes can detect and recapture the phonetic and cultural nuances of African names that have been lost in English translations. Anglophones omitted "ba" from the name. Therefore, Obalo-luwa became Ololuwa that, in turn, became Olo-loo-ay. Obaloluwa is an ilari house name that is still extant in Oyo. The name means that "where there is a king, the king is as God" or "the King is supreme," as confirmed by ilari Obaloluwa himself.[101]

Titled ilari had specific duties within the organization of the palace. Ikudefùn, for example, regulated the hunters and traders.[102] The house of Obaloluwa, which is more than five generations old, was a compound of warriors.[103] The fact that the house of Obaloluwa was a compound of warriors is significant, in light of the fact that Cudjo hailed from a farmstead that began to prepare boys to fight at the age of 14, and, during his initiation, he learned war tactics and songs such as "Ofu, ofu, tiggy, tiggy, tiggy, tiggy, batim, ofu ofu, tiggy, tiggy, tiggy, tiggy batim! Ofu batim en ko esse!"[104] Chief Alhaji Olatunde Iyanda, who resides in the Monsifa area of Oyo, asserts that the words should be Ofu, jigi, jigi, jigi...a song associated with Ifa, the Yoruba deity of wisdom, and sung as an aid in freeing someone from captivity.[105] It is very interesting that Cudjo would recall such a "freedom song" in Alabama, where he was in captivity and from which he wanted to be freed. In Whinney, being called to war was considered an honor, and Cudjo looked forward to fulfilling that duty with the exuberance of a young boy on the threshold of manhood. However, members of his farmstead, ordinarily a peaceful place, did not initiate wars; they trained for war as a measure of protection. Although they did not maintain a regular army, ilari houses and farmsteads were obligated to muster up contingencies of boys and men to swell the ranks of the Oyo army when necessary.[106]

The fact that the house of Obaloluwa was more than five generations old is also important, relative to what Cudjo said about his father and his grandfather. He said that his father was a chief who was not wealthy in terms of having a lot of material possessions. In Africa, however, one's wealth can be derived from one's political connections. For example, the ilari's wealth may not be independent of the Alafin's wealth. Wealth can also be defined in terms of having lots of wives and children. Although Cudjo was one of four children born to his mother, he was one of 14 born to his father who had three wives.[107] He said that his grandfather did not reside with him because he was one of the king's officers, and he accompanied the king everywhere he traveled.[108] The fact that Cudjo's grandfather traveled with the king on every occasion, indicates generally that he was a royal bodyguard. Only the Alafin would have had such bodyguards in the form of ilari and, more hierarchically, in the form of the *Ona Olu kun esin*. As one who accompanied the king, Cudjo's grandfather's high rank was reflected in the fact that he lived in his own compound, separately from Cudjo, and the king had given him a large amount of land, sheep, and goats.[109] If the land and animals were personal gifts bestowed upon him directly by the king, then his political title and position was more senior than that of the ilari who managed land for the Alafin. Thus, by way of both his grandfather, and his father, Cudjo was descended from royal lineages, and he was connected to wealth.

During my visit to the Afin, I spoke with the *Ona Olo kun Esin*, whose *oriki*, or praise name, is *Oloye Olo kun Esin Aroju bobaku lamo*, meaning "the chief that we know who manages to die with the king."[110] The *Ona Olo kun Esin* further described himself as the "male wife" of the Alafin. As such, he will act as his chief servant in the afterlife as he does in the present life.[111] He told me that the *Olo kun Esin*'s primary concern is the king's safety and palace security while the security of the royal farms was the responsibility of the ilari. Obakayeja, the titled ilari who oversaw the labor of subordinate ilari working on farms, said that slave raiders captured several ilari and their family members, especially wives and children.[112] Frequent raids on Oyo farms and territories increased the numbers of titled, royal persons included in many slave cargoes.

While some of their African names have been distorted, or completely lost, the *Clotilda* captives' facial cicatrices served as iconographic links to their respective cultures of origin. Some of the *Clotilda* captives wore three horizontal lines on each cheek (in combination with two vertical lines between the eyes).[113] The three horizontal lines, within the cultural and political milieux of southwestern Nigeria, are known as *Abaja* marks. Professor Olorundare Oguntomisin remarked that cicatrices helped Yoruba slave raiders identify members of their own cultural group so as to prevent them from capturing and selling their own people into slavery, a consideration that disappeared with the fall of the Old Oyo Empire.[114] Abaja cicatrices identify the wearers as hailing from royal lineages of Oyo.[115]

The attack on Cudjo's farmstead coincides not only with the death of King Ghezo and the rise of his son Glele in Dahomey, but with the death of Alafin Atiba and the rise of his son Adelu in Oyo. Preoccupied with the growing threat that was Ijaye in the late 1850s and early 1860s, Oyo's western and eastern territories were vulnerable to attack.[116] Dahomey saw this as an opportunity to pounce on Oyo, raiding its productive farms. Ilorin also raided Oyo farms at this time.[117] Professor Bolanle Awe asserted that attacks on Yoruba farms were severe.[118] On royal farmsteads, one finds hundreds of ilari cultivating the land. To the Dahomeans, the royal farmsteads were both sources of food and skilled cultivators who would be able to contribute to agriculture in Dahomey as well as in the Americas. On royal farmsteads, young farmers bunked together.[119] This sleeping arrangement increased the opportunities for slave raiders to grab significant numbers of young males, the most desirable commodities in the trans-Atlantic trade.

Agriculture and weaving were two of the most important endeavors in Yorubaland. Young cultivators and weavers were valuable commodities on both sides of the Atlantic, in addition to the products of their skilled labor. Cloth held tremendous cultural, political, and economic value in internal trade networks, and as an export, before, and during, the trans-Atlantic slave trade.[120] New Oyo was as a major center of cloth production. The cloth produced in New Oyo was a valuable element of tribute in Dahomey, where Oyo weavers were also in demand.[121] Men weave the cloth, while women spin the cotton from which the cloth was woven. This is the typical division of labor in Yoruba weaving centers. Cudjo discussed the fact that cotton cloth was woven by the men in his village.[122] In Yorubaland, the type and manner of dress varies by gender, age, and status. Cudjo discussed the fact that women wore a "square of cloth" around their waists while men wore a square of cloth draped over the left shoulder.[123] Indeed, these are traditional styles of dress in Yorubaland. However, women typically wear two wraps. The *buba* is worn on the upper body, while the *iro* is wrapped around the lower body.

New Oyo is located approximately 27 miles from Iseyin, another major center of cloth production, around which the Dahomeans launched seven successful raids.[124] Iseyin is linked to New Oyo via a major trade route that would have facilitated Dahomey's march into New Oyo's territories beyond

This Akesan market woman is wearing the Abaja cicatrice that signifies that she hails from Oyo. Photograph by Natalie S. Robertson, PhD (2003).

the Ogun River. Cudjo and other young males were vulnerable to attack on farms, in weaving centers, and in other significant centers of labor where young males are found in southwestern Nigeria. Slave raiding is only one aspect of the multidimensional process of enslavement. The second dimension involves evacuating captives to coastal markets, after capturing them in the interior. The Ogun River was an important hydrological link between the interior and the coastal markets.[125] It served often as a political, military, and economic line of demarcation in southwestern Nigeria. According to Ajetun-mobi, the Ogun River was the "most convenient" route to follow for anyone traveling from Oyo to coastal slave depots.[126]

While the Ogun River corridor would have been the most direct route to the sea, the Dahomeans did not carry Cudjo and his co-captives directly to coastal markets. Instead, they marched them in the direction of Cana. Being between 19 and 25 years of age, and as one who had been taught to hunt and survive in the bush by his elders prior to undergoing his first initiation rite into man-hood,[127] Cudjo had a good sense of geography and topography, as is the reality for many African men who are skilled hunters or long-distance travelers-traders. Thus, Cudjo was in the perfect position to observe and document cognitively the circuitous routes by which he was evacuated to the sea:

> Dey march us in de Dahomey and I see de house of de King...De house de King live in hisself, you understand me it made out of skull bones. Maybe it not made out de skull, but it lookee dat way to Cudjo, Oh Lor'! Dey got de white skull bone on de stick when dey come meet us, and de men whut march in front of us, dey got the fresh head high on de stick. De drum beat so much lookee lak de whole world is de drum dey beat on.[128]

Cudjo is referencing the Dahomean king's palace at Cana, located eight miles before Abomey. Cana is linked to Owinni via the Iseyin Road. Historically, Cana has served four important functions in the political economy of Dahomey: 1) a secondary palace for the kings of Dahomey; 2) a garrison for monitoring the movements of foreign traders who must obtain permission to pass from Cana to Abomey; 3) a sacred venue for Xwetanu (Annual Customs Ceremony); and 4) a place to celebrate war victories.

Of this last function, Cudjo and his co-captives were direct witnesses as war captives and as objects of celebration. In fact, it was customary for Glele and his predecessors to launch their annual slave-raiding campaigns from Cana and to bring their war captives there to decide their fate.[129] While interrogating Cudjo's king in the bush, King Glele was also purported to have said to him, "I take you to Dahomey, so people can see what I do with the man who insult my father."[130] Glele would have decapitated the king for the pleasure of his people at Cana, but he arrived at Cana with the severed head of the king

As a titled official, Prince Ganiyu Ojo wears double sets of Abaja cicatrices. Photograph by Natalie S. Robertson, PhD (2003).

in tow. Severed heads became war trophies and symbols of Dahomey's military strength.[131] King Ghezo's royal stool, exhibited at the Royal Palace Museum in Abomey, rests on the skulls of four Mahi chiefs who refused to pay tribute and who competed against Dahomey as suppliers of African captives to the trans-Atlantic trade.[132] When he sat on his royal stool, therefore, he sat on the heads of his enemies, a demonstration of power.

After throwing off the yoke of Oyo in 1821, according to Burton, "Gezo instituted a sacrifice at Kana, which opens as it were the customs [Xwetanu] of Agbome. The victims were made to personate in dress and avocation Oyos, a pastoral and agricultural people."[133] While some victims were made to impersonate Oyo captives, others were Oyo indigenes captured in slave raids. Dahomey maintained an annual tradition of executing 12 Oyo males in retaliation for vassalage.[134] This data helps to explain why Cudjo and his co-captives were marched to Cana before being sent to the coast. At Cana, Cudjo observed that some of the skulls were white (clean), while others were fresh (in various degrees of decay or newly cut, as in the head of Cudjo's king and those of his "relatives and friends" who were slaughtered in the raid on his farmstead).[135] Dahomean warriors were required to bring fresh heads for presentation to the king and as proof of their victories over their enemies. Cudjo recalled that during their evacuation, the Amazons stopped to smoke the heads severed from the bodies of his relatives and friends, in order to abate decomposition.[136] The Dahomeans also placed severed heads along their roads and in their market places so that, as King Kpengla asserted, "people may stumble upon them when they little expect such a sight. This gives a grandeur to my Customs [Xwetanu], far beyond the display of fine things which I buy...If I should neglect this indispensable duty, would my ancestors suffer me to live?"[137]

At Cana, those war captives who were not sacrificed to the ancestors during Xwetanu, and those who were not reduced to servitude in the Kingdom of Dahomey, were sent to the coastal markets where they were sold to slave traders. The Dahomeans celebrated their victory over Cudjo's people by drumming and feasting for several days at Cana before they marched him and his co-captives to the sea, called *Esoku* by Cudjo.[138] The trek from Cana to the sea required two to three days. Arrival at the coast signaled the end of Cudjo's and his co-captives' tortuous trek from their point of capture and the beginning of their preparation for their forced migration across the ocean, along with other Africans who had been captured in central Nigeria and in Benin.

CHAPTER 6

Central Nigeria

The Dahomeans did not march Cudjo and his co-captives directly to Whydah. Cudjo's map indicates that *Eko* was the first coastal region that they reached. *Eko* means "ecclectic gathering point," a place where diverse cultures converge to conduct business and trade. The fact that Cudjo used the word *Eko* to describe that place is significant, since he would have been familiar with that Yoruba word for Lagos. Eko is the southern terminus of an important north-south trade route that extends into the interior of Nigeria, where it connects with east-west routes.[1] From there, Cudjo and his co-captives were marched to Badagry. Support from the National Endowment for the Humanities facilitated my return to Nigeria in the summer of 2004. My research agenda included travel to Badagry, in order to enhance my knowledge of slave-trade protocol in that former slave depot. Unlike Eko, Badagry has become an important resource center for scholars seeking information about the slave trade in that area of the coast. Badagry was just as I imagined it to be, sandy, flat land with clusters of small-scaled buildings. It is a quaint little sea town with a treacherous history as a bustling slave depot. As such, its layout is similar to that of Whydah, divided into quarters reserved for foreign and indigenous slave traders.

In Badagry, I interviewed ViaVoh Mobee, a descendant of a prominent indigenous slave-trading family. Understanding that African surnames contain historical, cultural, and genealogical data, I asked ViaVoh to explain the origin and meaning of the surname Mobee. He replied by saying that the name is a combination of the Yoruba words *emun obi*.[2] Loosely translated, *emun obi* means "pick your kola nuts." His ancestors uttered these words when making the traditional West African offering of kola nuts to Portuguese slave buyers who, without being able to speak Gun, the local language, and after hearing those words so much when being greeted, converted *emun obi* to Mobi (currently spelled Mobee).[3] ViaVoh's ancestor, Boekoh, was the founding father of the Mobee slave-trading dynasty. Mobee descendants maintain a museum that houses chains and other relics from the slave trade. I placed some of those chains around my neck, as I had done 10 years earlier in Whydah. Ten years later, in Badagry, the chains seemed so much heavier. Perhaps it is because they were heavier and, because of that, the experience was much more emotional, when thinking of the extent to which people carried that weight on their bodies weakened by disease and suffering from exhaustion. There were chains for adults as well as children and infants. In fact, if a buyer were to purchase 10 to 20 Africans in Badagry, he received a bonus in the form of one to three children.[4]

Since Cudjo's map indicates that he and his co-captives were evacuated through Badagry, I wanted to know the extent to which the Dahomeans used that slave port as a connecting point in their evacuation route to Whydah. Such data would hold tremendous significance for this study, given the restrictions that were placed on the movements of outsiders relative to monopolizing the trade and protecting local peoples from slave raiders. Interestingly, the founding father of the Mobee slave-trading dynasty hailed originally from Whydah.[5] Badagry was a point of convergence and a neutral zone for traders who were willing to suspend their cultural differences to protect their business interests.[6] In this effort, "enemies" were known to form alliances. As members of the same Aja-speaking family, Gun and Fon peoples collaborated in the name of trade.

After my visit to two area museums, I got in a boat that conveyed me across the lagoon to the route that led to the beach. I, along with the interpretive guide and my research assistant, walked for 30 minutes on this route that was 1.4 kilometers long. This trek was reduced 17 minutes for captives who were forced to double their pace in route to the beach.[7] In the sweltering heat, I imagined what the whole scene must have been like—barracoons on the beach and huge ships waiting for their Black Gold in the form of African men, women, and children. Crude oil is the Black Gold that pollutes the beach today, my shoes permanently stained with it. I remained focused on the fact that the *Clotilda* captives had trekked this beach more than 144 years ago in route to Whydah.

In *The Dahomans*, Forbes noted that the king of Dahomey had claimed the beaches of Badagry and neighboring Porto Novo as Dahomean territories as early as 1849, making military excursions on both ports.[8] By the early 1860s, Dahomey had established a military garrison in Badagry.[9] Cudjo's map indicates that they traveled through Porto Novo, written by Roche as Adaché (Ajase is the Yoruba term for Porto Novo), in route to Ouidah. Thus, the question arose as to why Cudjo and his co-captives were not marched directly to Whydah from Cana, but were rerouted via Lagos and Badagry. According to Dayo Senami, an interpretive guide at Badagry, the Dahomeans not only passed through Badagry en route to Whydah, but they regularly purchased captives there before traveling on to Whydah.[10] Lagos is the southern terminus for the Ogun River, a major link to the hinterland. As there were strict laws against selling local people, captives in Lagos and Badagry came mainly from Oyo and Hausaland.[11] Generally, coastal merchants, rather than traveling to the hinterlands to capture Africans, purchased captives from hinterland slave raiders.

At one point in its history, Badagry was selling up to 300 Africans per day.[12] To fulfill the quotas and the quality demanded by foreign buyers awaiting cargoes in the Bight of Benin, African sellers engaged in inter-port trade between Lagos and Whydah. This means that some Africans were sold twice and thrice before they were placed into the hold of a slave ship. In other cases, and within the context of inter-port relations, some Africans were sold four times before leaving West Africa (sold first to a middleman, sold second to a coastal merchant, sold third to another coastal merchant, and sold fourth to a European or American buyer). The French consul at Bahia, Brazil, observed the identities of particular Africans and their ports of origin in the middle of the nineteenth century:

> The Nago [Yoruba] who probably form nine-tenths of the slaves in Bahia and are recognized by three deep transversal lines tattooed on each cheek. Nearly all of them embarked at Onim (Lagos) or at Porto Novo. The Hausas, most of whom are used in Bahia as black palanquin bearers; they nearly all come through Onim. The Gegé [Glexwe] or Dahomeans who form a powerful nation and are quite numerously represented in Bahia; they previously embarked at Whydah but today they come mostly through Porto Novo.[13]

This statement also highlights the extent to which the cultural origins of the captives might change by port, determined by the exigencies of the market, the buyers' preferences for certain Africans, slave-raiding productivity in the hinterland, and inter-port relations. A lagoon system that begins at Lagos, and is interrupted temporarily at Porto Novo, facilitated the movement of slave coffles in the inter-port traffic. At Porto Novo, slave coffles could be evacuated overland to Whydah.

Just as foreigners took a mixture of trade items to African traders, Africans marketed captives of diverse cultural backgrounds to satisfy buyers' preferences. Hausawa, Africans from Hausa-speaking regions in central and northern Nigeria, were considered intelligent by foreign buyers who desired them as "house slaves" and tanners. The *Clotilda* cargo was comprised of captives from the Hausa-speaking regions. Although the Dahomeans captured Cudjo and Albiné in Oyo, those *Clotilda* captives who originated in Hausa-speaking regions are more likely to have come into Dahomean possession by purchase, rather than by direct capture, central and northern Nigeria existing, generally, outside of Dahomey's slave-raiding range.

In order to elucidate the origins of those *Clotilda* captives taken from central Nigeria, also referred to as the Middle Belt, I traveled to that region. Doing so was, by far, the most ambitious thing I have ever done as a researcher. The Middle Belt is where Christianity meets Islam, and Jos, and other Middle Belt towns, had been experiencing ethnic and religious conflicts on the eve of my arrival in Nigeria on May 20. On several levels, Nigerian life is extremely volatile. I remember the fuel strikes and conflicts of the previous summer, and Nigeria Labor Congress leaders were threatening to launch another strike during the summer of 2004. Therefore, I had to proceed expeditiously, if I was going to collect data in the Middle Belt.

On June 3, we left Ibadan for Jos. It was an adventure in the truest sense of the term, four of us (an African American woman and three African men) traveling across Nigeria in a compact station wagon that was built in the 1980s. My derriere felt every bump, and my stomach felt every swerve, as we dodged the potholes and accidents on the road that connected Ibadan with Ogbomosho. There were no less than 50 police checkpoints along this route. Being stopped by Nigerian police with assault weapons drawn is always a tense experience, since one never knows the mindset or intent of police officers. Immediately upon being stopped, I instructed Olayinka to inform them that I was a researcher traveling between universities. He did so, but he embellished the story by telling the police that he and our two drivers were my students. Although they were not my students in the truest sense, the exigencies of that moment required that I not dispute his claim.

Indeed, I had selected my research assistant based upon his intelligence as well as his astute comprehension of political affairs and indigenous protocol. The spiel was constructed to prevent the police from detaining us and rifling through my cargo, something that they continued to do without ever asking me for my credentials or, in Nigerian military vernacular, "my particulars." At other times, I used my gold tooth to my advantage. In Yorubaland, a gold tooth signifies that the wearer has made the *hajj* or holy pilgrimage to Mecca, and

Yorubas have ancestral and cultural connections to East Africans. Thus, a female wearing a gold tooth is called *Al-haja*, respected as one who has made the *hajj*. Although I had not made the *hajj*, I began to smile when confronted by the police. This strategy made me a little less tense and the police more comfortable with my identity.

Although the journey exacted a heavy physical toll on the body, exposure to the spectacular sites, as we traveled from Ibadan to the open plains of the savannah, was a phenomenal psychological experience. Traveling through Kwara State, I could see the massive orange termite mounds, nature's architecture, that share the plains with small, well-organized hamlets occupied mainly by Fulani families. At Jebba, we reached the mighty river Niger. If I should lose my sight tomorrow, I have been blessed with the opportunity to see the ancient Niger River, legendary as a mode of transportation and as a route for evacuating Africans who were captured in the West African interior to coastal markets. The famous ancestor, Black Nationalist, and physician Martin Robison Delany led an expedition to the Niger River Valley more than 140 years ago.[14]

From Jebba, we proceeded through Niger to Kaduna State, where we checked into hotel Zakariya, on the Badiko Express By Pass, just before sunset. Kaduna State is called the "Centre of Learning," and it is the home of the world-renowned Amadu Bello University. Kaduna is also the home of excellent farmers who can be seen working their fields everywhere along the road leading to Jos. I am always amazed at the expansive tracts of land that extend as far as the eye can see. In the nineteenth century, Delany knew that Africa was a critical frontier for black Americans to empower themselves through landownership, and it remains so today. The topography changes dramatically between Niger and Jos (Plateau State), characterized by majestic rocky outcroppings that rise 4,200 feet above sea level. I was captivated by the hills and inselbergs of Kaduna State and Jos, since I had never seen anything quite as beautiful. Africa is where God and nature converge, and the various moments at which I witnessed and contemplated those convergences were almost always metaphysical, spiritual, and emotive.

In Jos, we proceeded to the University of Jos where I made contact with Dr. Joseph Jemkur, Dean of Arts and Professor of Archaeology. I did not have an appointment with him, yet he interrupted an important meeting to see me. Indeed, the ancestors were opening doors for me every step of the way, for it was Dr. Jemkur who gave me some important information regarding the direction that my research agenda should take in the Plateau-Kaduna region. Dr. Jemkur has conducted extensive archaeological research in southern Kaduna, and he is an expert on the history and culture of the peoples in that region. I told him that my data indicated that some of the *Clotilda* captives hailed from southern Kaduna, and that I wanted to concentrate my search for their geographical and cultural origins there. He asked me for the specific evidence that led me to that area. I informed him that my preliminary analyses revealed that those *Clotilda* Africans captured in the Middle Belt bore the names of the places in which they originated, and those toponyms correspond to locations in southern Kaduna.[15]

Since I did not possess large quantities of ethnographic data for those *Clotilda* Africans captured in the Middle Belt, and because those captives bore the names of the places from which they hailed, I utilized an onomastic methodological approach in southern Kaduna. Onomastics involves the study of toponyms, hydronyms, and other names that are not necessarily personal ones. In Africa, names embody important historical, cultural, political, and geographical data.[16] Apart from examining the extent to which my preliminary hunches were correct, I needed to understand the nature of slave raiding in southern Kaduna during the second half of the nineteenth century. Among the *Clotilda* Africans taken from the Middle Belt, there was an African female named Kanko. The name was one that I knew the least about. I had not been able to connect it to a specific place, based upon the information that I had available to me in the United States. Since its etymology had eluded me, I mentioned that name first.

Upon hearing that name, and after considering it within the context of my spiel regarding the direction of my research, Dr. Jemkur told me that the name Kanko was a distortion of the name *Kaninkon,* referring to a people, and their chiefdom, in southern Kaduna.[17] My reaction was a combination of excitement and anxiety. Although I had certain expectations for my research in that area, the differences between what one expects to find and what exists can be vast. The realities that one encounters in the field can support or negate original assumptions; research is only partially predictable. For these reasons, it is necessary to draw on the expertise and experiences of indigenes who know the language, customs, and geography of a particular area.

While the morphological similarity between the words Kanko and Kaninkon was recognizable, the significance that Kaninkon holds for this search for origins would become more apparent when I reached southern Kaduna. Initially, however, Dr. Jemkur's explanation of the name Kaninkon seemed to reinforce my preliminary assumptions regarding southern Kaduna as my primary research location. Since he had interrupted his meeting to see me, I did not want to impose upon him any further. Before I left, however, he invited me to return to the University of Jos to share my research findings. With honor, I accepted his invitation. Dr. Jemkur directed me to Professor

Simon Yohanna, the registrar of Kaduna State College of Education, who would further assist me in southern Kaduna that was less than one hour from Jos. We immediately proceeded there. Upon arrival, I began to see signs for villages of the Kagoro peoples, a very old culture that appeared in some of the journal articles that I obtained in the United States and that bears some relation to the peoples from whom I needed come to collect data. Therefore, I knew that I was in the right geographical and culture zones. We located Kaduna State College of Education, in Gidan Waya, Kafanchan, where I asked for Professor Yohanna, who was not available at the time. After a short wait, however, he appeared. I introduced myself, explaining the nature of my visit. As he was occupied at that particular time, he summoned Professor Sati Baba to assist me in my research endeavors. I was elated that he would serve as a liaison between members of the local community and me, not only because having an indigenous guide is necessary in Africa, but because Professor Baba is also the secretary to the Traditional Council of Kaninkon.

Sati was of tremendous assistance to me in Kafanchan, headquarters of the Jema'a Local Government Area (hereafter referred to as LGA). We checked into the New World Motel, located on Kagoro Road in Kafanchan. I arranged for Sati to meet us the following morning, in order to escort us to the Chiefdom of Kaninkon. The Chiefdom is located in Jema'a, accessed via the Kagoro Road. Upon entering the chiefdom, one sees extensive, nutrient-rich farmlands that are cultivated by both men and women. Kaninkon peoples are farmers by tradition. An indigene is not considered a true Kaninkon if he or she cannot farm.[18] The principal crops grown there are cassava, corn, sorghum, beans, and greens. Indeed, farming is at the center of the lives of the Kaninkon people. We proceeded to the palace of Mallam Tanko Tete (Tum Nikyob I), the Supreme Chief of Kaninkon. Upon arrival, we were met by palace security guards who allowed me and my research assistant to enter the palace courtyard, where we waited for Mallam Tanko Tete to receive us. At his request, we entered the palace. Mallam Tanko Tete entered the room, and we greeted him. Afterwards, the customary drink and kolas were offered to open the way for communication. I further pursued the etymology of the name Kaninkon. Regarding that name, Mallam Tanko Tete informed me that it refers to the indigenes as well as their language, although Hausa is spoken as a *lingua franca*.

Literally, *Ka nin Kon* means "come let us fight."[19] This was a challenge that Kaninkon peoples issued to their Hausa enemies who were encroaching upon their land. According to Mallam Tanko Tete, Hausa-Fulani groups were a persistent threat during the nineteenth century, seeking to control the fertile farms of the Kaninkon peoples.[20] From 1830 to 1865, the Middle Belt was

Like their ancestors, young farmers cultivate the land in Kaninkon where the Clotilda African named Kanko was captured. Photograph by Natalie S. Robertson, PhD (2004).

ravished by Hausa-Fulani jihadists who vassalized numerous non-Muslim towns and villages in the areas of Kaduna, Plateau, Abuja, Bauchi, Adamawa, Benue, and Taraba.[21] Vassalization of these territories occurred for reasons that superseded the obligation to impose Islam on non-Muslims, unless one understands the jihad as a component of Sokoto's political economy. Territories resting south, southwest, and southeast of Zaria held economic value for Sokoto, being connected to lucrative trade routes and rivers, along which caravans and canoes transported commodities that were taxed by the emirs.

In the middle of the nineteenth century, the Middle Belt was densely populated by cultivators, skilled craftsmen, metallurgists, hunters, and fishermen. The emirs taxed these occupations that were central to the livelihood of the indigenes.[22] Mallam Tanko Tete, who is writing a brief history of the Kaninkon people, confirmed this, saying that Kaninkon came under the control of the Emir of Jema'a, who levied taxes upon the indigenes. Taxes were assessed and demanded annually in the form of cowrie shells, as a flat rate. As rulers of provinces within Sokoto's geopolitical sphere of influence, the emirs were required to enrich the royal coffers by paying an annual tribute to the sultan. Africans soon replaced cowrie shells as the most important component of tributary payments.[23] To supply their own households with servants, and to satisfy the trans-Saharan and trans-Atlantic demands for laborers, emirs required vassal towns to supply large quantities of captives.[24]

The Jema'a Emirate, in collaboration with the Zaria Emirate, launched punitive raids against Kaninkon and other territories that did not pay their tribute, confiscating grains, livestock, and farmers.[25] To protect themselves from Hausa-Fulani slave raiders, Kaninkon indigenes sought refuge on the tops, and in the crevices, of area hills. Those hiding places were kept secret, and they remain so today. It was a sad moment when Mallam Tanko Tete said, "none of the Kaninkon captives came back to say what they had experienced or seen after they had been captured. They were gone forever."[26] Indeed, the *Clotilda* African named Kanko is gone forever. But her ancestral spirit has returned to Kaninkon by way of this research. Before we left the chiefdom, Sati Baba extended an open invitation to the *Clotilda* descendants to return to Kaninkon, the place of their ancestors' birth. Such an open invitation reinforces the spiritual mission of this research that establishes trans-Atlantic connections between the *Clotilda* captives and their homelands, and between the descendants and their West African cultural heritages.

Like their Kaninkon neighbors, Jaba peoples were the targets of several Hausa-Fulani punitive raids during the nineteenth century. The Jaba people were defiantly delinquent on their tributary payments, refusing to give into the demands of the Emir of Zaria.[27] Delinquent tribute always served as a pretext for slave raiding vassal towns. This, in part, explains the presence of an African called Jabba (also called J.B. in AfricaTown) in the *Clotilda* cargo. The Jaba Chiefdom is located approximately 25 miles west of Kafanchan, and it is less than one hour's drive from Kaninkon. My visit to southern Kaduna afforded me a spatial perspective that I could not have obtained without going to that area. Relative to its proximity to the Jaba Chiefdom, Kaninkon began to take on new meaning. I began to see a regional pattern emerge, with respect to the capture of those *Clotilda* Africans who hailed from southern Kaduna; they were captured in areas that were linked by the Kagoro Road. As my preliminary investigations indicated, those captives did bear the names of the places from which they hailed.

I traveled to Fada District (Kwoi), the headquarters of the Jaba Chiefdom. Upon arrival, I learned that the Supreme Chief had traveled. However, I met with two heads of districts within the Jaba Chiefdom, Dr. S.N. Sani, head of the Fada District, and Emmanuel I. Galadima, head of the District of Sabon Gari (Kwoi). Additionally, Chief Galadima is a kingmaker, one who has the authority to name a successor to the throne. The fact that they are district heads enhances their credibility as Jaba indigenes, insofar as they are steeped in the local history and lore of Jaba peoples. I asked the chiefs to discuss the meaning of the name Jaba. Dr. Sani told me that Hausas assigned the name Jaba to them, but their indigenous name is Ham.[28] I had seen this reference in some literature on Jaba peoples, but I wanted know if its etymology was traceable to Ham, one of Noah's sons.

My question ignited a discussion regarding the mythic curse of Ham and his progeny (Khemites, Cushites, and Canaanites). Apart from the mythic curse of Ham (mythic because the curse was originally placed on Ham's son, Canaan), distorted and exploited by Europeans as a justification for the enslavement of African peoples, the story of Ham reveals some important information about Ham's ancestry and progeny. If black people are the descendants of Ham, then Ham must have been black. If that is true, and because Ham is Noah's son, then Noah was also black. This reality is reinforced by the fact that the Garden of Eden was comprised of East Africa and what we currently call the Middle East. In these environs, the intensity of the sun requires humans to maintain considerable degrees of melanin in their skin for protection against ultraviolet rays; tropical man is necessarily a man of color. In fact, *Ham* means "Black" in the Hebrew language, and it is the root of *Kham* that is variantly spelled *Khem*.[29]

Biblical texts refer to East Africa as Cush. It is more appropriate, however, to refer to East Africa as Cush I, and to the Middle East as Cush II, since East Africa's geopolitical sphere of influence incorporated parts of the Middle East and extended into Asia. In fact, what is currently called Khuzistan is a reference to "Kush," and genealogical connections to Ham can be seen in names like Ham(m), Hamid, Hamdullah, Hamurabi, Muhammed, Abraham, and so on. The significance that this information holds for Jaba peoples is that their ancient ancestry, like that of the rest of the human population, is traceable to East Africa. The Jaba chiefs told me that they speak an indigenous language called Hyam. Extended research reveals that Hyam is derived from Hym (interchanged with Ham), a language that is traceable to the ancient Canaanite city of Ugarit that was extant as early as 6000 BCE.[30] In fact, the word "ham" is the root of Ras Shamra, an ancient name for Ugarit.[31]

It is not surprising that the ancestry of the Ham is traceable to East Africans, like that of all of humanity, who migrated across Africa and the rest of the world. Other Nigerian cultures have ancestral connections to East Africa and to the Middle East, including the Gobirawa, the Katsinawa, the Junkun, and the Chamba.[32] West Africa's antiquity is recorded in its artifacts as well as its technical traditions, some of which date to the period before Christ. The terracotta, microlith, and iron artifacts excavated at Nok, a Ham (Jaba) village not far from Kwoi, date to 900 BC. Travel to Nok represented one of the highlights of my research odyssey. At Nok, I saw a few terra-cotta heads and figurines that, in terms of their manufacture, style, and iconography, are exquisite examples of the artistic and technical skills that confirm the presence of civilization among the Ham peoples 500 years prior to the establishment of

Greece and 1,200 years before European nation-states emerged. They also demonstrate the Africans' ability to extract and manipulate natural and mineral resources in their immediate environments, one of the hallmarks of civilization. Nok is one of the earliest sites for the practice of metallurgy in West Africa, where metallurgy intersects with political and military affairs that provide the basis for the production of weapons of war, instruments of execution, and accoutrements of royal status. At Nok, I visited the inside of a cave, formed of massive boulders, where Jaba elders adjudicated trials against criminals who, if found guilty of murder or other capital offenses, were executed inside that cave.

After consuming some Maltina and puff-puff (a local pastry) with the Jaba chiefs, I began to inquire about slave-raiding activities in Jaba territories. Dr. Sani said that the principal slave raiders were Hausa horsemen. Because Jaba houses and villages are nestled among craggy gneissic rocks and inselbergs, however, Hausa horsemen needed the assistance of Jaba indigenes to flush other Jabas out of their hiding places in the cracks, crevices, and caves of local hills.[33] In addition to seeking refuge on the tops, and in the crevices of hills, the Jaba dug trenches, covering them with grasses, in order to trap horsemen. I was curious about the fact that the *Clotilda* African named Jabba, and his co-captives from the Middle Belt, retained the names of the places in which they were captured. Chief Galadima informed me that it is typical for Jaba peoples, as well as other Africans, who, when situated in foreign places, to identify themselves by the regions, towns, or quarters from which they hail.[34]

Even when Jaba indigenes are in another part of Nigeria, they will identify with their home quarters or *Angwam Jaba*. For example, one can find Jaba quarters as far away as Sokoto, where Jaba peoples conduct trade. "Jaba men will keep their name anywhere they go. If a Jaba is asked 'what is your name,' he or she is likely to re-interpret the question to mean 'where are you from,'" said Chief Galadima.[35] They will not identify themselves so much by personal names when they are in the company of strangers. This will hold true especially when they are in the midst of captives with whom they have no cultural affiliation. In captivity, toponyms are useful when an indigene is attempting to reconnect to his or her place of origin. Under those circumstances, African captives never forget their homeland. Instead, they conjure up images, remembrances, and discussions of that place, a psychological and emotional link that offers hope for return to their homes.

Names and traditions connect people to their homelands. Although I did not have much information about Jabba, I possessed one important kernel of ethnographic data about him. Jabba was a healer, according to Augustine

Sati Baba, Secretary to the Supreme Chief of Kaninkon, Mallam Tanko Tete, wears cicatrices that connect him to both Kaninkon and Jabaland, the home of the Clotilda captive named Jabba. Photograph by Natalie S. Robertson, PhD (2004).

Meaher, Tim's son.[36] Like their Kaninkon neighbors, Jaba peoples are farmers. In Africa, cultivation is another hallmark of civilization that dates to antiquity. Africans who are experienced cultivators know the properties and efficacies of various plants, trees, roots, and barks. It comes as no great surprise, therefore, that one finds excellent herbalists and healers in Africa. However, it is fascinating to find so many healers localized in one place, as in the case of Jaba peoples. Every Jaba household specializes in the development of a specific cure for a particular disease (they can even cure leprosy).[37] The ingredients for certain medicines are kept secret, transferred from one generation to the next within the same family. In the Jaba Chiefdom, not only is traditional medicine still extremely important, but Jaba peoples prefer their traditional medicines over Western pharmaceuticals.

When I asked the Jaba chiefs how they felt about their ancestors being sold into slavery, they offered the following comment:

> We are saddened by the slave trade that had negative consequences for our people who fought attempts to enslave them for refusing to pay tribute and taxes. Otherwise, we were peaceful people. But, it must be remembered that among the

Jaba farmers converse with the author at Nok. Photograph by Natalie S. Robertson, PhD (2004).

many people that the slave trade took away were many chiefs who were custo-dians of philosophy, indigenous knowledge, and science. We must not forget the millions of people who were lost on the way, on land and at sea, in addition to those who were landed.[38]

Dr. Sani, who is a veterinarian and a ranch owner, and Chief Galadima, who is an engineer, invited the *Clotilda* descendants to return to Jabaland to help them in their entrepreneurial efforts to develop the Jaba Chiefdom. Such an invitation is very important in the political scheme of things, since there is a need for improved relations and collaborations between continental Africans and African Americans. That invitation from the Jaba chiefs increased my optimism that relations between Africans and African Americans will be strengthened, for the uplift of our communities on both sides of the Atlantic.

In AfricaTown, Roche categorized the *Clotilda* Africans as "Tarkars."[39] However, the *Clotilda* cargo was culturally diverse. Rather than defining the entire cargo, the name "Tarkar" refers to a culture cluster within it. Roche does not define this name, nor does she link it to a specific place in West Africa. The *Clotilda* African called Abackey told Byers that she originated in what he recorded as *Ataka*.[40] But, Byers provides no further description of that place. In the historiography on the Middle Belt region, I found one minor reference to Ataka.[41] It is described as a small hamlet on the border that sepa-rates eastern Zaria and western Plateau State (formerly Plateau Province).

This border region is located in southern Kaduna. I aimed to discover the relationship between Tarkar and Ataka, if one existed, within the cultural-linguistic milieu of southern Kaduna. I mentioned the name Ataka to Sati who informed me that the place still existed, located east of Kafanchan. In order to gain some geographical and historical perspective on this place, relative to Kaninkon and Jaba, I traveled to Ataka.

Ataka is located in Kaura LGA. Access to Ataka is via the Kagoro Road where a sign reads: "Takad Chiefdom, Head Quarters, Fadan Attakar." The Takad Chiefdom is bordered on the east by Plateau State, and on the south and west by Jema'a LGA. As we drove to the headquarters, it became apparent that the word "Ataka" is a truncated version of the name *Attakar*, the headquarters of the Takad Chiefdom. And, rather than consisting of one hamlet, Attakar is comprised of a cluster of well-maintained hamlets enclosed by cactus hedges that served historically as protective barriers against invasion by slave raiders on horseback. Upon arrival at the headquarters, we met the wife of Tobias Nkom Wada, the Agwam Takad I, who informed us that the chief was not available. I left my business card, and I told her that I would return the following day. Meanwhile, I needed to hear my mother's voice; she had not heard from me for several days after I left Ibadan. In southern Kaduna, telephone and Internet access was extremely limited. While traveling back to New World Motel in Kafanchan, we made a sudden stop on the road. My research assistant spotted an opportunity to make a telephone call. I saw only three men in the middle of a field. When we got closer to the spot, it was, in fact, three young men standing on a stone square. The stone square had a pole attached to it; at the top of the pole was an umbrella to shield them from the sun. Three cellular phones dangled from the umbrella's ribs. The enterprising young men were pulling signals from distant satellites. In fact, they did dial my number, and I spoke to my mother from the middle of a field in southern Kaduna. Ingenious!

The following morning, we traveled back to the Takad Chiefdom where the Agwam awaited our arrival. After sharing some Maltina, I told him that my research led me to his chiefdom in search of information that would elucidate the origins of Africans whom I suspected had been captured in his region. The Agwam was very curious about the story of the *Clotilda* captives, and he was quite surprised that I had traveled so far to collect data. He was even more excited about the fact that I was an African American scholar, having very little to no contact with African Americans in that interior region of Nigeria. I told the Agwam that the *Clotilda* African called Abackey was captured in Ataka, a truncated version of that name Attakar. Therefore, I needed some information about that name. According to the Agwam, Attakar is a name that

Located in Attakar, this round house typifies those found on farmsteads throughout Nigeria. Photograph by Natalie S. Robertson, PhD (2004).

Hausa invaders imposed on the indigenes of that area, and European writers entered it into the historical record.[42] But the indigenes call themselves, and their language, Takad.

The Agwam told me that the history of the Takad people began with their ancestor A'Kat. It is not correct to say that A'Kat founded the Takad Chiefdom, since chieftancy, particularly as it is currently defined, is a relatively recent form of governance in Takadland. Before Takad was officially designated a chiefdom, indigenes were governed by five descendants of A'Kat (Akpi A'shong, Layam, Ajang, Kabekwai, and Mindong). Today, kingmakers or those elders who are responsible for selecting candidates for the title of Supreme Chief of Takad, hail from among these five clans that comprise the Takad Chiefdom.[43] The occupations of the Takad peoples are reflected in the colors of the Agwam's royal headdress. Red symbolizes authority, and brown represents the skin of a leopard.[44] A'Kat and his descendants were hunters of wild animals. Leopards were numerous, and they often attacked people. Any Takad hunter who killed a leopard was venerated as a brave hero. In fact, this is true for hunters in other African cultures that view leopards as symbols of power.

Leopards are still respected, and they have been adopted as a royal symbol of the Takad Chiefdom. Within the color scheme of the royal headdress, green signifies the fact that 80 percent of the Attakar people are cultivators.[45] Their principal crops are yams, corn, cassava, greens, beans, groundnuts, bananas, oranges, and mangoes. In Takad, one sees nothing but farmers cultivating the plains that extend to hills at the border of Plateau State. The white color of the royal crown symbolizes the easy spirit and peace-loving nature of the Takad peoples. In AfricaTown, Abackey described her people as being "peaceful farmers and villagers."[46] They were not warriors who could easily fend off slave raids by Hausa-Fulani horsemen. Looking out over the cultivated plains, one can imagine the horror that farmers felt when they saw the Hausa-Fulani slave raiders racing across the fields towards them, to run them down, to capture them, and to carry them off, never to be seen again.

Beyond launching poisoned arrows at their attackers, their best defense was to seek refuge in the hills on Takad's eastern boundary. At one time in their history, Takad peoples used the hills as their primary place of residence. The high elevations of those hills allowed them to engage in reconnaissance, to see approaching enemies. Like their Kaninkon neighbors, Takad peoples used caves at the base of the hills as hiding places. Access to them was restricted, and new settlers were required to live elsewhere.[47] In fact, Takad indigenes continue to occupy the hills, despite the Agwam's requests that they relocate to the plains below. Rather than ignoring the wishes of their current leader, they are honoring the legacy of their ancestors who occupied the hills before them. On the hills, they maintain a well-organized society in which they operate a school for their children, the Primary School of Anturung-Attakar.[48] Yet, they are not so remote from the affairs of the plains that they do not participate in the political affairs of Kaura LGA of which Attakar is a part.

Takads were enslaved in a variety of ways. In addition to falling victim to indiscriminate slave raids by Hausa-Fulani horsemen, families sold young males that they deemed "timid" or "unfit" for farm work.[49] Others were victims of punitive raids launched to collect delinquent revenues in a tax system that the emirs imposed on the indigenes. Takads were exported from southern Kaduna because they possessed agricultural and hunting skills that were useful to the emirs who owned farmland and to plantation owners in other parts of the world. Particular culture clusters that filled the holds of American and European slave ships in the nineteenth century were captured in Zaria Province, which was dubbed "Chief of Slaves,"[50] being one of the major suppliers of captives to the trans-Saharan and trans-Atlantic trades. In reality, the entire Middle Belt area was a great reservoir of potential captives for the slave trades.

Mr. and Mrs. Tobias Wada, the Agwam (Supreme Chief) of Attakar where Abache (Abackey) and other Clotilda captives were captured. Photograph by Natalie S. Robertson, PhD (2004).

The cultural identities of indigenes might be somewhat difficult to distinguish in southern Kaduna, where cultural boundaries are superseded for several reasons, intermarriage between groups being chief among them. Sati Baba, for example, was born in a Jaba household, but he lives among Kaninkon people. To signify his connection to both groups, he wears Jaba cicatrices consisting of three vertical lines on his right and left temples, and he wears one horizontal line that stretches from the bridge of his nose across the most prominent part of his left cheek, the traditional Kaninkon mark. However, a similar mark is worn by Gwari peoples in the Suleja-Abuja area of Niger State. In the middle of the nineteenth century, provincial and cultural boundaries were meaningless to various peoples seeking safe harbor from slave raiders. Culture clusters that exist in close proximity to one another share language and traditions. This is especially characteristic of the Middle Belt, where 79 percent of Nigeria's ethnic groups are clustered.[51] Moreover, the Middle Belt is geographically and culturally distinct from southwestern Nigeria.

Abackey's name was also spelled Abaché by Roche. The latter spelling identifies her as "a Bache" indigene from the Bache village area of western Plateau Province, on the Takad Chiefdom's eastern border (contemporaneously, indigenes prefer the name Bazu over Bache, the latter being a

These men reside in the Attakar hills once used as defensive sites during slave raids conducted by Hausa horsemen on the plains. Photograph by Benedict Kanyip for Natalie S. Robertson, PhD (2004).

corruption of the former). Byers names Ataka as Abackey's place of origin. Ataka and Attakar are one in the same places, the royal seat of the Takad Chiefdom. However, Attakar and its variant spellings (Atakar, Attaka, and Takat) are also classified as dialects of the Kataf peoples, the northern neighbors of the Takads, who were heavily raided in the second half of the nineteenth century. Therefore, when Roche attempted to categorize the *Clotilda* African as *Tarkars*, she did not comprehend the fact that the *Clotilda* cargo contained clusters of distinct cultures from various places in southwestern Nigeria, central Nigeria, and the Republic of Benin. Moreover, the cluster from southern Kaduna was more heterogeneous than the Yoruba cluster from southwestern Nigeria.

Roche also documented that the "Tarkar village" contained Filanee, Goombardi, and Ejasha visitors when it was raided.[52] These are modifications of the names Filani (also spelled Fulani), Gambari, and Ijesa. According to the Agwam, *Gambari* is a name that Yorubas used to refer to Hausa merchants.[53] One finds Fulani herdsmen and Gambari (and Ijesa-Yoruba) merchants plying their trades in various places in the Middle Belt. In general, southern Kaduna became what Jemkur describes as a "stronghold of Fulani settlement."[54] Fulani herdsmen can still be seen in the Takad Chiefdom, as well as in other places in southern Kaduna and Plateau (tsetse-free zone) with fertile, well-hydrated grazing lands. Interestingly, Fulani herdsmen's search for grazing lands coincided with slave raiding, during the dry season when they, and their Hausa co-raiders, could evacuate their captives along the network of "dry season tracks."[55] Takad and Zangon Kataf are located in a historic commercial center (*zangon*) connected to the Kagoro Road, an important link in the axis of trade routes that extend in the four cardinal points of direction.[56] Thus, it would have been a collecting point for Gambari merchants as well as other long-distance traders. Such commercial centers often contained quarters for traders who are not indigenous to the immediate area, such as Ijesa merchants from Yorubaland. Thousands of Takad, Kataf, Bache (Bazu), Jaba, and Kaninkon captives were evacuated along the various trade routes that radiated out of the aforementioned commercial center to trans-Saharan and coastal markets.

By traveling to southern Kaduna, I made some important discoveries regarding the cultural and geographical origins of those *Clotilda* Africans who originated in that area. It became apparent that Abackey, Jabba, Kanko, and their Attakar co-captives were captured within a 30-mile radius of Kafanchan, in hamlets, fields, and towns that are linked by the Kagoro Road. Secondly, they hailed from groups that were heavily raided by Hausa-Fulani horsemen during the nineteenth century. Thirdly, their indigenous descendants remain in those areas today. Before I left Takad, I asked the Agwam if he had a message for the *Clotilda* descendants in AfricaTown. He replied, "my wish for your research is that it would solidify, without a doubt, those trans-Atlantic links that will allow Attakar peoples to confidently think of the *Clotilda* descendants as brothers and sisters."[57] Lastly, he extended Takad land to the *Clotilda* descendants, just as the Kaninkon and Jaba chiefs had done. In addition to being spiritually moving, the offers of land by Africans to black Americans has historical precedence. During his exploratory mission to the Niger Valley made one year before the *Clotilda* smuggling venture occurred, Martin Delany secured land for the repatriation of black Americans on African soil. On October 25, 1859, King Dosunmu of Lagos gave Delany a deed to land in Okai Po.[58] Subsequently, Delany traveled to Abeokuta, where the Alake (king) Okukenu, Bashorun Somoye, and numerous Baloguns (warlords), signed and sealed a document granting black Americans the right to settle in Abeokuta among the Egba-Yoruba peoples and instructing them to use their education, intelligence, and knowledge of the arts and sciences to improve Abeokuta.[59]

Delany was able to secure West African lands for black Americans at a time of great upheaval, when powerful warlords were confiscating valuable, productive lands for themselves. In the middle of the nineteenth century, Hausa-Fulani jihadists confiscated fertile, well-hydrated, tsetse-free lands for their cattle and horses; they gained control over lucrative trade routes; they levied taxes on indigenes, launching punitive raids against those who were delinquent in their tax payments; and, they exported highly skilled cultivators, metallurgists, healers, and tanners to trans-Saharan and coastal Atlantic markets. Middle Belt captives came from distances that were much greater than those traveled by captives who were evacuated from southwestern Nigeria. In fact, the *Clotilda* African named Kazuma said that she was sold twice before she reached Whydah.[60] Her statement indicates that she originated in a distant place situated outside of Dahomey's slave-raiding range. Instead of being captured by the Dahomeans, she was sold to them. The Dahomeans preferred to purchase captives who originated outside of their slave-raiding range, particularly those originating in distant interior regions in Nigeria, from Yoruba and Gambari merchants.[61]

Given the fact that slave cargoes obtained in the Bight of Benin in the mid-nineteenth century were comprised, in part, of captives from Nigeria's Middle Belt, I suspected that Kazuma was linked to Zuma Rock. At least, her name strongly suggests that link. One of Nigeria's natural treasures, Zuma Rock is a massive gneissic outcropping in Abuja. We arrived in Abuja at sunset, traveling a short distance to Suleja, where we checked into City Link Palace Hotel. The next morning, my drivers staged a mutiny of sorts. Road weary, they wanted to return to Ibadan. My research assistant reminded them of their obligations to the contract. If they left the Middle Belt without me, they would not be paid for the return trip. After considering the financial consequences of such a move, my drivers quickly came to their senses. I, on the other hand, did not disregard the fact that they were experienced drivers with a keen sense of geography, and that kind of knowledge was extremely important to this research. Therefore, I needed them even more than they needed me.

After my drivers recommitted themselves to the mission, I met with Alhaji M. Mohammed, who is the director of Zuma Rock Nigerian Village. He informed me that the name Zuma is extant in West and South Africa.[62] Within the context of slave trading in the Bight in the second half of the nineteenth century, and given the large number of captives from central Nigeria in the coastal markets at that time, it seems improbable that Zuma originated in South Africa. In central Nigeria, the name Zuma consists of two Hausa words: *ezhu* means "guinea fowl" and *mwa* means "catching."[63] It refers to the fact that catching guinea fowl was a major activity in the area of Zuma Rock, where an abundance of guinea fowl can still be seen in that area. Seeking additional information, I traveled a short distance to Zuma-Chaci, a small Koro village in the local forest opposite Zuma Rock Nigerian Village, not far from the main road. I met with Abdullahi S. Gani, the chief of that village. The chief informed me that he, like his Koro ancestors, is the custodian of Zuma Rock and, by extension, the history of the village.[64] However, he declined to share additional information with me, insisting that I obtain a formal letter of introduction from the office of the Local Area Government. While my drivers spoke some Hausa, a *lingua franca* of West Africa, language, culture, and religion proved to be barriers for me in this Islamic village.

In AfricaTown, Kazuma wore a cicatrice that Roche described as "three deep gashes meeting at the bridge of the nose, and running diagonally across each cheek."[65] I continued to investigate the origins of this pattern, and I discovered, through the assistance of Olayinka, that in Niger State in general, but in the Zuma Rock area in particular, this cicatrice is called *Agbesa*.[66] It is worn by the Gwari (*Gbagiyi* more appropriately), the major cultural group in Niger and in neighboring Nassarawa State, where the same cicatrice is referred to as *Libe*. A variation of this cicatrice, one horizontal line that runs from the bridge of the nose across the cheek, called *Yokozi*, is also found in Niger.[67] Kazuma was described as having this mark, as well. To the extent that the Gwari are located across two or more states in a slave-raiding zone, sometimes due to the forced migrations created by slave-raiding activities in the Middle Belt, Gwari peoples would be included in those coffles of Africans evacuated to coastal ports during the second half of the nineteenth century.

During my third inquiry into Kazuma's origins, I learned that her name is derived from the Gwari name *Kayizuma*, the name given to the child that is "born on the day of worship of Zuma Rock."[68] Gwari, Koro, and other groups believe that their ancestors' spirits are manifest in Zuma Rock that stands as an

This Zuma Rock resident is wearing the Yokozi cicatrice that connects her to the cultural group known as Gwari from which the Clotilda African named Kazuma also hailed. Photograph by Natalie S. Robertson, PhD (2004).

awesome work of nature.[69] Zuma Rock, and surrounding forests, became shelters for various peoples fleeing slave raiders. In the nineteenth century, group identity became linked to hill sites that served as places of refuge.[70] Therefore, Kazuma's name connects her to a place, and to important events associated with that place, Zuma Rock. The peoples of that area developed a special day of worship of Zuma Rock, in remembrance of the slave raids conducted by the emirs that carried away so many of their people.[71] While Zuma Rock served as a place of refuge for various groups seeking protection against slave raiders, it served antithetically as a reservoir of potential captives. In fact, the emirs of Abuja also captured peoples within its environs as well as in Nasarawa.[72]

No one was safe from attacks by Hausa-Fulani jihadists, who confiscated lands and subjugated indigenous peoples north and south of the Benue River. Jukun captives were sold into the trans-Atlantic slave trade, along with Chamba peoples who reside principally in what is now called Taraba State, on Benue's eastern border. It is not unusual, therefore, that the *Clotilda* cargo included an African called Chamba. Fulani-controlled trade centers along the Benue and Niger rivers, as well as the rivers themselves, facilitated the evacuation of captives to coastal markets. In the second half of the nineteenth century, the volume of captives being transported along the Niger River, between the Niger-Benue confluence and the Delta, was so great that the river was observed as being "choked with slaves."[73]

Returning to Ibadan, I contemplated the long distances that captives had been forced to travel from the Middle Belt to the coast, distances that exceeded those traveled by Cudjo and his Oyo co-captives. The day following my return to Ibadan, a brief fuel strike was implemented. I was happy to be back in Ibadan, in large measure, because my health had declined. It was only later that I learned that I had contracted community-acquired pneumonia for a second time. Maintaining good health is one of the challenges of conducting research abroad. I sacrificed my health for the opportunity to see the natural beauty of the Middle Belt and the cultural beauty of the various peoples who reside there. To the degree that I have elucidated the geographical and cultural origins of those *Clotilda* ancestors who hailed from that area, where very little knowledge of those origins existed prior to this study, the research was a tremendous success.

Two members of the *Clotilda* cargo hailed from places inside of the Republic of Benin. The ancestor Booker T. Washington, a graduate of Hampton Institute (formerly Hampton Normal and Agricultural Institute) and founder of Tuskegee Institute, traveled from Tuskegee to AfricaTown to see the people who, in the first decade of the twentieth century, were still practicing their African folkways. Washington met a *Clotilda* African who, to his amazement, was "still passing by his African name."[74] That *Clotilda* African was called Ossie Keeby. About his encounter with Keeby, Washington wrote, "meeting this old man whose dreams carry him back to Africa, I felt as if I had discovered the link by which the old life in Africa was connected with the new life in America."[75] Indeed, Washington's visit to AfricaTown caused him to reflect upon his own linkages to the slave chains that connected him to an African past, for he had been born into slavery on a plantation in Franklin County, Virginia, in 1856.[76] Washington asked Keeby if he ever thought of returning to Africa, to which Keeby replied, "Yes, I goes back to Africa every night in my dreams."[77]

Almost 50 years after their capture, the memories of their West African homelands were still fresh in the *Clotilda* Africans' minds, reinforced by desires for return to those places. Keeby told Washington that he originated among "a hill people in the uplands of Dahomey, more than 300 miles in the interior of Benin."[78] Keeby's use of Dahomey as a landmark for identifying his place of origin is significant in his case, just as it was in the case of Cudjo. Neighboring peoples feared Dahomey as the home of treacherous slave raiders. However, precolonial Dahomey did not encompass the entire country that is contemporaneously known as the Republic of Benin. Rather, the term Dahomey referenced the empire of the Fon peoples in southern Benin.

Therefore, the name "Dahomey," as Keeby understood and used it, refers to that southern empire and, by extension, to its royal seat at Abomey. The names Dahomey and Abomey were interchangeably associated with terror in the minds of neighboring peoples, who constituted potential captives for Fon slave raiders.

Keeby's claim that he originated in the "uplands of Dahomey" means generally that he originated in a distant, interior region that is north of Abomey. The term uplands can also be a topographical reference, relating to hills, mountains, and plateaus. Benin is a tall country whose topography changes dramatically as the elevation increases in its interior regions. A possible origin for Keeby is the Borgu hills, based upon his description of his homeland and based upon the numerous clashes between Bariba, Fulani, and Yoruba warriors in that area during the second half of the nineteenth century. Comprised of ancient rocks that rise to 1,600 feet above sea level, the Borgu hills represent a topographically distinct region that stretches across northern Benin and extends into Bussa (the Bariba rulers' ancestral home in northern Nigeria). The Borgu hills of northeastern Benin encompass the cities of Nikki, Parakou, and Kandi. The Bariba is the principal group in these cities. In general, however, Borgu is a culturally diverse region, the result of what Asiwaju calls "ethnic interpenetration" by Yoruba and Fulani peoples seeking refuge from Oyo slave raiders.[79]

But, Bariba princes, or *Wasangari,* were launching raids of their own in northeastern Benin, where they depended on slave labor to cultivate their farms, selling the surplus captives into the trans-Atlantic slave trade.[80] The princes of Nikki, the second-ranked empire in Borgu, led the way in this regard, attacking and enslaving groups within Nikki's geographical limits. What increased the market value of Bariba and Yoruba captives was the fact that they were excellent metallurgists who specialized in the production of iron weapons and tools.[81] Moreover, there are historical, cultural, and linguistic connections between Bariba and Yoruba peoples. In AfricaTown, Ossie Keeby was also referred to as Olouale. Since most Yoruba words follow a noun-verb pattern, this name is more likely to have been Oluwale. The name means "a chief has come into the house," identifying the bearer as a member of a titled lineage.

Augustine Meaher wrote that, "Keba was named for a river."[82] Morphologically, and phonetically, the name Keeby resembles the word Kibi, the name of a river in Nikki. The name Ossie appears to be a modification of the Yoruba word *Osi,* which means "left." Because rivers are used as important hydrological landmarks for determining one's location in Africa, his name might indicate that he originated in an area on the left side of the river Kibi.

If this is correct, then his name, a variant spelling of which is *Kibbie*, rather than being a personal one, signifies his place of origin, following the pattern and function of the names of several members of the *Clotilda* cargo. The Borgu region of northeastern Benin had, at one time, been the political province of the Oyo Empire. That the Bariba had political ties to the Yoruba would have provided Dahomey with pretexts for sacking that region as it had done the Yoruba-frontier towns of Sabe, Ketu, and Dassa, situated on Dahomey's war-path. In fact, one of the *Clotilda* Africans bore the name Ardassa. The name could indicate that she was "a Dassa," or one who hailed from Dassa, which suffered severely during Glélé's rampage through Yoruba towns located within striking distance of Abomey. In AfricaTown, she was sometimes referred to as Adissa or Dissa. These spellings suggest that the name is derived from the Yoruba name Àdýsá, which means "the clear one," "one who speaks with clarity/certainty," or "one who is insightful/perceptive."[83] However, Keeby's origination in the uplands of Abomey seems to have placed him beyond Dahomey's slave-raiding range. Furthermore, the Dahomean infantry could not successfully battle Bariba cavalry lancers. Thus, it is more likely that the Dahomeans purchased Ossie Keeby from northern merchants who brought captives to coastal markets, although Dahomean merchants were also known to travel to Borgu to exchange rum and other merchandise for slaves.[84]

While some rulers imposed sanctions against selling their fellow citizens into the trans-Atlantic slave trade, that protection had disappeared by the middle of the nineteenth century. Dahomean traders sold Fon nationals into slavery, some of whom were acquired in intraethnic conflicts in the Weme River valley in southeastern Benin.[85] Titled persons were also exported as a form of punishment for committing minor offenses against the society or grave, seditious ones against the Dahomean state. Within the economic framework of the Atlantic slave trade, however, there was much diversity in the objectification of Africans. While most Africans were sold as merchandise, some were given as gifts to foreign traders who, in turn, gave them as gifts to royal persons who used them as dining and bedroom fixtures, the source of sexual scandals in the houses of de Medici and other prominent European families.[86] Therefore, Europeans have ancient, and more recent, genealogical connections to African peoples. In fact, the word *Caucasian* is derived from three Ethiopian words, *caer cush aur*,[87] indicating the mutation of Cushites (Ethiopians) into fair-skinned peoples after migrating to, and living in, colder climates such as that which is found in the Caucasus Mountains (located on Russia's southwestern border that is the threshold to that portion of the cradle of civilization that comprises Cush II).

It was customary for Dahomeans to give Africans as gifts to foreign traders.[88] When talking to whites, the *Clotilda* African named Gumpa described his predicament by saying, "my people sold me and your people bought me."[89] But Gumpa was not sold into the trans-Atlantic slave trade. The stout prince of Dahomey gave Gumpa to Captain Foster.[90] Recall that the 250-pound prince was the first high official that Foster encountered in Whydah. In fact, the "ebony prince," as Foster described him, was the only high official with whom Foster negotiated to purchase slaves. During King Glélé's reign, Prince Sodaaton served in the capacity of *yovogan,* or chief in charge of relations with whites at Whydah. To be considered worthy of being given away as a gift, Gumpa had to exhibit special or unusual qualities. He was described as "one of Dahomey's tribe."[91] In other words, Gumpa was *Danxomenu* (one who was of Fon descent) and, as Roche asserted, "nearly related" to the prince that gave him to Foster.[92] Although the nature of this relationship is not clear, being "one of Dahomey's tribe" conferred upon him political rank that increased his value as a gift. Therefore, Captain Foster was able to accept Gumpa as a special souvenir from the Kingdom of Dahomey.

As a Fon national of rank, Gumpa was considered to be royalty by his shipmates. In Alabama, he came to be known as African Peter, or Peter Lee. The chimney that was once attached to Gumpa's house stands in the yard of a house that belonged to his great-granddaughter, Mrs. Josephine Lee Marshall. With pride, she talked proudly about her ancestor who, she thought, was a prince in West Africa, emphasizing the respect that others accorded him in AfricaTown because of his royal status.[93] In fact, Gumpa was held in such high esteem that a street was named for him in AfricaTown (Peter Lee Street).

Gumpa possessed a keen awareness of the military prowess of Dahomean warriors, and he exhibited the kind of patriotism that might only be expressed by one who was Danxomenu. He rebuffed one investigator's claims that Dahomey had been defeated by the French in 1892, saying, "No, No! No man whip Dahomah [king of Dahomey]. Got 'em too much men, got 'em too much fight-women [female warriors]. No man whip Dahomah."[94]

After several battles with King Behanzin, The Shark King, the French defeated Dahomey in 1892. The French found in Behanzin a formidable foe who was shrewd and resilient, two characteristics that he inherited from his father Glélé. Behanzin refused to let the French encroach upon Dahomey's sovereignty, rejecting their requests to plant the French flag at Abomey.[95] The French launched a punitive campaign against Dahomey, led by General Alfred Amédée Dodds, who was the progeny of a Senegalese woman and a Frenchman.[96] When the Dahomean warriors attacked the French before dawn, Dodds counterattacked with Senegalese sharpshooters who understood the military strategies of their Fon opponents.[97] Dodds's African ancestry contributed to his success over Dahomey, but it was a source of hatred by French nationals, who refused to credit him with the victory.[98] Instead of dying as a French hero, Dodds died as a despised pawn in a pernicious chess match that pitted him against his fellow Africans.

As a final demonstration of imperialistic power, the French sent Dahomean warriors to the Chicago World's Columbian Exposition of 1893, where they were exhibited as trophies of war. Specifically, they were installed in a Dahomean Village, one component of an exhibition entitled "White City." They, and other groups, were arranged in racial hierarchical order along the midway.[99] Fair-skinned peoples were placed closest to the White City, being considered more intelligent than those individuals whose skin possessed higher dosages of melanin.[100] The Dahomeans were installed the farthest from the White City, a location that was meant to convey the notion that darker-hued peoples were savages. Their placement at the bottom of this racial hierarchy justified their colonization and subsequent objectification in the minds of spectators.

Rooted in slavery, the objectification and debasement of black people became a regular feature of world's fairs and museum exhibits that etched in the psyches of millions of Europeans and Americans the notion that African-descended peoples were subhuman. Ota Benga, a "pygmie" (derogatory reference to one who descends from the Twa cultural group) who had been abducted from the Kongo, was placed on exhibit at the St. Louis World's Fair in 1904. When the fair closed in 1906, Ota Benga was transferred to the Bronx Zoo, where he was incarcerated in the monkey house. Ota Benga, "the Black ape man," became the most popular attraction at the zoo. On one occasion, visitors chased him about the grounds of the zoo, as if they were on a safari hunt.[101]

The terrorization of Ota Benga is consistent with the pathology of sadistic racists who debased and mutilated the black body for pleasure, for sport, for fear, and for fetish. In 1810, Europeans took Saartjie Baartman, a member of the Khoi-San culture of South Africa, to Britain where she became a traveling exhibition of "racial inferiority and savage sexuality."[102] After four years of physical and psychological abuse, she died in France. Subsequently, the butchers removed her genitalia, placing them on display in the Musée de l'Homme.[103] Such was the pathology of the architects of slavery that, in its psychosexual dimension, provided a platform for the perpetration of heinous perversions against the black body.

Rather than proving that blacks were subhuman, the aforementioned atrocities only exposed the sadism of their perpetrators who aimed not only to justify slavery but to amuse themselves with the destruction of black lives that were considered expendable by "superior" individuals with a collective God-complex, one of the dangerous consequences of racial categorization and codification. For quite some time after they were deposited in Alabama, the *Clotilda* Africans remained on exhibit. From the perspectives of their smugglers, and of the pseudoscientists of the day, they were savages who deserved to be enslaved. Savagery and ignorance, however, did not characterize the lives of the *Clotilda* captives in AfricaTown where they would supersede the lowly expectations that the creators of the word "nigger" had for them.

CHAPTER 7

The Founding of AfricaTown

Whether or not the *Clotilda* Africans became slaves has, heretofore, remained open to interpretation. Those who reject the notion that they were made slaves contend that Tim Meaher abandoned the *Clotilda* Africans. Certainly, they were illegal commodities to which Tim Meaher made no immediate, public, or legal claims of ownership. But, Roche asserts that Tim Meaher considered his portion of the *Clotilda* cargo as his property.[1] What is not questionable is that all of the *Clotilda* Africans were victims of a crime, having been forcibly taken from a foreign place; held captive in the hold of the slaver *Clotilda* that had been illegally fitted out for slaving; transported from a foreign place into the United States; transferred from the *Clotilda* to other vessels involved in the smuggling scheme within the United States; and held against their will by their captors and buyers, each component of the smuggling scheme violating the provisions of the Anti-Slave Trade Act of 1807.

For some time after they were pulled from the fetid hold of the *Clotilda*, Cudjo and his co-captives remained terrified of their unfamiliar surroundings in Alabama. After being deposited on Tim Meaher's land at Magazine Point-Plateau, Albiné refused to eat. She feared that the extra weight would make her attractive to whites who would cannibalize her.[2] Such fears, although they appear to be irrational, haunted newly imported Africans who had no plausible explanations for their captivity and the horrors associated with it. Those fears were compounded by others that developed when they were thrown into the midst of acculturated blacks. In this case, as in others involving contact between *bozale* (newly arrived) Africans and seasoned blacks, the two groups did not have an instant affinity for one another.

The *Clotilda* Africans had arrived in Alabama wearing nothing more than their filed teeth and cicatrices that identified them as Fon, Oyo-Yoruba (titled and nontitled), Attakar, Kaninkon, Jaba, Bache, Gwari, and Chamba peoples. Their appearance was a source of ridicule for seasoned blacks in Magazine Point-Plateau.[3] The sociology of slavery must not be viewed myopically as a conflict between blacks and whites; several conflicts developed between blacks themselves. Black slave drivers used brutality to force newly arrived Africans into compliance with plantation protocol, pitting both groups against each other from the outset. Thus, one slave's quest for legitimacy was often achieved at the expense of a fellow slave. If seasoned blacks defined themselves as different from or, in some cases, superior to newly arrived Africans, their perceptions of themselves could not override the reality that the larger society relegated all of them, newly arrived or not, to the status of chattels who were mere extensions of the plantations to which they were shackled.

The seasoning process produced a change in the consciousness of some blacks for whom Africa became a refracted image in their minds, poisoned by the ideology of slavery that defined all things African as primitive. Consequently, some blacks purposefully discarded elements of their African heritages. Newly arrived captives did not hold such base views of their African heritages that continued to hold cultural, political, and spiritual relevancy for some time after they were enslaved. The fact that the relationship between the *bozale* Africans and seasoned blacks remained tenuous is not to argue that seasoned blacks had no compassion for, or that they did not understand the plight of, the newly arrived Africans, for one of the most spiritual aspects of the black community is its willingness to adjust its boundaries to accommodate those in need.[4]

If the *Clotilda* Africans were to secure shelter, food, and other necessities, therefore, they would have to rely on the local blacks for whom they had been a source of ridicule.[5] That was the humiliating and precarious situation in which the *Clotilda* Africans found themselves in Alabama in 1860. According to Cudjo, the Meahers charged their seasoned field hands with the responsibility of explaining American planting techniques to the *Clotilda* Africans, in part because the *Clotilda* Africans could not understand the English language, impeding communication with the Meahers.[6]

Although they hailed from agricultural societies, they were unfamiliar with some of the farming methods that were used on Meahers' farms and plantations at Magazine Point-Plateau and along the Alabama, Tensaw, and

Tombigbee rivers. "We astonish to see mule behind the plow to pull. We so surprised to see man pushee and mule pulee," said Cudjo.[7] This method of tilling contrasted sharply with the one that is implemented by West African cultivators, who used handheld hoes and other indigenous technologies to cultivate the soil.

As it was for slaves who did not commit suicide to escape the horrors of perpetual enslavement, to preserve their dignity, and to seek a nobler place among the ancestors, the *Clotilda* Africans' adjustment to plantation labor was both difficult and dehumanizing. The production of cotton was labor-intensive, requiring slaves to work from sunrise to sunset. Cudjo recalled particular moments in his life as a slave:

> Cap'n Tim and Cap'n Burns [Byrnes] Mehear workee dey folks hard. Dey got overseer wid de whip. One man try whippee one my country women and dey all jump on him and takee de whip way from him and lashee him wid it. He doan never try whip African women no mo.[8]

This recollection contains five important elements. First, existence on the Meahers' plantations was as harsh as it was on others. The Meahers owned slaves individually and collectively, as in the case of the firm J.M. and T. Meaher. Their slaves, like others, absconded from their bondage. A slave named Andrew is described as the "bona fide property of J.M. and T. Meaher" in the Runaway Slave Book for Mobile County.[9] Second, in addition to being unfamiliar with plantation labor and practices, the *Clotilda* Africans were also unfamiliar with the concept of being disfranchised and being forced to labor entirely for the benefit of others under brutal conditions. Some of the *Clotilda* captives descended from titled families, and they would not accept abuse at the hands of others. The argument that Africans acquiesced in, and enjoyed, their conditions as slaves is a specious one advanced by slaveowners in an attempt to exorcise the guilt that they experienced as a result of their inhumane treatments of African men, women, and children. Third, Africans formed important bonds along cultural, national, and situational lines for the sake of protection against inhumane treatment. Fourth, Africans have never been passive peoples, but they were always prepared to meet, and exceed, directly and indirectly, the violence that was being perpetrated against them. Fifth, black men defended, and protected, black women.

In addition to being field hands, some of the *Clotilda* men labored on the Meahers' steamboats. Cudjo could recall the name of every landing that the steamboats serviced between Mobile and Montgomery, where he carried bales of cotton, freight, and wood for the boats' furnaces.[10] In southern parlance, the black men who stoked the furnaces of steamboats, and who used their strength to push boats over sandbars, were known collectively as the "nigger engine." Recognizing the injustice of slavery, Cudjo complained constantly about having to work long hours under the constant threat of the lash and without proper sleep or compensation, saying "I sho appreciate they free us."[11] But, freedom would not come until three years after the *Clotilda* African's arrival. The Confiscation Act of 1861 and the Emancipation Proclamation of 1863 were war strategies designed to divest the Confederates of their ability to use slaves in their military efforts against the Union.[12] For this reason, the Emancipation Proclamation freed only those blacks enslaved in the rebellious states. Because the Confederate states lay outside the jurisdiction of the Union, the federal government could not, in reality, enforce the Emancipation Proclamation. Once enslaved persons discovered that the measure granted them their freedom, however, they walked away from their masters and plantations. Thus, for the Union, the intended outcome was achieved.

The extent to which slaves could exercise that freedom varied from state to state and from plantation to plantation, with intimidation, death threats, and the lack of adequate resources to facilitate their independence being major deterrents. For the *Clotilda* Africans, who had been in Alabama for only three years when the Emancipation Proclamation was issued, the situation was even more precarious. They were far less familiar with Alabama customs than other blacks enslaved there prior to their arrival. This was true not merely due to the limitations of time, but due to the fact their languages, practices, and other elements of their indigenous African heritages were still visible, thwarting their movement beyond their immediate environments and situation. To both white and black communities, they would always remain oddities, savages, and the targets of insults.

Like the Emancipation Proclamation, the Thirteenth Amendment must not be relished as a humanitarian legislative act. The very fact that it is an amendment means that Congress was obligated to do in 1865, after a war had destroyed the national security, what it should have done in 1787 when the proslavery, slaveowning congressmen were more concerned with maintaining slavery for their own economic well-being and that of their posterity. The Thirteenth Amendment could not guarantee the safety or prosperity of blacks in the post-slavery period. Without land or gainful employment, many blacks were forced to remain on the plantations of their former masters. This was a viable option, in some cases, not only because the plantation continued to provide them with basic necessities, but because it also provided them with a modicum of protection against lynching. As brutal as the institution of slavery was, Americans did not habitually kill their slaves, who held value for plantation, industrial, and household economies. Within the context of slavery, the black man in particular, and black people in general, comprised a political economy, dominating political thought, influencing legislation, and serving as the basis for wealth in the nation. As long as Americans could own and control black people, they were "pro-Black," at least, from an economic perspective.

When slaveowners lost control of black people, the one possession that defined their economic, social, and political status, they avenged the loss by unleashing a murderous campaign against black people and their supporters. Leading the campaign were former slaveowners, Confederates, and their sympathizers who sought recognition and honor as the first terrorist groups on U.S. soil. Among the disaffected was John Wilkes Booth, the ancestor of Cherie Booth who is the wife of Tony Blair, the former Prime Minister of the United Kingdom. John's father, Junius, moved to the United States in 1821, after England had abolished new importations of slaves into her territories. However, blacks continued to be held in bondage in those territories. Thus, abolition of new importations did not limit Booth's ability to own slaves in United States. Apart from their reputation as accomplished actors, members of the Booth family had made a name for themselves on the basis of subjugating black people.

Booth assassinated President Lincoln to "avenge" the South's loss of its "niggers." One year before he murdered Lincoln, he wrote the following about the institution of slavery:

> This country was formed for the white not the black man. And looking Upon African slavery from the same stand-point, as held by those noble framers of our Constitution, I for one, have ever considered it one of the greatest blessings (both for themselves and us) that God ever bestowed upon a favored nation.[13]

Booth, like other Americans, had made a religion of slavery, and those who protected the institution were worshipped as patriots. In the post-slavery period, however, patriotism involved annihilating black people not merely as competitors for valuable resources, but as threats to the "white race" itself. If the proliferation of miscegenation was the excuse that proslavery advocates gave for keeping blacks in slavery, it became a dangerous pretext for killing blacks after they were freed.

Slavery was supported by a series of antimiscegenation laws designed to protect the institution, on the one hand, and abate the destruction of the "pure white race," on the other. Thomas Jefferson and other slaveowners regularly violated antimiscegenation laws. Furthermore, sexual intercourse between white men and black women was defined as exotic, and because it symbolized the white man's dominion over his human property, the practice was both accepted and cherished. Sex between white men and black women was far more tolerable than that between black men and white women, in great measure, because the white woman was, and continues to be, viewed as the symbol of virtue and as the gatekeeper of white racial purity. The language of antimiscegenation laws emphasized the role of white women in avoiding sexual penetration by black men, to avoid tainting her offspring with black blood or any signs of African genetic influence.

As a child bearer, the burden of keeping the white race pure and free of "negro blood" fell squarely on the loins of the white women who have been portrayed, by and large, as victims of black male sexual aggression and violence. Historically, white women played active roles in the Africanization and "browning" of Greek, Roman, and other European populations by abandoning their own men in favor of African explorers, mercenaries, and conquerors. This phenomenon was such a scourge on the English populace that Shakespeare found it suitable material his play entitled *Othello.* The envy that Iago expressed towards Othello had less to do with the fact that Othello was of a higher military rank than he, and far more to do with the fact that Othello, a Moor from North Africa, was the husband of a white woman. This was the psychosexual crisis in which Europeans continuously found themselves before and after the fall of the Moorish Empire in 1492. Additional evidence of African genetic and cultural influence can be seen in European surnames such as Blackamoor, Blackmore, and Blakemore.

The Africanization, "browning," or "blackening" of Europeans persisted in North America, where miscegenation threatened the ideology of slavery and the complexion of the white population. Miscegenation produced children whose "Negroid" features and "one drop of Negro blood" would relegate them to the Black category within the United States' bifurcated social system of race. Such a classification reduces the numbers of whites—or, at least, that was white supremacists' perception of the matter. When white women failed to uphold the eugenicist ideology of white supremacists, simultaneously failing to uphold society's image of them as virtuous, innocent beings, black men became the scapegoats for her failures in Greenwood, Rosewood, Mariana, Omaha, Little Rock, Waco, Jasper, Rome (GA), Eagle (CO), or AnyApplePie-Town, USA. As such, black men were not only lynched, but they were castrated in massive numbers, from the time of slavery, when castration was also a form of punishment for runaways, to, and beyond, the heinous murder of Emmit Till.[14]

More than being a form of punishment, castration was a manifestation of the sadistic pathology of racism; castration removed the threat of having black men, symbols of "filth" and "immorality," penetrate white women, symbols of "virtue" and "racial purity." In fact, there are two ways in which white supremacists removed the perceived threat. They killed blacks who were already in existence, and they carved fetuses out of mothers' stomachs.[15] Lynchings were ritual killings in which the murderers made a fetish of destroying black peoples' bodies by stripping them naked, severing penises, testicles, "nigger toes," "nigger fingers," and retaining those body parts as cherished souvenirs meant to help the killers recall, relive, and fantasize about the event. As late as 1981, Michael Donald, a black male, was lynched by two klansmen who cut his throat before hanging his body from a tree on Herndon Avenue in Mobile.[16] On behalf of Donald's mother, Attorney Michael A. Figures, a civil rights leader and Mobile County's first black senator, won $7 million in damages against the klan.[17] As a memorial to the victim, Herndon Avenue was changed to Michael Donald Avenue (intersects with Springhill Avenue) where the tree still stands as a reminder of the racial hatred and violence that blacks have faced, and continue to face, in the United States. Today, black athletes, at the high school, college, and professional levels, continue to receive hate mail threatening to castrate and set them on fire if they do not abandon the practice of dating white women.[18]

After 1865, the "Negro Question" or the "Nigger Problem" was defined in sexual and economic terms. The Civil War ended, but cotton continued to grow. There remained a tremendous need for labor to refurbish plantations left fallow or destroyed during the war. The problem hinged on forcing newly freed blacks back onto plantations. The solution, once again, resided in the U.S. Constitution. Thus, Section One of the Thirteenth Amendment provides for the re-enslavement of blacks as a *punishment for a crime whereof the party shall have been duly convicted.* Any serious student of American history must analyze the letter of the law, its intent, and the agenda, or motives, of its designers. *Qui Bono* or who benefits from the manner in which the language of the law is framed? The Thirteenth Amendment was both a help and a hindrance to black freedom, its well-crafted language providing for the re-enslavement of blacks who had been "duly convicted" of a crime. In an environment in which judges, ex-Confederates, and owners of mills, mines, and plantations are one and the same persons, they would regard all convictions against blacks as *duly.* Vagrancy laws were expediently constructed to capitalize on the fact that blacks lacked property, shelter, and gainful employment. Arrested as vagrants, blacks were forced to labor in lieu of paying fines paid by business owners in need of cheap labor.[19]

Rather than facilitating the upward mobility of newly freed blacks and their descendants, Reconstruction was a period of re-enslavement. Federal and state statutes designed specifically to re-enslave blacks worked in tandem with the prison system, buttressed by domestic terrorism. Where slavery ends, prisons begin to warehouse large numbers of blacks for the sake of exploitation while ridding white society of what it defined as "roving sexual predators." The 1865 Alabama constitution made it "the duty of the general assembly to periodically enact laws prohibiting intermarriage between whites and blacks, or with persons of mixed blood, and to establish penalties."[20]

Fulfilling that duty, the 1867 Alabama state code established penalties for intermarriage and cohabitation between blacks and whites. Black violators were confined to hard labor in the Alabama State Penitentiary for two to seven years.[21] Individuals who performed a marriage between, or issued a marriage license to, a "mixed-race" couple, were fined $100 to $1,000, or they were imprisoned for six months, or both. Demonstrating the extent of the fear of miscegenation, Alabama enacted a law that prevented white nurses from caring for black male patients, in an effort to prevent white females from seeing or touching the genitalia of the black male patients.[22]

Alabama's Ella Barrett Ligon, a white physician who claimed to "know the negro question in all of its aspects," expressed the fear and the psychosis surrounding sexual relations between black men and white women in the following warning:

> Let all the world listen while the south calls on you to hear: The white woman is the coveted desire of the negro man. The despoiling of the white woman is his chosen vengeance. The white woman must be saved! All philanthropical claims can be fully met mentally and morally without taking the negro, even the best negro, into the home. It makes no difference that social equality is asked for only those who are worthy. The social recognition of one good negro stimulates in thousands of black devils resentment at not being similarly treated, and rouses them to fresh insults and outrages aimed at the southern white woman.[23]

Guess who's *not* coming to dinner? Not only is, as Ligon warns her fellow white supremacists, the "best negro" to be kept out of the home circle, but as Alabama law required, he is to be arrested and incarcerated for trying to penetrate the white woman's *home*. Indeed, large numbers of black men were rounded up on the charge of "having sex with white women." In keeping with both the letter and the spirit of the Thirteenth Amendment to the U.S. Constitution, Article I, Section 34 of Alabama's 1865 state constitution provided for the re-enslavement of blacks *duly* convicted of crimes.

Re-enslavement was facilitated by Alabama's convict-lease system that yielded profits that were split between wardens, mayors, and business owners,[24] much in the same way that prosecutors, police officers, judges, and other court officials derive salaries, promotions, and political positions from blacks who become ensnared by the current penal system, in which many prisons are privately owned, publicly traded enterprises, in part, due to a general ignorance of that system as a political economy that generates profits to the owners who can afford to send their children to Harvard and Yale while too many blacks languish in jail. As W.H. Oates, an Alabama State Prison inspector, exclaimed, "our jails are money-making machines."[25] In the twenty-first century, it is imperative that blacks understand the historical and economic ramifications of prisons that are extensions of the plantation and sources of profit for the governments and the private citizens that own them.

On April 12, 1865, Union soldiers informed Cudjo and those working aboard one of James Meaher's steamboats at the time that they were free.[26] Up to that point, the *Clotilda* Africans had relied on the assistance of local people like Free George and Tom Lewis, from whom Cudjo, Char-Lee, and Chamba acquired their European surname.[27] Polee and Gumpa adopted the surnames Allen and Lee, respectively. As free persons, however, they would need to rely more on themselves. The *Clotilda* Africans never accepted the racist conditions under which they were forced to exist in Alabama.

From the time that they emerged from the belly of the *Clotilda,* and throughout their ordeal as enslaved persons, their collective consciousness was focused on Africa. Although they were now free, they did not want to remain on American soil, where they were dispossessed of land and where blacks continued to face rampant discrimination and violence. The *Clotilda* group decided to prepare for their return to West Africa. To pay for their passage back across the Atlantic, they agreed to take jobs and to save the money that they made. The *Clotilda* men took jobs in Meaher's mill and shingle yard.[28] Alabama became a center for lumber and resin production, due to the abundance of pine, oak, gum, elm, and cypress trees. In some cases, the *Clotilda* men were working alongside convicts who had been leased to mill owners and who were living in labor camps like the one that existed in the "piney woods" near Tim Meaher's mill.[29] Meaher's mills were so productive that they received recognition in the proslavery publication *De Bow's Review* as manufacturing 2,000,000 feet of lumber and 1,200,000 shingles in 1859.[30]

Ivory Hill, Polee's granddaughter who currently resides in AfricaTown, discussed the terms of their labor contracts:

> Polee, Cudjo, and others worked in the mills for eleven hours each day for which they were paid a wage. But, Meaher and other mill owners did not compensate them for the eleventh hour, an hour of free labor that they were forced to give in exchange for the opportunity to work in the mill.[31]

This exploitative measure was universally employed by mill owners, in order to maximize profits. Rather than allowing the *Clotilda* men to walk in the road when traveling to and from the Meaher's sawmill, the Meahers forced them to walk in the ditch, according to Mary Pogue, who is the granddaughter of

Polee and the sister of Ivory Hill.[32] In slavery and in freedom, ditches are synonymous with degradation. Not only were blacks made to walk in ditches to show deference to whites by yielding the streets, sidewalks, and "right-of-ways" to them, blacks were made to dig ditches, urinate in the waist-high water in which they were working, and draw their drinking water from those same ditches.[33]

The *Clotilda* men were not accustomed to the dehumanizing treatment that they experienced at the hands of the Meahers before and after slavery. They only made one dollar per day as mill workers.[34] Although they attempted to pool their resources to pay their passage back to West Africa, they fell short of their financial goal. Economic exigencies forced them to remain in Alabama, where the acquisition of land would be tantamount to their continued survival. Understanding the importance of land acquisition to their general welfare, the *Clotilda* Africans chose Cudjo, their outspoken leader, to convey their wishes to Tim Meaher.[35] Cudjo approached Tim Meaher, arguing that he had dispossessed the *Clotilda* Africans of their ancestral land by bringing them to Alabama where he made them slaves.[36] On behalf of the *Clotilda* group, Cudjo asked Meaher for land upon which they could build their own community. Meaher refused to give them land, requiring them to pay rent for parcels that he allowed them to carve out for themselves on his land in Magazine Point-Plateau.[37]

Collectively, those parcels became what, in Cudjo's dialect, was referred to as "Afficky Town" in 1868.[38] That community is currently called AfricaTown. Mr. Henry C. Williams, an historian and a former resident of AfricaTown, described the community's boundaries this way:

> Its boundaries within the city of Mobile include a point north of Duck Lake, east to Spanish River. The boundary continues south to northeast section of Polecat Bay, and moves further south to the mouth of Polecat Bay. Its borders are marked west to Conception Street and around the southeastern section of the Davis Avenue landfill site to Stone Street; from Stone Street northwest to Craft Highway; north on Craft Highway to Meaher Street. The boundary ends east to Timothy Street and Telegraph Road; north on Telegraph Road, east to Chickasabogue Creek; and, north to Duck Lake.[39]

Some of AfricaTown's street names clearly locate that community within the parameters of Timothy Meaher's property, including Chickasabogue Creek, where he maintained his shipyard. Over the years, AfricaTown's boundaries expanded so that it now encompasses a much larger region than it did when it was established.

With the founding of AfricaTown, 1868 was a pivotal year in the *Clotilda* Africans' social and political history. They became leaders of their own community, which they would develop and govern by their African values. AfricaTown's internal governance, to some extent, was linked to the larger question of citizenship. Realizing that they would likely remain displaced Africans in Alabama for the remainder of their lives, the *Clotilda* Africans sought to become naturalized citizens of the United States and of the state wherein they were smuggled and enslaved. They had met the residency requirements for naturalization, albeit under the worst of circumstances. On July 13, 1868, Alabama's legislature ratified the Fourteenth Amendment to the U.S. Constitution. In October of that year, six of the *Clotilda* Africans appeared before a judge in Mobile's City Court to declare their intentions to become naturalized citizens of the United States, the first step in the naturalization process for aliens. Court records identify them as Cudjo Lewis, Chamber [Chamba] Lewis, Polee Allen, Ossa Kibbe [Ossie Keeby], Toney Thomas, and Archie Thomas.[40] Court records list Cudjo, Polee, and Ossie as being 21 years of age, the age required to declare an intention to become a citizen or to vote. Judging by Cudjo's age at the time that he was imported into the United States, however, he was much older than 21 in 1868. Toney and Archie Thomas were listed as being 28 and 25 years of age, respectively. More significant than their ages was their place of origin in the court records that described all of them as "aliens" from "Africa."[41]

None of the *Clotilda* women appeared in court to declare their intention to become citizens, in large measure, because women acquired their citizenship though their husbands (children through their parents). Declaring their intent to become citizens was an affirmative action on the part of the *Clotilda* men, who deemed it important to be classified as citizens of the United States, since they had no real prospects for returning to Africa. They demonstrated courage in the face of those determined to disfranchise freedmen and their descendants. "Nigger citizenship," as Booth dubbed it, was one of the principal fears that drove him to murder Lincoln.[42] Booth and others defined both democracy and citizenship in racial terms, reserved only for whites.

By declaring their intent to become citizens, Cudjo and his shipmates took affirmative action to improve the quality of their lives and to control their destiny, relative to political empowerment. In doing so, they exercised their mobility as freedmen, generating a sense of entitlement and sparking the desire for access to other important resources such as land.

To rent land is one thing, to own land is real empowerment. The *Clotilda* Africans did not agree with the notion of renting property, hailing from West African societies where they had access to free communal land that they cultivated for their own subsistence and economic development. In 1870, the *Clotilda* Africans began to use the money that they made in the mills to purchase land, a powerful move considering the fact that only 10 years prior, they had emerged from the belly of the *Clotilda* as captives. Miss Lorna Woods maintains that her ancestor, Char-Lee Lewis, purchased land from his former owner, Colonel Thomas Buford.[43] Indeed, Mobile Probate Court records indicate that Char-Lee and Jaba purchased seven acres of land that "lies on the west side of Three Mile Creek and West and nearly contiguous to touching the Mobile & Ohio Railbroad, and in the County of Mobile," for which he paid Thomas Buford $200.00.[44] Located behind Gulf Lumber Company, that area is still extant as Lewis' Quarters, where some of Char-Lee's descendants currently reside.

In 1872, Polee [spelled Paulee in the deed] Allen purchased two acres of Tim Meaher's land, further described as being situated between No. 6 & 7 of the Owen, Griffin, Earle, and Simms Division of the St Louis Tract, for which he paid $200.00.[45] In that same year, Ossie Keeby [spelled Ossa Kibee in the deed] purchased two acres of Meaher's land, located also between No. 6 & 7 of the Owen, Griffin, Earle, and Simms Division of the St. Louis Tract, for which he paid $150.00.[46] Hence, Polee and Keeby lived in close proximity to one another. In 1872, Cudjo also purchased approximately two acres of Lorenzo M. Wilson's land, described as Lot #15 of the St. Louis Tract, for which he paid $100.00.[47] In 1904, Cudjo sold a parcel of land to Mobile Light and Railroad Company.[48] The *Clotilda* Africans possessed deeds to their own land. The power of possessing the deed, as a legal instrument, is that it certifies ownership, and it protects the holder's rights in the property. Monabee, who was listed as "Head of House," owned her house "free and clear."[49]

The deed is also a symbol of economic power and stability, something that can be transferred to one's heirs as a way of providing a strong economic foundation on which their descendants might continue to build the wealth they inherited from their ancestors. Cudjo became a land prospector, acquiring an additional acre of land, described as Lot #2 in No. 6 of the Owen, Griffin, Earle, and Simms subdivision of the St. Louis Tract, for which he paid $64.50.[50] Samuel Johnson asserts that, "there is no subject in which the Yoruba man is more sensitive than in that of land."[51] This sensitivity characterizes most Africans who are agriculturalists and herbalists. It is a sensitivity that is magnified tenfold when one is dispossessed of it and, subsequently, made to perpetually cultivate a foreigner's land for the foreigner's benefit. These were the feelings and the experiences of the *Clotilda* Africans who endeavored to acquire as much land as they could afford. With deeds in hand, the *Clotilda* Africans continued the process of community building. In Africa, the importance of community building is reflected in the fact that a descriptive exists for that process in several languages. In Yoruba, it is called Ibagbepo; in

Kiswahili, Ujima; and in Bantu, Ubuntu. With no prospects for returning to their West African homelands, the *Clotilda* Africans needed to establish a safe, permanent haven for themselves. AfricaTown emerged out of exigencies of the *Clotilda* Africans' transatlantic ordeal. As members of the same illegal cargo, they formed a strong bond, a collective consciousness, and a spirit of cooperation that generated a sense of security and fostered their development.

Linguistic and cultural homogeneity facilitated communication, thereby promoting cohesion and communalism among AfricaTown's founders. They "talked that African language to each other," according to Clara Eva Bell Allen Jones, Polee's daughter, who was also referred to as Mama Eva.[52] Yoruba and Hausa constituted the two major West African language clusters in the *Clotilda* cargo. In general, most West Africans are multilingual, speaking Yoruba and Hausa as indigenous languages or using them as *lingua franca.* The *Clotilda* Africans continued to speak their indigenous languages for more than 30 years after they arrived in Magazine Point-Plateau, whose topography resembled that of the hilly regions in Benin and Nigeria where the architectural forms and functions are dictated by the landscape, climate, materials, status, and occupation. The *Clotilda* men built 30 small houses on approximately 1.5 square miles of land that comprised AfricaTown.[53] From Africa to America, environmental changes shaped the architectural design and the nature of the materials employed.

Cudjo encased his house with the eight-gate wall system reminiscent of the wall systems of New Oyo, fastening the main gate with a linchpin, a technique that Hurston described as "ingenious."[54] Indeed, the profundity of inventions and ideas is really to be found in their simplicity or in their essence, not their complexity. As someone who understood and respected black culture, Hurston understood that genius crossed the Atlantic with black people, and profit-motivated slave traders understood that too. Cudjo constructed a square single-room log house, filling the cracks with lime and sand.[55] This house differed architecturally from the palm frond–roofed, conical clay house in which he dwelled in his Whinney, and which are typically found on farmsteads.[56] Insulation consisted of newspaper that was plastered on the interior walls, and he covered the roof with some of the cypress shingles that he made in Meaher's lumber mills.[57] To warm the house during the winter months, he added a fireplace. Polee modeled his house on the single "shotgun" type,[58] a wood construction with a tin gable roof. The dimensions of shotgun houses tend to be 12 feet wide by 12 to 16 feet long, simulating those of houses constructed by Yoruba peoples in Nigeria.[59] Ivory Hill, Polee's granddaughter, said that he carried his wood on his back when he traveled from Meaher's mill to the site where he built his house.[60] The other 28 houses constructed in AfricaTown modeled the two examples built by Cudjo and Polee.

The building of AfricaTown is to be regarded as a major achievement for the *Clotilda* Africans, one that embodies the genius and the resiliency of Africans in the Americas, given the fact that they began their lives as captives dispossessed of all things material. What they did possess, however, was a desire to rise above their circumstances. Speaking proudly of the affirmative action that the *Clotilda* Africans took to establish their community, Cudjo said, "we doan pay nobody build our houses. We all go together and buildee de house for one 'nother."[61] The *Clotilda* Africans had transitioned from lying in their own feces in the hold of a slave ship, to being forced to sleep under the houses of their captors,[62] to relying on the generosity of other blacks who provided them shelter, to building their own community.

To outsiders, AfricaTown stood merely as a curious exhibit of the last Africans to be smuggled into Alabama, attracting several onlookers eager to get a glimpse of the "savages." In fact, Augustine Meaher escorted ethnographer Henry Romeyn to the *Clotilda* settlement, being very familiar with its exact location on his father's property.[63] Romeyn published his findings in

Cudjo sits in front of the fireplace in the house that he built in AfricaTown. Erik Overbey Collection, University of South Alabama Archives (circa 1930).

Southern Workman, a publication of Hampton Normal and Agricultural Institute (currently known as Hampton University). Delineating the *Clotilda* Africans' geographical and cultural origins to greater degrees of specificity than had been accomplished by previous writers is significant not only for anchoring them in time and space, but for establishing baselines for measuring the continuity or discontinuity of specific aspects of their West African heritages in AfricaTown.

Miss Lorna Woods, a fifth-generation descendant of Char-Lee, described the *Clotilda* Africans as being insular; they understood, respected, and kept, their social boundaries, requiring neighbors on the margins of AfricaTown to do the same.[64] That is, in large measure, how they maintained a respectable and viable community. According to the 1880 Census Report for Mobile County, the *Clotilda* households contained two parents. While they remained heavily influenced by West African concepts and values, they did dispense with the practice of polygamy that characterized their family structures in West Africa.[65] Cudjo used the following allegory to describe polygamy as he understood it:

> Cudjo he been married for three years for example...His wife says: "Cudjo, I am growing old. I am tired—I will bring you another wife." Before speaking thus she has already one in mind—some girl who attracts her and whom Cudjo has never seen. The wife goes out and finds the girl—maybe in a public square, maybe in the market place and she asks: "You know Cudjo?" The girl answers "I have heard of him." The wife says: "Cudjo is good. He is kind. I would like you to be his wife." The girl answers: "Come with me to my parents." They go together; questions are asked on both sides and if they are satisfied the parents say: "We give our daughter into your care. She is ours no more. You be good to her."[66]

There are four culturally significant aspects of this allegory: 1) in Yoruba communities, the first wife can select the second and subsequent wives, based upon the needs of the household; 2) the public square and the marketplace, the domain of female vendors, are excellent places to meet candidates; 3) as heads of the *Ebi* (family-lineage-profession), the parents and grandparents determine the appropriateness of the marriage when two *Ebi* are joined;[67] and 4) once parents have supported their daughter's choice, and once she has moved into her husband's house, they do not want her to return home in consequence of her spouse not being able to fulfill his roles as husband and father. In Africa, it is a disgrace for adults to neglect their familial responsibilities. Consequentely, the *Clotilda* Africans upheld those duties in Alabama.

The *Clotilda* Africans rendered mutual aid to one another, and they reached major social, political, and economic milestones together: they applied for naturalization together; they purchased real estate at approximately the same time; they helped build each other's houses; and many of them married in the same year. With few exceptions, marriages were arranged primarily between members of the *Clotilda* cargo. That the *Clotilda* cargo was divided almost equally between the two sexes means that they could form several heterosexual bonds in AfricaTown. Polee married his shipmate named Rosalie.[68] They had six daughters and one son (Clara, Maggie, Martha, Mary, Nancie, Viola, and Clarence). Char-Lee married his shipmate named Maggie. They had three daughters and two sons (Maggie, Mary, Martha, Joseph, and Richard). Ossie Keeby married his shipmate named Anna. They had eight children (Sarah, Fannie, Luvenia, Aaron, Simon, William, Pat, and Siloie). Cudjo married his shipmate Albiné, whose name is more accurately spelled Abila.[69] It is a Yoruba name that means "one who is born to the rich." She had been captured in Whinney with Cudjo, and her name indicates that she was connected to wealth as was others captured in what the research confirms was Owinni. In AfricaTown, Abila was called Celie.

A captive aboard the *Clotilda,* Char-Lee resided in Lewis's Quarters, where he owned property. Mobile Public Library, Local History and Genealogy Division (circa 1912). Courtesy of the Mobile Public Library. All rights reserved. Reprinted with permission.

The 1880 Census Report lists Cudjo and Celie as originating in Africa, and their children are listed as born in Alabama.[70] Aleck, their first born, is listed as being age 14. Since Cudjo was between 19 and 25 years old when he was smuggled into Alabama, and he was between 25 and 31 years old when his first child was born. Census taking was not scientific, and there was no real effort to collect accurate information where blacks were concerned. Moreover, African peoples had indigenous ways of reckoning time and age that did not always involve maintaining paper records of births. They did keep culture-specific records of important human events, nonetheless.

Cudjo and Abila had four other sons (Cudjo, James, Polyon, David) and one daughter (Celie, sometimes interchanged with Celia). In the late nineteenth century, Romeyn observed that there were "no mulatto children among them."[71] The slow rate of acculturation is attributable to the Clotilda Africans' selective insularity and to the insularity that resulted from the fact that Africa-Town was, in addition to being carved out of Meaher's land, surrounded by Meaher's land. Therefore, most of the contact that they had with whites was with the Meahers. The slow rate of acculturation is also attributed to the fact that the Clotilda Africans made a conscious effort to keep aspects of their African heritages intact. "We give our children two names. One name because we not furgit our home; den another name for Americky soil so it won't be too crooked [difficult] to call," said Cudjo.[72] Africans continue to give their children two names. The European name facilitates communication and movement in Europe and the United States. The African name maintains cultural connections to their African ancestral land and lineages.

A captive aboard the Clotilda, Polee Allen became a landowner, a farmer, and a beekeeper in AfricaTown. Drawing by Emma Langdon Roche, author of Historic Sketches of the South (circa 1912).

When giving their children Yoruba names in Alabama, Cudjo and Abila held a Yoruba naming ceremony called *Ikomojade,* which means "giving the child a crown." That *Ikomojade* transpires over the course of several days speaks to the importance of naming a child. Names not only convey messages about the child's character, economic or political status, or religion, but names speak to, and guide, the destiny of the child. This is precisely why parents should refrain from giving their children names whose morphologies are too close to the name "demon," foreshadowing something ominous and destructive. To the contrary, Cudjo and Abila gave their children positive names connected to God. Both of Cudjo's parents' names reflect a connection to God. Recall that his father's name was Obaloluwa (God is King). Hurston recorded Cudjo's mother's name as Ny Fond lo loo.[73] This is more accurately spelled *Ninfoluwa,* a Yoruba name that means "have something for God; give something to God; make gifts to God."

Cudjo and Abila pay homage to God via the names that they gave to their children. For example, they gave Aleck a Yoruba name that Hurston recorded as Yah-Jimmy.[74] It is more accurately spelled *Iyayemi* (God has blessed me with good birth even in a time of suffering); Polyon was named Poeleedahoo; James was named Ahnonotoe; David was named AhtennyAh (*Ateniola* means "God has made wealth; made of the wealth of God"); Cudjo Jr. was named Fisheeton (*Feyisheton* means "God makes the history or destiny of this person good or positive"); and Celie was named Ee-bew-o-see (*Ebunosi* means "a thankful gift from God").

While Cudjo, Char-Lee, and Polee married women who had been their co-captives aboard the *Clotilda,* some members of the cargo married blacks who were living in Alabama when they arrived. Gumpa married Clara Dozier, and they had two children (Mamie, who bore Sydney Robert Lee, and Clara, who bore a daughter Josephine).[75] Chamba married Hales Wigerfall, and Abackey married Sam Turner.[76] However, information about their family histories is scant. Monabee (possibly Omolabi), who was referred to as Kattie Cooper in AfricaTown, is listed in the census as "Head of House."[77] Monabee had one child whose name was not listed. Kazuma married John Livingston (sometimes interchanged with Levinson and Leverson), although not much is known of him.[78] They had five children in their household. Jabba married a woman named Polly, although she could have also used the name Ellen. They had two daughters and one son (Mary, Mary Ann, and Willie). Kanko married James Dennison, Byrnes Meaher's slave who assisted in the transference of the captives from the *Clotilda* to the *Czar* that transported them to Mount Vernon where they were hidden from the U.S. marshal and the Mobile revenue collectors. The *Clotilda* Africans were unfamiliar with laws permitting "marriage by license." In their West African homelands, marriage was governed by indigenous religion, parental and elder discretion, and brides' wealth. For many reasons, not the least of which involves the stigma attached to divorce, marriages were not to be hastily arranged. Initially, Kanko refrained from having intimate relations with Dennison.[79] Over time, however, they had three children (Willie, Napoleon, and Equilla who died of lockjaw at the age of 13).

The Yoruba say, *Aladugbo eni ni omo iya eni* or "one's neighbors are one's brothers or sisters: it is one's neighbors who will do the duties of one's brothers or sisters when they are not near."[80] In this spirit of African communalism, they extend their family structures to solve certain problems. For example,

This is a rare image of Abache (Abackey) standing with her shipmate Cudjo in AfricaTown. Mobile Public Library, Local History and Genealogy Division (circa 1912). Courtesy of the Mobile Public Library. All rights reserved. Reprinted with permission.

Kazuma became a surrogate mother for Mary Allen, whose mother Rosalie died.[81] Kazuma incorporated Mary Allen into her family, despite the fact that she was physically disabled, and she already had five children of her own (George, Alee, Martin, in addition to Mary J and John).[82] John and Mary J were twins. Several sets of twins were born in AfricaTown. Gumpa's descendants produced one set of twins in 1916.[83] A high rate of twinning occurs among Yoruba groups that accord special rites to living and deceased twins.[84] Martha and Mary, Cudjo's great-granddaughters, are twins.

Africans gave birth to the human family, and fertility issues are paramount across the continent. Children are considered gifts from God. They contribute to the spiritual, social, and economic well-being of the household, compound, or village. Children are cherished, but elders rule. The *Clotilda* Africans' descendancy from *ilari,* chiefs, and other titled officials shaped the age-grade system of governance that they implemented AfricaTown. In such systems of governance, elders rule over the affairs of the community.[85] Cudjo, Char-Lee, Gumpa, and Polee served as AfricaTown's governors. Because Jabba had been a healer in West Africa, he was accorded high status in AfricaTown, where he also served as governor.[86] Younger cohorts were forced to show respect to their elders by addressing them as *mama, papa, aunt,* and *uncle.* They used these references on both sides of the Atlantic, even when those elders were not their blood relatives.[87] Therefore, children who lived in, and outside of, AfricaTown addressed Cudjo as "Uncle Cudjo," Char-Lee as "Big Poppa," and Kazuma as "Aunt Zuma."[88] Children were expected to behave in a manner that was appropriate for their age group. The *Clotilda* Africans did not negotiate with their children, nor did they allow their children to hold them hostage with threats of calling the authorities. They were the authorities! They accepted their parental responsibilities, and they controlled their children's behavior. As Ms. Ivory Hill asserted, "they meant what they said, and if they told you to move or to perform a task, you doggone better be moving. They were disciplinarians, so we didn't get into trouble."[89]

The *Clotilda* Africans honored their West African, and royal, heritages by maintaining an exemplary character and appearance. Lorna Woods described them as prideful people who dressed well and who possessed a dignified countenance.[90] The *Clotilda* Africans brought indigenous value systems to Alabama. Mr. Spencer Williams, who, as a child, interacted with the *Clotilda* Africans, discussed the strict moral codes by which they lived:

> Uncle Cudjo was a good old man, but he was strict. Those old folks were straight; they believed in living right. They didn't believe in no robbing or stealing or nothing like that. You could leave your house wide open, and no one would bother your things. Today, thieves will come into your house while you're in it.[91]

Cudjo embraces his twin granddaughters, Martha and Mary, in AfricaTown. Yoruba peoples have one of the highest rates of twinning in the world. Erik Overbey Collection, University of South Alabama Archives (circa 1930).

Cudjo and his co-captives hailed from societies whose members relied on an honor system, one that allowed them to take food or other products from an unoccupied market stall, roadside stand, or veranda and leave the money in its place. Cudjo explained the situation in his usual allegorical style when he said, "Suppose I had left my purse in town in a public square. To-day I have not the time to go for it—nor tomorrow—am I worried? No. for I know when I go I will find it where I left it. Could you do that in America?"[92] This is Cudjo's second reference to the public square that was some distance from his farmstead. The public square (*aganju*), as a center of trade and communications, is a prominent architectural feature of Yoruba towns like New Oyo.

If Cudjo left his purse in a public square, he could expect it to remain where he left it not only due to the honor system, but because of the strong sanctions

Cudjo's face reflects the seriousness with which he approached life and his role as a leader within the *Clotilda* group. Erik Overbey Collection, University of South Alabama Archives (circa 1930).

against theft in West African societies where thieves are severely punished. Soyinka asserted that, "theft is the ultimate betrayal of friendship."[93] Theft is also a betrayal of family and community. One of my first experiences in Cotonou included witnessing the beating of a man who stole something from a local vendor. That was social justice, the African way. Cudjo repudiated individuals who stole his property, as discussed by Mr. John C. Randolph:

> Cudjo did not tolerate stealing from his garden. If he caught you stealing, he terminated his relationship with you. Their [*Clotilda* Africans] moral standards were way beyond those that are being displayed by our current generation. They were very straightforward individuals.[94]

The *Clotilda* Africans served collectively as moral compasses for their children, guiding and teaching them how to live and behave as upstanding citizens. As Mama Eva testified, "you didn't steal and you didn't lie. I was carefully reared."[95] Theft continues to be morally offensive in African America, where one finds the vernacular sayings "she looked at me like I stole something" or "he ran like he stole something." In other words, she gave a look of strong disapproval, and he ran to avoid "catching a beat down."

AfricaTown was characterized by moral order that, as a gift from God, belongs to the spirit realm according to several West African religious belief systems.[96] Sango, the god of thunder, lightning, and fire, acts as an agent of social control, and he is both respected and feared as a powerful enforcer of moral order. These sacred and secular forms of justice continued to be honored and applied in the New World, helping to regulate behavior in black communities before conversion to foreign religions that could not fulfill the spiritual or regulatory needs of those communities. Moral order had to be maintained by word, by deed, and by sanction. The *Clotilda* Africans were not afraid to punish those who broke the moral and social codes. Normally, Char-Lee, Gumpa, or Jaba meted out the punishment. However, their power was not absolute; they were not beyond reproach. If Cudjo and his coleaders breached the codes, community members voiced their disapproval.[97]

Murder is the worst moral offense that one individual can commit against another or the community. Unlike American *juris prudence,* indigenous African courts did not allow murderers to plea bargain, as Cudjo explained:

> If it would be my son. He kills a man. I have money—I want to buy my son. I go before the King, and say "Oh, King, my son has killed, but I have money." The King would reply, "Here is the Law, read." I read and say, "Yes, King, the Law says Death." And the King would answer, "That is the Law, and I am the King. Shut your eyes, give up your son—money cannot buy."[98]

Most murderers were executed in Yoruba, Fon, and other West African societies. As Polee asserted, "Money don't plea you there."[99] In some cases, they were sold into slavery or sentenced to hard labor for the benefit of the victim's family.[100] Nevertheless, they were held responsible for their actions. Egregious offenses such as theft and murder were adjudicated before the Oba or the Ogboni Society in Yorubaland, where Sango assisted in meting out punishment to the offenders.

The *Clotilda* Africans and their descendants also took on the responsibility of guarding their community against destructive elements. While they maintained strict control over the internal affairs of the community, they could not control external forces.

Tragedy struck the AfricaTown community when Cudjo Lewis Jr. was indicted on charges of first-degree manslaughter.[101] The reasons for the murder remain speculative.[102] According to Cudjo, the *Clotilda* Africans remained the target of insults and harassments by blacks living on the periphery of AfricaTown, who called them ignorant savages, monkeys, and cannibals.[103] He had raised his children to be respectable people, but included in that respectability was the responsibility to defend the family against insults, harkening back to the reality that African peoples have never been passive in the face of threats. Recall the defiance demonstrated by the king of Cudjo's farmstead, and recall King Glélé's reaction to that defiance. Moreover, Cudjo and his descendants hailed from royal lineages whose members were obligated to defend their position, integrity, rights, and land.

In the case of Cudjo Jr., persistent altercations with individuals on the periphery of AfricaTown may have led to the charge of murder, to which he pled "not guilty."[104] In Jim Crow Alabama, one has to question whether or not Cudjo Jr. received a fair trial. Included in the majority-white jury was Frank A. Cazalas Jr.[105] Cazalas was the son of Mobile's sheriff, charged with aiding and abetting the murder of a black man named Richard Robertson who was shot, stripped naked, and hanged from a tree in downtown Mobile.[106] AfricaTown was surrounded by danger at the turn of the twentieth century and in its first decade. Lynching was rampant. In fact, three black men were lynched in the immediate vicinity of Plateau, on the accusations of rape.[107] As naturalized citizens, the *Clotilda* Africans were entitled to equal protection of the laws and due process of law in theory, but there was no guarantee that they would receive those protections in practice. The other danger that threatened the safety of the *Clotilda* Africans was being thrown into the Mobile County Jail on trumped-up charges. Nonetheless, according to his indigenous laws, and according to the laws of Alabama, Cudjo Sr. had to give up his son to the criminal justice system.

County Probate Courts and jails were feeders into the Alabama State Penitentiary, also known as "The Walls." On two occasions, I witnessed a Mobile County Jail guard escort a black "trustee" prisoner up to the second floor of the archives where I was conducting my research. The racial demarcations were very clear: the guard was white, the prisoner was black, and the people for whom he had come to give a day of virtually free labor were white. I could not help but observe that although the prisoner's uniforms have changed from black-and-white stripes to orange, the racial divisions of the criminal justice system, and the extent to which prisoners are exploited by that system, have not changed. Again, such issues are magnified tenfold when you are in the Deep South. Although the prisoners were trustees, they were candidates for the Alabama State Penitentiary, simply by virtue of being in the Mobile County Jail system.

It is through the probate courts that "The Walls" were able to receive and hold blacks for exploitation by mining companies that signed contracts with the Alabama state government that received monetary payments for the convicts' labor.[108]

After being convicted of first-degree manslaughter, the court ordered that Cudjo Jr. be held by the sheriff of Mobile County until he could be delivered to the warden of the penitentiary of the state of Alabama to serve a five-year sentence.[109] Mines were major beneficiaries of convict-labor in the nineteenth and early twentieth centuries. Cudjo Jr., like many "convicts" who found themselves inside "The Walls" of the Alabama State Penitentiary via Mobile Probate Court, labored at Pratt Mines, located in Jefferson County. In *Rules and Regulations for the Government of the Convict System of Alabama,* approved by the governor on March 22, 1886, customs at Pratt Mines mimicked those on the plantations—the main rule—only white persons shall control or guard convicts, but colored persons may instruct or direct them in their work.[110] Eighty-five percent of the convicts sent to Pratt Mines were black. Like the slave trade and the contemporary prison-industrial complex, the convict-lease system desired young laborers. Forty-eight percent of all convicts were between 20 and 30 years of age.[111]

Cudjo's life was in jeopardy. The Pratt Mines constituted a death trap where black "convicts" were forced to work 10–14 hours per day as they had done on plantations before 1865. At Pratt Mines, convicts slept in beds suspended by iron rods.[112] It was as if they were stacked on tiers of lumber planks in the hold of a slave ship. The convicts "breathed and drank their bodily exhalations and excrement," according to R.M. Cunningham, a physician employed by Pratt contractors from 1881–1885.[113] Black men were sent to Pratt Mines to work and die of bacillus tuberculosis, typhoid fever, pneumonia, lung infections and abcesses, meningitis, scurvy, dysentery, asphyxiation from gaseous explosions, and murder at the hands of fellow convicts and white supremacist guards.

Cudjo Jr. did not perish at Pratt Mines, only because he received a pardon issued in 1901 at the request of Augustine Meaher, a cadre of deputy sheriffs (M.J. Goldsmith, J.W. Murphy, and Frank Douglas), and a contingent of jurors who petitioned for his release on the claim that, as the petition reads, there was "some provocation for the act" and that Cudjo Jr., up to the point that he committed the alleged murder, had been "a man of excellent character, and had stood well with all the people who knew him, white or colored."[114] By the turn of the century, Augustine Meaher had inherited Timothy Meaher's property that engulfed the AfricaTown community. He also inherited the legacy of the *Clotilda* smuggling venture in which his father played a major role. Had it not been for the commission of that crime, Cudjo Sr. would not have been in the predicament of struggling to free his son from incarceration. Thus, rather than casting a cloud over AfricaTown, the case of Cudjo Jr. demonstrated how challenging it was for the *Clotilda* descendants to maintain their morals and exemplary behavior when surrounded by hostility. Despite the fact that they constituted an exhibit to outsiders who mocked them as savages, and despite the fact that Cudjo Jr. was convicted of a serious crime, the *Clotilda* Africans maintained their dignity under these and other treacherous circumstances. In the tradition of their ancestors, this was an obligation that they would not, and could not, neglect, especially if they, and their children, were going to survive. The residents of AfricaTown rejoiced at Cudjo's pardon, thanked God for blessings, and moved forward with their lives.

CHAPTER 8

Spirit of Our Ancestors

The *Clotilda* Africans persevered despite the tragedy of Cudjo Jr.'s incarceration. The first tragedy was that they had been displaced, enslaved peoples at all. Scholars have questioned why Africans were targeted for massive enslavement over Europeans who, from a geographical perspective, might have been more economical to transport to the Americas.[1] But, the economics of slavery encompassed more than labor. Europeans did not possess the knowledge and skill sets that Africans brought to plantation and industrial economies, thereby contributing to their success. Specifically, Africans came to the Americas endowed with certain artistic, metallurgical, and agricultural (crop rotation, terracing, fallowing, irrigation, and fertilization) skills that Europeans lacked. Consequently, the political economy of American slavery was based upon the free labor, knowledge, and skills of Africans rather than Europeans. For example, British and Irish planters depended upon Senegambian, Ibo, and Yoruba Africans from the Grain and Slave coasts who knew the intricacies of planting indigo and rice, the cash crops in the Carolina-Georgia region.

Although some blacks discarded elements of their Africanity in an attempt to assimilate Euro-American societies, many more were compelled to rely on aspects of their indigenous African heritages that they applied to their new world situations. Indigenous African knowledge and skillsets not only contributed to the success of plantation and industrial economies in the Americas, but they ensured the survival of the enslaved Africans themselves. This does not attenuate the oppressive nature of life in American slave systems in a way that negates the fact that Africans were reduced to the status of chattels, denied access to resources, and divested of their social, economic, and political mobility, by law and by force, for the benefit of their owners. Rather, it is to acknowledge and, to some extent, to celebrate the Africans' intellectual, artistic, and technical abilities to triumph over such an ordeal by relying on aspects of their African heritages. As with other dislocated, disfranchised, and enslaved peoples, the *Clotilda* Africans raised improvisation to the level of a high art. Or, in the African American vernacular, "they made a way out of no way."

AfricaTown is a study in the transference and application of ancestral genius and indigenous knowledge. The *Clotilda* Africans were respectful, hard-working folks who paid their own way. The men supplemented their wages from the mills by working as carpenters, selling furniture and crafts that they carved with their own hands.[2] "Char-Lee could fix anything with his hands. In fact, all of them [*Clotilda* Africans] were smart and industrious," said Lorna Woods.[3] In every black community, there are people like Char-Lee, talented craftsmen who can fix anything. The *Clotilda* Africans descended from Fon, Yoruba, and Jaba peoples, who specialize in carving, sculpting, forging, and die-casting several materials that they extract from their immediate environments and fashion into useful objects.

The *Clotilda* men's carving skills were known throughout AfricaTown and the surrounding communities. Mr. Randolph said, "those Africans were good at carving wood. Old man Polee [Polee] would always carve walking sticks."[4] Walking sticks, which often featured zoomorphic icons, became regular features of the material culture of African-descended peoples throughout the diaspora, due to their wide applicability as canes, conjuring paraphernalia, and dance props.[5] The *Clotilda* men also carved single- and multiple-log boats, or "dugout canoes."[6] Dugout canoes are carved in various places in Africa where they serve as a mode of transportation along lagoon and river systems.

The *Clotilda* men transferred their carving and hunting skills to Alabama. Fon, Yoruba, Jaba, Kaninkon, Attakar (Takad), Bache (Bazu), Gwari, and Chamba peoples record hunting traditions as important characteristics of their cultures or lineages. On Ajia road (Ibadan), I encountered a hunter who emerged from the bush. He was wearing nothing more than shorts, no shoes or shirt, and he was armed with a machete and what seemed to be a cartouche of quivers. He said hello to our group, and he disappeared into the bush as quickly as he had appeared. The bush is a mysterious, sacred place where spirits reside. Therefore, hunting is a sacred endeavor replete with its own deities and rites. In Africa, oral traditions attribute the founding of important towns to courageous hunters who are held in high esteem.[7] Cudjo hailed from

Lorna Woods, the great, great granddaughter of Char-Lee, stands in the doorway of his house in Lewis' Quarters. Photograph by Natalie S. Robertson, PhD (2005).

a society of "great hunters."[8] He had been taught to hunt animals during his first initiation into manhood in Yorubaland. He continued to hunt and trap animals in Alabama, including opossums, rabbits, and raccoons.[9]

Cudjo also raised chickens, cows, and hogs, as his people had done in West Africa. However, agriculture continued to be the most important endeavor in which the *Clotilda* Africans engaged in AfricaTown, where they cultivated their own gardens. Mr. Randolph discussed Cudjo's agricultural skills and his generosity:

> He was a very generous person. If you would ask for something from his garden, he would give it to you. I imagine that where he came from in Africa, he was familiar with raising his own food, so that was not a hard task for him in Plateau.[10]

Indeed, Cudjo hailed from a very productive farmstead in Whinny. As a culti-vator, he was steeped in the knowledge of plant material. As members of Yoruba, Fon, Bache, Chamba, Attakar, Jaba, Kaninkon, and Gwari societies, all of the *Clotilda* Africans possessed important agricultural knowledge rela-tive to crop rotation, terracing, fallowing, and fertilization. In Africa, fertilizer consisted primarily of manure, as it did in Lewis' Quarters where the *Clotilda* men made their own fertilizer pits.[11]

Fertile, nutrient-rich soil coupled with South Alabama's humid, temperate climate were conditions that allowed them to cultivate some of the same crops that they had grown in West Africa. In AfricaTown, Cudjo grew corn, beans, blackberries, figs, scuppernong grapes, peaches, black-eyed peas, and sweet potatoes.[12] Black-eyed peas are West African transplants. Often called *yams* in the African diaspora, sweet potatoes differ from the yam grown in West Africa. Like the West African yam, however, the sweet potato is a tuber. Because sweet potatoes were also grown in West Africa, they remained an important staple in the diets of African-descended peoples in the diaspora. In general, the yam was a sacred crop for which festivals are held to give thanks to the gods and the ancestors for a bountiful harvest.

There was much in Cudjo's garden that reminded him of his ancestral farmstead. As in West African agricultural societies, the crops are connected to fertility issues, and nature is often used to explain human behavior. Israel Lewis III, a fifth-generation descendant of Cudjo, said that Cudjo used okra as a metaphor for secrecy and for introspection, maintaining that, "okra is more than just food, when opened you see the seeds inside, man should open himself up to see what's inside of him [explore his intelligence and investigate his integrity], and okra symbolizes that a man's and a woman's face does not reveal what is going on inside."[13] Cudjo also grew sugar cane (also grown in Yorubaland), especially for his great-granddaughters Martha and Mary, who were fond of eating it.[14] Apparently, other people were fond of eating his food as well, often without his permission. Cudjo shared his food with those who knew how to ask for it. But, local people regularly raided his garden. Mrs. Thelma "Mama" Shamburger, a midwife who, with the assistance of her mother, delivered over 900 babies in Plateau —or, as the vernacular phrase goes, she used to "catch babies"—stole peaches from Cudjo, who chased her on several occasions yelling, "Gittee out, Gittee outa me yard."[15] Mama Shamburger recalled that because the *Clotilda* Africans did not bother anyone, they expected others to leave them alone. It is not difficult to see how the theft of his crops in AfricaTown would remind him of the events associated with the raid on his farmstead in Whinny.

Mrs. Ivory Hill said that her ancestor Polee cultivated a variety of fruits and vegetables, some of which he sold to his neighbors. He grew onions, garlic, pears, plums, apples, figs, scuppernong grapes, peanuts, watermelons, canta-loupes, bananas, and okra (a West African transplant).[16] Mama Eva recalled her father's dedication to agriculture:

> I'd help Daddy in the garden in the evenings. Momma say, "Supper's ready," and Daddy say, "Tell Momma I can eat by lamp light, but I can't do this planting by lamp light." And, he'd stay out there till seven or eight and I'd stay with him. Lord Jesus, that's the best life I ever lived. Jesus, I loved it.[17]

In West Africa, farmers remained in their fields until late in the evening, in order to take advantage of the sunlight. Ikudefun informed me that the name Polee is derived from the Yoruba names Kupolu, Kupolusi, or Kupolokun, abiso names that mean "one born after the death of the *Olu* (chief) of the house."[18] Operating in the spirit and legacy of chieftancy, Polee was a leader, a hard worker, and a provider for his people in Alabama. In the tradition of Yoruba peoples, as well as other West Africans, he raised bees from which he extracted honey that has both nutritional and medicinal value.[19] He kept much of the honey for himself, sharing the surplus with his neighbors.

Mama Eva recalled some of the Yoruba words that Polee spoke, such as *bontee* and *joko*. She understood the words to mean "apron" and "love," respectively.[20] Bontee is a modification of the word *bante,* an apron worn by prepubescent males in Yoruba cultures.[21] *Joko*, as it was used by Mama Eva, is a Yoruba verb that means "to sit." If she understood the word to mean "love," perhaps Polee used the word as a shortened version of the name *Banjoko*, given to *Abiku* children or those who repeat the tragedy of dying at early age.[22] In this context, Banjoko means "stay or remain with me." In fact, some of the *Clotilda* Africans wore three horizontal cicatrices on their cheeks, in combination with two vertical cicatrices between their eyebrows.[23] To break the death cycle of *Abiku*, Ifa, the Yoruba deity of wisdom, recommends marking the individual with this combination of cicatrices.[24]

Mama Eva was one of the most memorable descendants of the *Clotilda* family, and she worked tirelessly to keep its legacy alive. In my father's opinion, the black community could not have survived slavery without the strength and wisdom of the black woman, who is the backbone of black history and culture, from antiquity to the present. She was a coruler of the Khemetic dynasties; she sat on the throne as an independent ruler in Ethiopia; she has served as an administrator in kings' courts; she fought alongside men in wars; she has led men into war; she is the essence of her culture; and she is the nurturer of her family. Under the oppressive conditions of a Eurocentric patriarchal model, however, there has been an assault on her industriousness, a quality that is purposely misconstrued and vilified as an emasculator of black men. AfricaTown and other black communities were successful not in spite of the black women, but because of black women's contributions to the intellectual, cultural, and financial uplift of those communities.

As a champion of the rights of blacks, Senator George F. Hoar said, "above all, let the Negro know that the elevation of his race can come only and will come surely through the elevation of its women." In AfricaTown, the *Clotilda* men did not subscribe to the Eurocentric patriarchal model that limits the rights and mobility of women, relegating them to a marginal position or making them scapegoats for the problems and injustices of the larger society. Instead, they shared the responsibility of making AfricaTown a viable community with their women. In West African societies, both men and women cultivate the land, but women manage the markets where food and other commodities are vended.[25] To a great extent, the *Clotilda* Africans maintained that traditional division of labor in AfricaTown. The *Clotilda* men worked in local mills for more than 15 years. Cudjo and his son, Aleck, were shingle makers.[26] Cudjo's son, James, was a shingle stacker. Polee stacked lumber at Dixie Mill Company, owned by Uriah Blacksher.[27] Within the labor hierarchy of the sawmill, skilled and semiskilled jobs were reserved for whites, while blacks were given menial positions like felling trees, rolling logs, and stacking shingles.[28]

The *Clotilda* Africans possessed an entrepreneurial savvy, the same that caused black people to create some of America's greatest inventions like the traffic light, the gas mask, the filament for the light bulb, peanut butter (thank you, Mr. Carver), and jazz. They worked in the mills, and sold meals during the day, but they did not neglect their gardens, which they tended till dusk. The *Clotilda* women sold the fresh vegetables that they harvested from their gardens to their neighbors.[29] Because AfricaTown was surrounded by lumber yards, veneer mills, and railroads, they had a built-in market for their goods. Living in the midst of several industries was somewhat dangerous, and, in 1903, Cudjo Sr. was hit by a train as he attempted to cross the tracks of the Louisville and Nashville Railroad that runs through the eastern boundary of AfricaTown, down to Government Street. After suing L & N Railroad Company, and after winning a $650 judgment at the Mobile Circuit Court, the Alabama Supreme Court overturned the judgment.[30]

One cannot speak of a typical day in lives of the *Clotilda* Africans, who were very diverse, industrious, and creative. But there are some constants that characterize African communities, like sweeping the yard as the first order of business for the day. True to West African tradition, the *Clotilda* women began their day by sweeping their yards.[31] Afterwards, they prepared food to be carried to their small marketplaces. Like their West African sisters, they transported their commodities on their heads.[32] In keeping with the way in which fruits, vegetables, and spices are sold in West African markets, the *Clotilda* women used quart-size containers to measure their figs and spices.[33] The *Clotilda* women also cooked meals that they sold in designated places, typical of West African women. Kazuma sold hot meals to mill workers. "The white folks would just love to eat her cooking," said Viola Allen, who was Polee's granddaughter.[34]

The *Clotilda* Africans developed a reputation for being excellent cooks. As Mr. Spencer Williams recalled, "those old folks could cook good. They raised their own food. They didn't beg white folks for nothing."[35] Instead, whites purchased food and other goods from them. By this example, there was never any doubt that black people could possess, and prosper from, an entrepreneurial spirit. The problem has always been gaining access to necessary resources. What they did not have, they created for themselves. Such improvisation is typical of African peoples on the African continent and in the diaspora. The *Clotilda* Africans passed their knowledge and their skills to their children, teaching them how to cook and vend. Mary Allen, Polee's daughter, sold meals to workers at R.H. Benner's veneer mill, meals consisting typically of fish, chicken, gumbo, peas, rice, and cornbread.[36] But, the *Clotilda* women were not the only ones who could cook. Mary Pogue said that Polee liked to prepare a corn-based gruel called "mush."[37] Mama Shamburger received mush from the *Clotilda* Africans, describing the dish as consisting of corn meal, onions, salt, and pepper.[38] Gruels made of cassava, also called *gaàri*, are a popular morning meal in Yorubaland. Polee also cooked "greens" and peas in big pots in his fireplace, roasting potatoes and peanuts in the ashes.[39]

Gumbo and other stews continued to be important dishes in the diaspora, because they constituted an economical way of feeding several people at once. Africans not only maintained preferences for the same foods that they consumed in their homelands, but West African influences can also be seen in the ways that foods are prepared and consumed. In West Africa, various stews are prepared with fish. Mrs. Josephine Marshall recalled that Gumpa put salmon, onions, and tomatoes in his stews.[40] Mama Eva put tomatoes and fish or chicken in her stew.[41] The *Clotilda* Africans made hoe-cakes and other corn-based breads that they used to "sop-up" their stews and collard greens.[42] The *Clotilda* descendants say that the appropriate way to eat greens is with one's fingers, in the tradition of their ancestors. Indeed, that is the African way, for Fon and Yoruba peoples use their fingers to consume stew, along with pounded yam or yam-flour.

The *Clotilda* descendants continued to apply the agricultural skills that they inherited from their ancestors. Like her ancestor Gumpa, Mrs. Marshall cultivated a garden. Ivory Hill, Polee's granddaughter, continues to cultivate herbs, pears, and figs from which she makes preserves. Canning fig preserves is popular among the descendants, including Mrs. Vernetta Henson, whose maternal grandmother, Mrs. Ora Anna Ellis Floyd, was the granddaughter of Polee Allen. Mrs. Henson, a great-great-granddaughter of Polee, makes the best cornbread in Mobile, and the descendants continue to share garden produce, and home-cooked meals, with one another. "You see, Natalie, this is what it's all about—the simple pleasure of good food and family," said Mrs. Henson.[43] Communalism and mutual aid continue to exist as cultural hallmarks not only of AfricaTown, but of the descendants wherever they might reside. As Mr. John Peoples put it, "we never go hungry in AfricaTown."[44]

Food, and the production thereof, is both a social and a political endeavor. A people who lack a basic knowledge of how to cultivate the land, and who are dependent upon others for the delivery of their food, are vulnerable to strategic starvation and poisoning. This kind of dependency was not an option for, or a desire of, the *Clotilda* Africans. Indeed, the agricultural knowledge that they brought to Alabama contributed to their survival. The Yoruba say, *Ko si orisa ti ko ni igbe* (there is no orisa or deity that has no bush, trees, roots, and leaves).[45] West African peoples who are steeped in the knowledge of plant material possess extensive knowledge of the medicinal properties of that plant material and other natural substances. In Whydah, Eulie De Souza, my African mother, prepared an herbal tea from the leaves of a particular plant that is efficacious in the treatment of constipation. I drank the tea, which was so effective that it produced the opposite result, being too strong for my system. In West Africa, one should err on the side of caution: drink half! Her malarial tea, which was also prepared from a bush in her yard, would have been more effective than my chloroquine that did not prevent me from contracting malaria.

Alabama's swamps were fertile breeding grounds for mosquitoes that transmitted malaria and yellow fever. The *Clotilda* Africans survived various fevers and infections by using their own herbal medicines. Although Jabba had been an herbalist in West Africa, little is known of his specific practices in AfricaTown. Polee, on the other hand, developed several medicines from the plants and herbs that he gathered from his own garden and neighboring fields. "He had something for every complaint. They all [*Clotilda* Africans] knew about them things [herbs]. They'd all gather that stuff, and if one give out, they'd go to another and borrow some," said Mama Eva.[46] Polee made "life-everlasting tea," meant to relieve fevers and congestion.[47] Prepared throughout the diaspora, life-everlasting tea is made from plants that are thought to extend life by curing and preventing illness.[48] Yellow Top plant was the main ingredient in Polee's recipe for life-everlasting tea. In Benin, some plants with yellow tops are also employed in the preparation of teas that reduce fevers.[49] Yellow top is a bitter weed. Polee sweetened his tea with sorghum, a West African transplant that was grown in AfricaTown, and with the honey, an immune system booster, that he extracted from his bee hives.

Bitter plants, barks, gums, and resins are astringents that draw out infections, impurities, or pain.[50] The *Clotilda* Africans used the twigs of the prickly ash to clean their teeth and to treat toothaches. To cure toothaches, they also used red oak bark and alum.[51] Yoruba peoples also chew bitter or peppery twigs to clean their teeth and to treat toothaches.[52] Bitter plants and barks were also efficacious in the treatment of gonorrhea. Yoruba and Hausa herbalists view gonorrhea as a sign that "dirt is in the blood" or that the blood has become contaminated.[53] The *Clotilda* Africans concocted "blood-medicine" from popgum elder and poke-salad, used to rid the blood of harmful bacteria.[54] Blacks cured themselves when Western-trained doctors could not, or would not, treat them. Moreover, blacks refused to let white doctors treat them because they lacked the understanding of healing as a holistic process meant to improve the mind, body, and soul.[55] But, whites often consulted black herbalists for cures for various diseases including syphilis, which is a nondiscriminatory infector.[56]

Since spirits reside in the bush, herbal medicine belongs to the spiritual realm in West African belief systems that provide devotees with a myriad of options for solving worldly problems. Some of the *Clotilda* women were known to throw their newborn babies into the river. If the infants struggled to remain afloat, their mothers retrieved them. Conversely, drowning was an acceptable remedy for those children who demonstrated any weakness from which they would not recover, in the opinion of their parents.[57] Several West African groups perform this trial by ordeal to address birth defects and diseases. Among Attakar peoples, for example, a priest will throw children with incurable diseases into the Kaduna River, where they are allowed to drown.[58]

Among Fon peoples, children who are born hermaphroditic or macrocephalic are called *toxosu*.[59] As abnormal children, they are thought to belong to the river spirits. A priest of the toxosu determines if the child will be a help or a hindrance to the family. Priests recommended that children with insurmountable handicaps be "sent back" to the river spirits from which they came. Before that is done, however, they are taken to the riverbank, where their parents perform specific rituals. Abandonment cannot occur without the support of the gods. Since African peoples view children as gifts from God, they do not abandon them for superficial reasons. Some children who have been ordered to return to the river cry out in protest, indicating that they refuse to accept the verdict. In this case, the priest may order the mother to retrieve and rear the child.[60]

The *Clotilda* Africans' behavior and practices must have appeared strange to blacks on the fringes of the AfricaTown community. Of course, there is a tendency to reduce to witchcraft that which we do not understand or that about which we have lost sensible, cultural understanding. For many years after they arrived in Alabama, the *Clotilda* Africans continued to draw on their indigenous belief systems that sustained their lives under the treachery of slavery and oppression. Because some of them were Islamic, their religious beliefs clashed with those of their enslavers. Kazuma frequently expressed her objection to Eurocentric Christianity by drawing a cross on the ground and spitting on it.[61] Her reaction cannot be explained merely as a clash between her Hausa-Islamic influences and Eurocentric Christianity; it was a conscious rejection and protest of the hypocrisy of those who used Christianity as a justification for enslavement. Kazuma had come from one of the Hausa-speaking regions of West Africa that was coveted by slave buyers as producers of good "house servants." As a Muslim, however, Kazuma would not acquiesce in the idea and practice of chattel slavery. Moreover, her name served as a constant reminder of both the place of her Gwari ancestors and the ungodly, inhumane circumstances that brought her out of the Zuma Rock region and into Alabama.

West Africans drew their strength from their indigenous religions to which they held tenaciously in a world that aimed to destroy their humanity. For eight years after they arrived in Alabama, the *Clotilda* Africans propitiated the deities that comprised their West African pantheons. They held religious meetings in their homes that offered privacy in an environment hostile to West African deities, allowing them to plan their sacred and secular affairs in seclusion. They also held religious gatherings on what was referred to as the "Praying Ground," adjacent to Cudjo's yard.[62] Gatherings on the Praying Ground were akin to brush arbors, secret religious meetings held in wooded areas. In the absence of buildings, brush arbors constituted appropriate sanctuaries because spirits dwell in the bush.[63] Brush arbors also provided a safe haven for West African religious practices that were outlawed in many states, primarily because their indigenous pantheons consisted of powerful, warrior deities that would not only reject enslavement, but would demand rebellion against it.

For these reasons, indigenous religions were always more fulfilling spiritually and politically than foreign ones, particularly *vis-à-vis* foreign aggression. Hence, the primary goal of enslavers and colonizers was to destroy all vestiges of indigenous religion, understanding that doing so removes the power base of the target group.[64] Wherever Africans were dispersed in the world, they carried their pantheons that consist of a Supreme Being and a series of lesser deities. Roche documents that the *Clotilda* Africans propitiated Ahla-bady-oleelay as a "malevolent spirit" in AfricaTown.[65] Instead of being one deity, however, this is a trinity of deities known as *Alasa, Gbade,* and *Akele*. They are assistants to *Xevioso,* the Fon deity of thunder, lightning, and fire.[66]

Alasa, Gbade, and *Akele* have dual natures, possessing good and bad qualities. Alasa is an agent of social control, meting out punishment to thieves and other offenders of the moral and social order. Gbade, the youngest of the three deities, is undisciplined. He destroys fields, houses, and humans by throwing bolts of lightning to the earth. Akele, on the other hand, does not kill humans. He "holds the cord of rain," pulling water up from the sea to the sky, returning that water to earth in the form of rain that nourishes the fields that, in turn, yield food for humans.[67] Thus, Akele stabilizes the relationship between the powerful, often vengeful, thunder gods and humans.

Thunder and lightning are ubiquitous forces that are revered, feared, and consistently placated in Africa and throughout the African diaspora. West African–descended peoples in St. Lucia refer to their thunder deity as *Kele* (derived from Akele).[68] Although Akele is an assistant to Xevioso, Akele is also interchanged with Sango, who is the Yoruba counterpart to Xevioso. To the extent that Fon peoples share a geographical boundary with their Yoruba neighbors, cross-cultural exchanges occur between them. In general, the thunder deities are placated throughout West Africa, and Sango is recognized by various peoples who live outside of southwestern Nigeria. This is due, in part, to the fact that Yoruba honor Sango as a deified ancestor, the fourth Aláfin of the Oyo Empire. Yoruba oral tradition also documents that Sango used a chain to ascend to heaven.[69] In both Yoruba and Fon traditions, therefore, the thunder deities are linked to the earth by a chord or chain, symbolizing the important tie between heaven and earth.

Because thunder deities have the ability to send harmful lightning to the earth, they must be placated. In African America, the notion that thunder and lightning are instruments of God is still extant. For African Americans, thunder and lightning signify that "the Lord is doing his work," during which time one is obligated to show respect by remaining still and quiet. Irreverence incurs the wrath of God in the form of a lightning strike, God's most powerful demonstration of his anger towards humans. "I hope God may strike you dead" is a vernacular saying that expresses the worst physical/spiritual harm that one person can wish upon another. In another context, being "struck dead" by God has been accepted as a sign that initiates the process of religious conversion for "seekers" or those desiring to "know God." Many African Americans have testified that they became Christians after being "struck by the power" of God.[70] Symbolically, their experiences are akin to being struck by lightning, since the prospective convert or "seeker" often claims to see a flash of light that causes him or her to "pass out." In their unconscious state, the converts hear the "thunderous" voice of God, who instructs them to take specific actions to complete the conversion. Ultimately, being "struck dead" by God legitimizes the process of conversion to a "new life" as a Christian.

For African and African-descended peoples, therefore, being struck by lightning, physically or metaphysically, is no ordinary event. The experience may be seen as a blessing or a curse. If the latter is so, and in cases where the lightning has caused loss of life or property, victims are given special rites by priests and priestesses who are devoted to Sango or Xevioso. In AfricaTown, Cudjo and other *Clotilda* Africans showed reverence to the thunder deities by kneeling and crossing their arms over their breasts, saying "we will be good."[71] Crossing the arms over the breasts forms an "X" icon that imitates the shape of the *edun ara,* or neolithic celts that are said to appear on the ground after lightning strikes the earth.

The "X" icon is repeated in the manner in which cowrie shells are worn criss-crossed over the breasts of Sango priests and priestesses who carry dance wands, *oshe Sango,* which embody the same symbol. Sango priestesses wear two *yata* (beaded dance panels) and bags on the right and left sides.[72] The bands that support the panels and bags form the "X" icon over the breasts of the priestesses (some Yoruba chiefs wear two *pakato,* strips of beaded cloth, criss-crossed over their chests). Thus, the icon serializes in the following way:

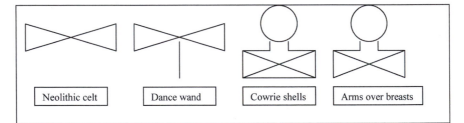

| Neolithic celt | Dance wand | Cowrie shells | Arms over breasts |

Kneeling and bowing are the traditional greetings for Sango as well as his living representative, the Alaafin.[73] Traditionally, men would prostrate fully, 180°, with their bodies parallel to the ground. This was not an appropriate position for women who, rather than prostrating themselves fully, would kneel forward and cross their arms over their breasts, according to the Olo kun Esin.[74] Kneeling is a cultural and political gesture in carvings that depict women making offerings to Sango. Kneeling before the Alafin, they would utter "Ká biyè si," a greeting that means "you are the highest, we cannot ask anything of you."[75] Idowu interprets the greeting to mean "His Majesty–here on earth."[76] In Khemet, kings are often depicted with their arms crossed, grasping the crook and the flail. The "X" is an icon of Ausaru (Osiris to the

Henson, Hill, and Doris Lee exhibit their handmade quilt embued with the "x" icon. Photograph by Natalie S. Robertson, PhD (2005).

Greeks), symbolizing his resurrection from the underworld after which he is considered a deified manifestation of God on earth.[77]

The "X" represents the crossroads, the point of metamorphosis, uncertainty, and unpredictability. Because humans are vulnerable to the forces of nature, various gods must be placated not only to help humans choose a righteous path, but to allow them to walk the path at all, with the full knowledge of the role of the ancestors in that design; gods-nature-humans-ancestors are linked to the same spiritual cipher. Indigenous Yoruba culture makes no distinction between religion and politics. The latter exists because of, and in service to, the former. Heaven and earth are also inseparable in African religious belief systems. Some of the *Clotilda* Africans made references to a deity whose name was transcribed as *Elaha*.[78] This is a reference to the Yoruba deity Èlà, invoked as a savior or one who will restore order during a time of crisis.[79] It is under-standable that the Yoruba members of the *Clotilda* group would invoke this deity to help them cope with enslavement. It is for this reason that West African pantheons remained in tact, in one form or another, for longer periods of time, and under the most oppressive situations, than other elements of culture. In 1868, the *Clotilda* Africans were invited to join Stone Street Baptist Church, whose congregation, like most black churches, formed out of a "brush arbor."[80]

Four years later, Cudjo led efforts to establish Old Union Baptist Church in AfricaTown, now known as Union Baptist Church, erected on the site of the

Praying Ground. Cudjo served as its caretaker, ringing the bell that summoned members to worship.[81] Mama Eva recalled the pride with which he worked to preserve Union Baptist Church:

> Every week Uncle Cudjo had a bench out there at the church. He would take all the lamps out there and set them on that bench. He'd wash the globes and fill the lamps and take them back in the church. Those lamps would be sparkling clean. I'd get down on my little knees with a bucket and somebody else's children, and we would scrub that church. Uncle Cudjo and his wife would fix them lamps and wash them benches off and have them beautiful. And we enjoyed it. Yes we did. It was beautiful.[82]

When blacks built their own facilities in which to hold "church," that building became a focal point of the community, an educational center, a meeting place for political activism, and a symbol of pride. In keeping with the tradition of rural black churches, but rooted in African forms of governance, the polity of Union Baptist was gerontocratic. The senior male members of the *Clotilda* group became its leaders. Thus, Cudjo was referred to as "Elder Lewis," and Polee was called "Elder Allen."[83]

Union Baptist held midweek Bible study and prayer meetings.[84] Mama Eva remembered the *Clotilda* Africans' dedication to religion:

Ivory Hill, Vernetta Henson, and Mary Pogue are proud descendants of Polee Allen. Photograph by Natalie S. Robertson, PhD (2007).

> Them old people pray day and night for their children. I don't know of no other place they went for enjoyment but the house of prayer. They'd have service there every Wednesday night, every Friday night, and every Sunday night. On Sunday morning we went to prayer meeting, praying until dark.[85]

The Bible was the only text that Polee could read, according to his descendants. He delivered sermons with the help of an interpreter. "Rather than preaching 'fire and brimstone' sermons, he used the power of persuasion to convey his biblical stories and spiritual messages," said Ivory Hill.[86] Cudjo could not read the Bible, but he could recall from memory all of the Biblical stories that he had learned.[87] As was the case for many blacks, the Bible was the first text to which the *Clotilda* Africans had access, slaves being denied, by law, access to Eurocentric education.

The *Clotilda* Africans embraced some of the basic tenets of Christianity because they resembled aspects of their West African belief systems. Cudjo said, "we know in Africa dat it a God, but we not know he got a Son."[88] Cudjo and others accepted Jesus as the son of God because the Trinity, like West African pantheons, is stratified. In fact, the original Holy Trinity and ideas regarding judgment, the afterlife, and resurrection were first conceptualized by blacks in East Africa before the rest of the world adopted them. Therefore, it is not difficult to comprehend why Cudjo accepted the notion of heaven as the final resting place, saying to Roche, "When they tell you Kazoola is dead, say No! Kazoola is not dead. He has gone to heaven to rest."[89] Cudjo believed, as many West Africans do, that death signifies the end of a worldly existence and the beginning of a spiritual one as an ancestor.

Baptism cleanses the soul, signifying the beginning of a new life as a Christian. Water is universally used as a purifier, having the ability to wash sins and malevolent spirits away. Union Baptist Church was not equipped to facilitate baptisms that were held in local creeks and rivers. Mama Eva was baptized in Three Mile Creek, for example.[90] Holding baptisms in local creeks was a fitting West African response to a religious dilemma, since, in Africa, lakes, rivers, and waterfalls are considered to be sacred, and they are used as religious objects.[91] The religion that the *Clotilda* Africans practiced after 1868 can best be described as syncretic, incorporating African and European ideas and customs. It is important to note that when one speaks of "the Black Church," one is not referencing a building constructed for religious events. Rather, the Black Church encompasses a people and their worldviews and practices, many of which are rooted in African cultural traditions.[92]

The *Clotilda* Africans and their descendants, like many African-descended peoples, worshipped God in a spirited way. "Shouting" was a regular feature of their religious practices, derived from the ring-shout in which Fon, Yoruba, and other West Africans dance counterclockwise in a circle during religious ceremonies.[93] Viola Allen, the granddaughter of Polee, described the manner in which she "confessed religion" at Union Baptist Church:

> It came a time I couldn't hold my feet sturdy and I was wriggling on the bench and trying to hold my feet to the floor. And I began wondering how I was going to get out of there because I wasn't going to get up. And when I knew anything, I was up! I was going up and down the aisle, and I was saying, "thank you, thank you." And when I found myself, I couldn't control myself no longer.[94]

Reinterpretations of the ring-shout (dancing, stomping, or running up and down the aisles) signify that the spirit being invoked has manifested itself in the presence of the congregant(s).[95] The inflections in the preacher's voice and his dramatic exhortations set the tempo of the sermon, emotive forces that bring about a myriad of responses from the congregants. These practices are still extant among Union Baptist congregants, who continue to worship God in a spirited way.

In keeping with the traditions of most independent black churches, Union Baptist served the spiritual and educational needs of its members. Rosalie Allen, Polee's wife, became the first Sunday school teacher, and the *Clotilda* Africans made Sunday school compulsory for their children.[96] By 1893, the *Clotilda* Africans had established a regular day school, taught by black women from Mobile, for their children, who received instruction in various subjects, including geography.[97] By most accounts, and for that time, the descendants were well educated, as one investigator observed:

> In [Little] Africa, a girl of eleven, who acted as interpreter when their [*Clotilda* Africans] English failed, showed not only knowledge of African geography but of the United States as well, and used good language in her translations, and her name, written in my note book, was in clear, legible, well-formed letters.[98]

The writer is surprised to encounter this young, educated *Clotilda* descendant, particularly at a time when many blacks were still being denied access to educational opportunities in, and by, the greater society. Alabama's 1875 constitution provided that "separate schools be provided for the children of citizens of African descent," reinforced by a 1901 constitutional provision that "no child of either race to be permitted to attend a school of the other race."[99] Of course, these constitutional mandates are extensions of Section 31 of the Alabama Slavery Code prohibiting persons from teaching free blacks and slaves to read, write, or spell.

The writer also emphasizes the fact that the *Clotilda* descendant demonstrated proficiency in oral and written communications. The most powerful tool that an individual can possess is the power of communication, more powerful than all the riches in the world. For a wealthy individual who cannot articulate his or her concerns, despite his or her wealth, remains a fool in the eyes of the public and a disgrace in those of children. Understanding this, the *Clotilda* Africans took the responsibility of educating their own children. For this reason, and for others, AfricaTown is an important microcosm for contemporary African Americans to study the manner in which black people took affirmative actions to provide resources for themselves and for their children when the larger society refused to do so. Cudjo articulated the responsibility in this way:

> We Africans try to raise our children right. When day say we ig'nant we go together and build de school house. Den de county send us a teacher. We Afficky men doan wait lak do other colored people till de white folks gitee ready to build us a school. We build one for ourself den astee de county to send us a teacher.[100]

The importance of literacy is seen in the fact that laws and brutality were used to deny blacks that skill. What is the value of literacy beyond gaining access to information? Literacy helps one develop insight into the workings of people/events; to develop a comparative perspective that would allow the reader to better navigate life, manipulate events in one's favor, outwit an opponent, and understand the ways of the world and the ways of humans. All of these qualities are threats to the body politic, whose power and wealth depend upon the exploitation of masses of ignorant people.

When the state of Alabama refused to fund the establishment of a public high school, Isaac Green and Jeff Giles, also residents of Plateau, donated land for a school for blacks in Plateau.[101] Their donation contributed to the establishment of Mobile County Training School, the first public high school for blacks in Mobile County (erected in 1910). Plateau residents petitioned the state for funds to pay the teachers' salaries, but the state rejected the petition because they did not possess a deed for the land.[102] In fact, no white lawyer would draft the deed. Isaiah J. Whitley, the school's first principal, made himself a notary. Afterwards, he drafted, and signed, the deed.[103] Consequently, Whitley obtained state aid for the school's programs.

Booker T. Washington encouraged Julius Rosenwald, the president of Sears and Roebuck, to give additional monies to the school. Rosenwald was eager to assist. After he witnessed a lynching of a black American in his hometown of Springfield, Illinois, Rosenwald began working for the uplift of oppressed blacks.[104] He had funded several training schools for blacks in Alabama. In 1926, Mobile County Training School obtained accreditation, offering courses in "Domestic Science" and "Shop" or industrial arts.[105] Dr. Benjamin F. Baker, who became the school's principal in 1926, added a sociology course to the curriculum. The ideas that were espoused in the sociology course were based upon a theoretical framework that had been developed by Dr. W.E.B. Du

Bois,[106] one of the greatest intellectuals in American history. Dr. Baker had received his training in sociology under Du Bois's professorship at Atlanta University, transferring his knowledge to Mobile County Training School.[107] In 1926, Dr. Baker issued the first high school diploma to be awarded to a black American in Mobile County.[108] Mobile County Training School is still extant in AfricaTown. Gumpa's grandson, Sydney Robert Lee, was a member of the school's first graduating class. Another of his descendants, James Lee, produced the highest score on the SAT in 1989. In general, many of the *Clotilda* descendants excelled at education, advancing to the college level.

The *Clotilda* descendants, and the children who lived in the vicinity of AfricaTown, learned some of their most valuable lessons not in school, but from Cudjo himself. Children, and adults, adored Cudjo for his ability to tell, and animate, folktales, as recalled by Mr. John C. Randolph:

> He was a nice, generous person. He was always willing to talk to the children. Although we didn't understand much of what he was saying, we enjoyed his company. He was known to tell stories and make gestures. I enjoyed talking with him because he was able to talk that tribal language. He spoke English pretty well before he died.[109]

Cudjo was charismatic, gregarious, and extremely intelligent. He was not only the most outspoken member of the *Clotilda* group, but he was the consummate griot. In 1925, Arthur H. Fauset, an African American folklorist, collected one of Cudjo's folktales called *T'appin* (terrapin).[110] Although tortoise tales are told in several West and Central African cultures, they are very popular among Yoruba peoples.[111]

The tortoise is a trickster who solves his problems by manipulating his environment and the people in it. In *T'appin*, the tortoise tricks other animals into giving him food to feed his family during a famine. The animals comply. But when the tortoise tries to feed the entire village, he loses his ability to feed his own family. The main lesson of the tale, however, is that while it is important to share what you have with others, it is equally important to practice thrift during difficult times. The tortoise also learns to avoid taking advantage of people who offer their assistance. The tortoise loses his ability to feed his own family, but he gains wisdom in the process. Therefore, the tortoise "wins by losing," a recurrent theme in the tortoise tales told by Yoruba peoples.[112]

"Frequently, these old mothers [and fathers] were very clever in story telling, so that Uncle Remus, Brer Fox, and Brer Rabbit were familiar to the children of the South, both white and black, many years before they were in print," said Robert Russa Moton, speaking of the value of his mother in the nineteenth century, in particular, and parents, in general, who used African-influenced folktales to instill intelligence and survival skills in their children, who emerged as adults equipped with the tools not only for survival, but for success.[113] In the twentieth century, Earl Graves, the archetypal symbol of entrepreneurial success in America, included in his book, *How to Succeed in Business Without Being White,* a quote from Bob Holland, the first African American CEO of a publicly traded company (Ben & Jerry's) who, in turn, quotes Bre'r Rabbit, saying, "No matter where you is or what you is, be what you is, 'cause if you is what you ain't, you isn't."[114] Like the *Clotilda* Africans, you must maintain a sense of cultural identity and pride in that identity, which is both the driving and the sustaining force in one's life. One's identity is a source of cultural and economic wealth, if one has the courage to accept it and the discipline to mine it. Return to Bre'r Rabbit and the use of folklore to tap, excavate, and nurture that ancestral genius in children.

The values that Cudjo imparted through his allegories and folktales live on in his descendants. Israel Lewis III maintains a list of maxims that were given to him by his father. Most of these maxims extol the virtues of hard work, community service, reverence for God, and rising above victimization.[115] Indeed, these were the virtues that contributed to the survival of the *Clotilda* Africans, and to that of their descendants, in Alabama. In 1935, Cudjo was

Israel Lewis III is a fifth-generation descendant of Cudjo. Photograph by Natalie S. Robertson, PhD (2007).

asked to appear in a vaudeville show in New York.[116] But, he rejected the invitation for political and moral reasons. He was conscious of the fact that he had already been the object of one man's crime; he would not be objectified or exploited for a second time. He, and his shipmates, has suffered a terrible fate. And, as courageously as the *Clotilda* Africans had lived their lives in Alabama, Cudjo would not allow their history to be reduced to a minstrel show for the amusement of spectators who would pay money to fulfill their bizarre psychological need to see the *primitive darkie.*

Although they became captives in a foreign land, the *Clotilda* Africans survived the ordeal of slavery by their own efforts and by the grace of God. "One ob dese days, I tek time to die," said Cudjo in his final interview.[117] Cudjo was prepared to face the inevitable, with dignity and grace. He spent a portion of his life struggling to return to his ancestral lands, never accomplishing that goal. What Uncle Cudjo did not accomplish physically, he achieved spiritually when he crossed over into ancestorhood in July 1935, 75 years after he was smuggled into the United States. He was between 94 and 100 years of age. His death certificate names the cause of death as artereosclerosis.[118] One could say that he died of a lonely heart. He was preceded in death by his wife and children. His only daughter, his beloved, Celie, died at 15 years of age in 1893, the year of the Chicago World's Columbian Exposition. Cudjo had this to say about her death:

> Dat de first time in de Americky soil dat death find where my door is. But we from cross de water knows dat he come in de ship wid us. Derefo' when we build our church, we buy the ground to bury ourselves. It is on de hill facin' de church.[119]

Cudjo personifies death as a captive that traveled in the hold of the *Clotilda* alongside of him and his shipmates. For too many Africans, slavery was equated with death. From a different perspective, death was inevitable. The *Clotilda* Africans understood that so they, as Cudjo said, bought land with which they established Plateau Cemetery.

The second time that death found its way to Cudjo's door, he called for Cudjo Jr., who suffered a gunshot wound to the neck from which he never recovered, and for which the perpetrator, the pastor of Hay Chapel Church in Plateau, was never indicted.[120] David was killed by a train in Plateau, his head severed.[121] The horror of that sight must have forced Cudjo to revisit those heinous images of the severed heads of family, friends, and strangers decapitated by the Dahomeans. James passed away subsequent to David's death. After more than 28 years of marriage, Abila died in 1908. Abila was an excellent mother, a devoted wife, and Cudjo loved her "all de time."[122] All of the *Clotilda* Africans loved each other and their children. They provided for them, and they sacrificed for one another. Aleck, Cudjo's first born, died after his mother. After his wife and five of his children had passed away, Cudjo expressed his loneliness this way:

> Den I jes lak I come from de Afficky soil. I got nobody but de daughter-in-law, Mary and de grandchillun. I tellee her [Mary] she my son's [Aleck] wife so she stay in de compound and she take de land when I go wid Seely and our children.[123]

But, Cudjo died intestate. After Abila died, Cudjo sold the land he had acquired from Wilson to Thomas L. Dawson, realizing a $75 profit. The deed was notarized by none other than Isaiah J. Whitley.[124] In 1926, he sold another parcel of land for $108 to Mobile County.[125]

At the time of his death, Cudjo owned property valued at $750.[126] Among the individuals listed as his heirs were Polie [Polyon] Lewis, who was last known to be living in Guatamala; Annie Lewis Black, a granddaughter (daughter of James); Gertrude Lewis Bennett, a granddaughter (daughter of James); Angelina Lewis Singleton, a granddaughter (daughter of Alex); James Lewis, a grandson (son of Alex); and Elcania Lewis Mills, a granddaughter (daughter of Cudjo Jr.). Thus, most of his heirs were grandchildren, since most of his children were deceased. Joe Lewis, a descendant of Char-Lee, had filed a petition to become administrator of Cudjo's estate, but his petition was challenged by Annie Lewis Black on the grounds that she, not he, was entitled to become administrator as Cudjo's next of kin.[127]

Although the deeds that the *Clotilda* Africans possessed warranted against claims made by the heirs of the seller, the transfer of property rights is not guaranteed without a will. Consequently, a scramble ensued for Cudjo's property. In Cudjo's defense, Thomas L. Dawson, to whom Cudjo sold property for the establishment of the Elks Lodge that still stands on Bay Bridge Road, Harry M. Touart, the tax assessor of Mobile, and others who had known Cudjo throughout his life came forward to testify that he was the rightful owner of his property, emphasizing the manner in which he had used the eight-gate enclosure to define the parameters of his property.[128] S.P. Gaillard filed to become administrator of Cudjo's estate. But, this posed a conflict of interest, because Gaillard was married to one of the heirs of Lorenzo M. Wilson, from whom Cudjo had purchased land in 1872.[129] Although Cudjo sold that land in 1920, Wilson's heirs were now making claims against that property via S.P. Gaillard. When one dies intestate, any stranger can apply to become the executor of an estate controlled by probate court. Joe Lewis's, Annie Lewis Black's, and S.P. Gaillard's petitions to become administrator of Cudjo's estate were rejected. Interestingly, Walter F. Gaillard became the adminstrator of Cudjo's estate, and his property was sold to J.F. Pate, who, in turn, paid Gaillard $1,200 for property originally appraised at $750.

It does not appear that Cudjo's heirs received anything from his estate. In fact, congregants were forced to take up a collection at his funeral held at

Union Baptist, the church that he founded.[130] His funeral was well attended by both white and black citizens who came to honor the homegoing of Cudjo's ancestral spirit.[131] It was a tremendous outpouring of emotion by all who attended and who had the blessing of knowing Cudjo, who served the remainder of his life as he did the beginning of his life in Alabama, as the honorable spokesman for the *Clotilda* group. Despite the criminal circumstances that brought him to Alabama, Cudjo lived a righteous life, characterized in the following excerpt from the preacher's eulogy:

> Uncle Cudjo was a good ol' man. Deah nevah was a woman in his cabin aftuh de sun went down. We all must be bohn again. Uncle Cudjo is bein' bohn again, but he knew no wrong and nevah done no wrong. Uncle Cudjo twarn't no back slider. Dat's de trouble wid de woild. Deah's too much stuff (deceit) 'round heah. Deah's too much sayin' you is what you ain't.[132]

Cudjo maintained a sense of identity as an African man, he never tried to be what he was not. It has been 13 years since I first interviewed Israel Lewis, and I recently asked him what Cudjo meant to his life. He replied, "Cudjo was my link to the creator."[133] That is a response that emanates from one who is "conscious"—one who is spiritually aware of his ancestral connections that are not only physical, but metaphysical. I also asked Israel what he learned from Cudjo, a question to which he replied, "how to be a good parent. Cudjo set the example, he encouraged harmony, and he kept the African culture in tact. He maintained a profound respect for African culture."[134] Israel is quite artistic, with drawings and paintings displayed on the walls of the various archives throughout Mobile. In the tradition of his ancestor, he has plans to cultivate a garden in which he will plant corn, watermelon, and turnips. Some of the descendants may not have inherited their ancestor's property, but they inherited a powerful, prideful legacy.

In celebration of his life, the *Literary Digest* dubbed Cudjo as "The Most Historic Negro in the United States."[135] First and last, Cudjo was a symbol of humanity, although he was the victim of an inhumane crime; he was a symbol of decency, although he was the target of indecent acts; he was a symbol of strength, despite others' attempts to break his spirit; and he was a symbol of the cultural genius of the African people, contrary to others' description of him and his co-captives as ignorant savages. Cudjo's remains, along with those of many of his shipmates, and, according to local lore, the female house slave of U.S. President William McKinley, are buried in Plateau Cemetery. He was survived by five grandchildren and nine great-grandchildren.[136] At the time of his death, Cudjo was the last member of the *Clotilda* cargo. His death certificate recorded his birthplace: Nigeria, Africa. Long live the ancestral spirits of Cudjo and those of his shipmates.

CHAPTER 9

Crossroads

The *Clotilda* Africans never fulfilled their dream of returning to their ancestral lands. What they did not accomplish physically, this research has achieved spiritually by reconnecting many of them to their places and cultures of origin. At the conclusion of my second research mission to Nigeria in 2004, Oyeronke Aduke Oladipupo, the mother of Olayinka and a princess in the royal palace of Oba Yunusa Bankole Oladoja Ogundipe Arapasowu I, the Olubadan (ruler of Ibadan), invited me to sit courtside for the Egungun Festival, an important cultural and spiritual event by which Yoruba peoples pay homage to their ancestors. One by one, from near and far, princes, princesses, chiefs, and royal wives came to take their places on the Olubadan's veranda. They were elaborately dressed in their finest agbadas, wraps, and geles that befitted the occasion, which symbolized their status, and that reflected the beauty of black people. Such a sight made me contemplate the culturally enriched and regal heritages out of which some of the *Clotilda* Africans had come, only to be reduced to the status of slaves in the United States.

Attending the Egungun festival was a fitting capstone to my research, since it is the ancestors who have guided this entire project from the beginning to a new beginning in which the *Clotilda* descendants can discover, and reevaluate, the geographical and cultural origins of their ancestors. To the extent that this research has enhanced the *Clotilda* descendants' knowledge of their West African ancestries, the project has been an historical and cultural success.

Primary data from Timothy Meaher's descendants would have balanced out this discussion of AfricaTown's history relative to the *Clotilda* smuggling venture. I invited Augustine Meaher III, the great-grandson of Timothy Meaher, to lend his perspective to this research. However, he has not responded to my invitations.[1] Possibly, an admission of his ancestor's complicity in the smuggling venture could expose the Meaher estate to claims for reparations by the *Clotilda* descendants who exist as the human evidence of the *Clotilda* smuggling crime. That the Meaher brothers, and their co-smugglers, were negligent in their treatment of the *Clotilda* Africans by detaining them as captives aboard a U.S.-registered vessel; by transporting them from a foreign place; by importing them into the United States contrary to federal anti-importation laws; by transferring them from one vessel to another; by concealing the captives from local and federal authorities; by plying the federal authorities with liquor, thereby obstructing search efforts; by failing to pay customs duties on a vessel involved in slave smuggling; by burning the vessel as evidence; by failing to appear in court when officially summoned; by dislocating, holding, and enslaving a portion of the captives against their will; and by selling the balance of the cargo to American slave buyers is well documented in Alabama's historiography.

No case for reparations, however, can be argued solely on the basis that slavery was an enterprise that violated the human rights of Africans and their descendants whose bodies, labor, ideas, and skills were exploited for the economic, social, political, and psychosexual benefits of their owners. But, the case must be argued on the strength of specific evidence of complicity in slave trading, owning, brokering, mortgaging, renting, taxing, prostituting, and other fiduciary, legal, and political aspects of this exploitative enterprise at the federal, state, local, corporate, or individual levels. At the federal level, Constitutional language was left open for U.S. citizens to interpret according to their desires to enrich themselves via the importation, taxation, exploitation, and retrieval (in the case of runaways) of Africans who were *held to service* in the United States.

In *Dred Scott v. John F.A. Sanford*, Chief Justice Roger B. Taney confirmed that Constitutional language protected the institution of slavery:

> But there are two clauses in the Constitution which point directly and specifically to the negro race as a separate class of persons, and show clearly that they were not regarded as a portion of the people or citizens of the Government then formed. One of these clauses reserves to each of the thirteen States the right to import slaves until the year 1808, if it thinks proper. And the importation which it thus sanctions was unquestionably of persons of the race of which we are speaking, as the traffic in slaves in the United States has always been confined to

them...no one of that race had ever migrated to the United States voluntarily; all of them had been brought here as articles of merchandise...And this traffic was openly carried on, and fortunes accumulated by it, without reproach from the peoples of the States where they resided.[2]

As a slaveowner, and as Chief Justice of the U.S. Supreme Court, Taney possessed intimate knowledge of slavery's design, its target group, its political economy, and its legal framework. His bias in favor of slavery undermined his ability to render an impartial decision in the Dred Scott case. Instead, his decision destroyed blacks' chances for gaining their freedom while further stigmatizing them as slaves and as condemned peoples in the view of the U.S. Supreme Court, setting a dangerous precedent for lower courts to follow when adjudicating cases concerning the rights of black people, the ramifications of which are still being felt. Yet, Taney's opinion reflected the prevailing bias of American democracy and jurisprudence that denied freedom to human beings in order to profit from their labor, ideas, knowledge, and skills.

Federal judges have expressed their awareness of the fact that certain Articles of the U.S. Constitution applied to the process of enslavement and to the regulation of slaves. They were also cognizant of the fact that the Constitution's language was, by design, left open so as to be manipulated for those purposes. Speaking of the Fugitive Slave Law, Judge Samuel Nelson, associate justice of the U.S. Supreme Court, gave the following instructions to a grand jury in anticipation of, and in preparation for, several cases involving runaway slaves coming before the U.S. Circuit Court of the Southern District of New York:

> The act, as you are aware, was passed for the purpose of carrying more effectually into execution a provision of the Constitution of the United States; namely, a part of the second section of the fourth article. That provision is as follows: "No person held to service or labor in one state under the laws thereof, escaping into another, shall, in consequence of any law or regulation therein, be discharged from such service or labor, but shall be delivered up on claim of the party to whom such service or labor may be due"...This act has been on the statute book and in operation for more than fifty-seven years. Its constitutionality has been recognized and affirmed by the courts of Massachusetts, Pennsylvania and New York, and by the supreme court of the United States in Prigg v. Pennsylvania, 16 Pet. [41 U.S.] 539, and has never been denied by any court, with the qualification that will be presently noticed.[3]

It must be remembered that the Fugitive Slave Laws of 1850 and of 1793 were acts of Congress that denied enslaved black people their freedom. These acts also threatened the liberty of quasi-free blacks who were, in accordance with Article IV, Section 2 of the U.S. Constitution, to be delivered up on claim of the party to whom such service or labor may be due. This language opened the flood gates of false claims that became the basis for arresting black people in large numbers, a scheme that has continued to this very day on the American legal and economic landscapes.

The U.S. Capitol and the White House stand as symbols of the intimate relationship between the federal government, slavery, and capitalism. In fact, the federal government outsourced the construction of the U.S. Capitol to slaveowners who forced slaves to do the work. In 2005, almost two decades after he witnessed the historic Twinning Ceremony that officially recognized the trans-Atlantic link between AfricaTown and Whydah, Representative John R. Lewis led a task force that researched and exposed the extent to which rented slaves helped build the U.S. Capitol.[4] Not only did U.S. presidents, congressmen, and federal judges profit personally from their ownership of black men, women, and children, but judges were federally compensated to decide cases involving runaway slaves. Moreover, the federal government established a U.S. commission to hear cases involving runaway slaves. The commissioners were paid more money if they ruled in favor of the slave masters, representing a direct conflict of interest on behalf of the U.S. government, which played a role in returning slaves to bondage. The federal government also retained the proceeds from sales of African captives confiscated from condemned slave ships during the illegal period in the trans-Atlantic slave trade.[5]

The federal government's culpability in the fiduciary aspects of American slavery is reflected in the transactions of the Bank of the United States, overlooked in the historiography on slavery. The Bank of the United States was established by congressional charter "to serve as government fiscal agents and as depositories for federal funds."[6] Some of those funds were derived from interest gained on bank notes advanced to individuals for the purpose of purchasing slaves. In *Fleckner, Plaintiff in Error, v. The President, Directors, and Company of the Bank of The United States, Defendants in Error*, adjudicated in the U.S. Supreme Court in 1823, the Bank of the United States purchased a promissory note held originally by the Planters' Bank of New Orleans that advanced the note to William Fleckner for the stated purpose of purchasing a plantation and slaves from John Nelder.[7] In addition to discounting the note, the Bank of the United States deducted interest from the sum advanced at the time the discount was made. This means that the U.S. government, through the Bank of the United States, collected interest on monies loaned via its branch bank at New Orleans, for the purpose of buying slaves.

When borrowers defaulted on their mortgages or loans, the Bank of the United States was empowered to bring suit, and execute levies, against property in the form of buildings, land, and slaves. In *Bank of the United States v. Smith,* adjudicated in the Circuit Court of the District of Columbia on March 1836, the Bank of the United States acquired two deeds, the first for five slaves and the second for three slaves.[8] Both deeds were securities against rent due on the City Hotel, located in Washington, DC. When the rent was not paid, the bailiff of the bank sold the slaves (on the premises of the property levied against). The net proceeds in the amount of $1,262.04 were paid to the bank.[9] Therefore, the U.S. government, through the Bank of the United States, profited from the sale of slaves.

The Bank of the United States profited from the sale of slaves through its branch banks operating in slave states. In *Branch Bank at Montgomery vs. L.D. Hallonquist, James G. Birney,* the bank levied on the property of the aforementioned individuals. The property, consisting of black men, named Peter and Morris, a black woman named Vinlett, and a black girl named Sarah, were to be sold to the public on the front of the Mobile County courthouse. Jacob S. March, deputy agent for the bank, recorded that he received, on behalf of the bank, a $190 bid for the Negro named Peter.[10]

At the state and local levels, ledgers record the fiduciary transactions of banks and corporations that financed slaving ventures, that approved mortgages on slaves, and that sold slaves at public sales. The commodification, and collateralization, of blacks as slaves is well documented in Probate Court records of Estate Sales from which numerous municipal banks collected fees from the proceeds. In *Willis & Co. v. The Planters' & Merchants' Bank of Mobile,* adjudicated in the Supreme Court of Alabama in January 1851, slaves were levied on under an execution in favor of the bank.[11] *Dunn & Wife, ET. AL. v. The Bank of Mobile, ET. AL.,* adjudicated in the Supreme Court of Alabama, January 1841, reveals the manner in which black people were defined as both property and "inheritance," transferred in a deed, from one owner to another. The slaves were subsequently levied on by the Bank of Mobile.[12]

One year before the *Clotilda* embarked upon her smuggling venture, the Bank of Mobile announced its intention to sell 77 black men, women, and children (the oldest being 74 years of age, the youngest being one year of age, and including a set of twins, Charles and Julia), all belonging to John P. Broun.[13] The terms of the sale were described as follows:

> One half cash, the balance in one, two and three years, all the payments negotiable and payable at the Bank of Mobile, bearing 8 per Ct. interest payable annually, the Cash payment to be made before the negroes are delivered, by Mobile acceptance, the other payments in Negotiable Notes jointly and severably, with two approved securities. Bills of Sale given as soon as the Cash payment is made, warranting the Titles, but nothing farther.[14]

Not only was the economics of slavery far more complex than supply and demand, but the institution was a political economy upon, and around, which owners of slaves and allied businesses built reputations and fortunes. As the example above demonstrates, the collateralization of slaves generated income and residual income for banks that wrote mortgages for slaves and that collected interest on those mortgages and slave sales. State and municipal governments collected duties and taxes on various transactions related to slave trading and slaveownership. The taxation of Africans at the state level was sanctioned by Article 1, Section 9 of the U.S. Constitution. At the municipal level, the city of Mobile collected taxes on slaves owned by its residents.[15]

State and local governments' culpability in the exploitation of black men, women, and children for capital gain continued in the post-1865 period, particularly via convict-leasing schemes that allowed private companies to enter contract agreements with state-run penitentiaries, their wardens, and governors.[16] In Alabama, the main scheme worked as follows: 1) Black males were sentenced to "hard labor," often on trumped-up charges; 2) those convicts were processed through probate courts that sent convicts to "The Walls" of the Alabama State Penitentiary; 3) private companies such as Pratt Coal and Iron Company, Comer & McCurdy, J.F.B. Jackson, Milner Coal & Railroad Company, and L.D. Rouse, to name a few, entered into contracts with the state of Alabama (assisted by the Court of Commissioners and the Probate Courts of each county), pursuant to Alabama state code, to lease the convicts at prices agreed upon in the contracts; and 4) the private companies paid the original monies, and 20 percent interest accrued on defaulted contracts and escapees, to the state of Alabama, its governor, and the penitentiary warden.[17] Alabama State Penitentiary is listed on the National Register of Historic Places. Classified a "National Treasure," the penitentiary was a critical component of the convict-leasing schemes that contributed to the profits of mines, mills, and railroads and contributed to the early deaths of many blacks.

Some existing corporations are descended from parent companies with ties to slavery and convict-leasing schemes. Pratt Coal and Coke Company merged with Tennessee Coal and Iron Company, known today as U.S. Steel. Owning black people was far more lucrative than selling and transporting them, for two important reasons. First, blacks, as property, constituted collateral against which money could be borrowed from banks. Americans desirous of becoming owners of black people could, with the right credentials, obtain a mortgage on them, paying the bank back at a predetermined rate of interest. On its corporate Web page, Wachovia admitted that its predecessor companies, the Georgia Railroad and Banking Company and the Bank of Charleston, owned slaves as both collateral and as property confiscated from clients who had defaulted on their loans.[18] In another case of corporate slaveowning, two Louisiana-based banks, Citizen Bank and Canal Bank, both predecessors of JP Morgan Chase & Company, held black people as collateral and confiscated blacks as property when customers defaulted on their loans.[19]

In *Deadria Farmer-Paellmann v. FleetBoston Financial Corporation, Aetna Inc., CSX*, a class-action lawsuit filed in the U.S. District Court for the Eastern District of New York, it is alleged that "FleetBoston is the successor in interest to Providence Bank which was founded by Rhode Island Businessman John Brown."[20] The lawsuit alleged that "Providence Bank lent substantial sums to Brown, thus financing and profiting from the founder's illegal slave trading."[21] It further alleged that CSX is a successor in interests to several railroads that benefited from slave labor and that Aetna Inc., a major insurance company, insured slavers and their human cargoes.[22] This case was dismissed because the plaintiff, the court argued, could not demonstrate specific ways in which descendants of slaves had been wronged, something that must be done necessarily. In an indirect way, the court argued that descendants were not entitled to reparations because they had received assistance from the Freedmen's Bureau and from the passing of civil rights legislation.

While efforts have been made to get the U.S. government to openly acknowledge its culpability in the enslavement of Africans and their descendants, not to mention efforts to get the federal government to compensate the victims of slavery, slaveowners have received reparations from the federal government. Between 1854 and 1856, the federal government issued Compensation Bonds to slaveowners who emancipated their slaves. However, an important document that confirms the issuance of Compensation Bonds to slaveowners is currently classified as "missing" from the National Archives.[23] As the reparations debate intensifies, the chances that certain documents will go missing from files will also increase. However, there are other instances in which slave masters have received reparations for the loss of their slaves. Under the District of Columbia Emancipation Act of 1862, the U.S. Treasury Department compensated slave masters for each person "held to service or labor within the District of Columbia by reason of African descent."[24] Once *such persons* had been appraised, and their values determined, the slave master presented the appraisals to the appropriate commissioners, who paid the owners up to $300 per slave.[25] The federal government also set aside $1,204,000 to compensate masters whose slaves were both captured by the British and who absconded to British vessels during the War of 1812.[26]

The British remained involved in America's political and economic affairs far beyond 1812. Indeed, the British textile factories were major consumers of cotton produced in Alabama and other Southern states. For this reason, British industrialists had a vested interest in helping to preserve the institution of slavery in the United States. Toward the preservation of slavery, industrialists continued to purchase U.S. cotton. The evidence shows that Timothy Meaher's ship, the *William R. Hallett*, transported a load of cotton to Liverpool.[27] British shipbuilders in Liverpool also supplied the Confederates with munitions, war ships, and blockade runners, including the CSS *Alabama*, during the Civil War.[28] British banks also contributed finances to the Confederate cause. Those transatlantic fiduciary connections are reflected in the architecture of Liverpool's banking and commercial buildings embellished with symbols of Raphael Semmes and the CSS *Alabama* at Rumford Place, and with images of "negro" boys holding ship anchors in the entrance of Martins Bank (now called Barclays). Many foreign banks and corporations thrive today based upon their past exploitation of enslaved Africans. Lloyd's of London, for example, underwrote insurance policies for numerous slaving ventures.[29] Thus, the reparations equation must be expanded to factor in the roles that Britain and other foreign countries played in the enslavement of Africans and their descendants, not to forget the fiduciary roles that the financial houses of Britain, Venice, and Genoa played in backing early investors in the slave trade such as John Hawkins and Queen Elizabeth I.

While it is true that individuals who comprise the current generation did not enslave anyone, as many of them are quick to argue in defense of themselves or in objection to reparations for descendants of enslaved Africans, it is also true that many of those individuals are the beneficiaries of "old money" converted into real estate, trust funds, degrees from prestigious universities, and, albeit less tangible, political status and access. The evidence of specific families' involvement in slavery, and of the extent to which old money was converted into contemporary collateral, is recorded in probate records and personal papers that provide information regarding their property (land and slaves), their professions and allied enterprises, the names of their descendants, and the nature of their educational or occupational accomplishments. In addition to being the founder of Providence Bank and a slave trader, for example, John Brown was an opium trader, a rum distiller, a plantation owner, and proprietor of the slave ships *Delight, Hope,* and *Mary*.[30] His descendants inherited the wealth generated by those businesses. They also acquired land, some of which they donated to Rhode Island College. In recognition of their generous gifts, the name of that college was changed to Brown University.[31] Current generations are benefiting, even from the opportunity to walk the hallowed halls of Brown, Harvard, and Yale, which were endowed in part with monies derived from slave trading.[32]

The architectural and material evidence of slavery exists as wealth *in plain view*, from the north to the Gulf shores. Boston's Faneuil Hall was donated by Peter Faneuil, a Yankee slave trader and co-owner of the slave ship *Jolly Batchelor* that returned to New England with 20 slaves after being sea-jacked on the West African coast. The slaves were sold for the equivalent of 1,624.[33] In 1743, *Jolly Batchelor* was sea-jacked by black pirates who killed the Captain (Cutler), throwing his body overboard. The pirates plundered the *Jolly Batchelor*'s cargo, including the slaves in her hold.[34]

If Alabama's, Mississippi's, and what remains of Louisiana's plantation mansions can serve collectively as a visual, architectural record of the amount of wealth that slave masters accumulated, then American slaveowners reaped tremendous profits from slavery. Their descendants continue to reap residual profits from these plantation estates, converted into bed-and-breakfast establishments, historic mansions, and gardens. Today, the Meahers hold prominent professional positions as lawyers, bankers, and homebuilders. They have been designated "the largest landholding family in the Mobile-Tensaw Delta."[35] Their "Land For Lease" signs can be seen throughout Plateau, Magazine Point, Pritchard, and Saraland. They gave land for the establishment of Meaher State Park. In tradition of their ancestors, they control valuable waterfront properties with access to the Gulf of Mexico. Meaher industrial sites consist of prime real estate along the Mobile River, sites that are valuable to industrialists engaged in trans-Atlantic shipping, logistics, manufacturing, packaging, and storage.[36]

Within the context of the reparations debate, particularly when assessing the extent of individual liability in slavery, recognition must be given to the fact that the black children of white masters also inherited property in the form of slaves. Any master or mistress, irrespective of racial self-identification or categorization, or religious affiliation, who enslaved another human being and, in doing so, also denied that human being opportunities for educational, social, political, and economic advancement, so as to be injurious to those human beings and their descendants, and any descendant of that master or mistress who benefited from the enslavement, directly or indirectly, are culpable, and liable, based upon specific evidence. However, an admission that a small percentage of blacks and Native Americans owned slaves does not negate the fact that the federal government, and the states within the Union, codified, implemented, and enforced systems of slavery from which they derived profits.

Regarding the culpability of the U.S. government in the enslavement of Africans and their descendants, the questions are whether or not the U.S. government knowingly and willfully held persons to service and labor within its jurisdictions; whether it designed or utilized laws to support, ensure, or protect the practice of holding persons to service or labor; whether or not Africans and their descendants belonged to that class of individuals held to service or labor; whether or not, in holding Africans and their descendants to service or labor, the holders deprived them of their freedom; and whether or not, by holding them to labor or service, their holders, according to federal laws, codes, and statues, or according to laws, codes, and statues of the various states that comprise the Union or the United States, derived a profit from the labor and products of the intellect of those held to service or labor in ways that deprived the laborers of compensation and advancement and that deprived their descendants of inheritance; whether or not their holders continued to hold them, and their descendants, to service and labor for numerous and successive generations of their lives in the United States; whether or not the U.S. Congress enacted laws to bring members of that class of individuals held to service, but who had escaped their bondage in search of freedom, back to bondage; whether or not the aggregate of the aforementioned actions perpetrated by the U.S. government separately, and in concert with its slave states, prevented those held to service from achieving liberty in accordance with its democratic design, and that would, in any manner, deny them, and their descendants, prosperity, enfranchisement, and advancement? To all of these questions, the answers are in the affirmative.

That blacks survived slavery and its aftermath was attributed, in great measure, to God's grace and to the slaves' application of their West African folk traditions, intellect, ingenuity, and talents to their New World situations. These were the actions that blacks affirmed for themselves. They did not wait for others to affirm anything for them because America's policies, public and private, were never ones of benevolent, affirmative action on behalf of black people. In the twenty-first century, blacks must act in the affirmative towards themselves, their families, and their communities. As the ancestor Martin Robison Delany asserted in his *Official Report of the Niger Valley Exploring Party,* "We must make an issue, create an event, and establish a position *for ourselves.* It is glorious to think of, but even more glorious to carry out." Thus, following in the tradition of the *Clotilda* Africans and other ancestors, blacks must redefine the concept of affirmative action as that which one implements for the empowerment of one's self, one's family, and one's community. Within this redefinition, strategies should entail all, or part, of the following objectives for cultural, social, and economic development: 1) study the ancient and global dimensions of black history, in order to understand that the experiences and achievements of black people are not limited to slavery; 2) expand the definition of spirituality to incorporate a respect for ancestors, elders, nature, and indigenous African philosophies and values; 3) explore the manner in which Africans applied their indigenous knowledge and talents in practical ways that improved, sustained, and protected the quality of their lives; 4) avoid the traps set by criminal justice systems and the prison-industrial complex; 5) develop the economic infrastructure of black communities through intellectual entrepreneurship and the creation of micro- and macro-level enterprises, especially in the areas of education, food supply, elder care, and real estate acquisition (residential and commercial secured by deeds, wills, and trusts); and 6) form cooperatives and corporations to purchase as much real estate as possible, as soon as possible, because real estate has multiple uses, it appreciates in value, and it yields residual resources in perpetuity as plantation mansions have demonstrated.

Cumulatively, these affirmative actions towards, and within, the black community will be far more beneficial than reparations since blacks possess the intelligence to develop local cooperatives into a national economic network that collateralizes and leverages their $500 billion net worth in order to build *generational wealth.* Throughout America's social and political history, blacks have been viewed and discussed as "problems" that plague the American body politic. If blacks constitute a problem for American society, then they represent a problem that America made for itself in its effort to gain wealth on the backs of enslaved peoples who were denied access to education and important resources necessary for their social and economic development. The fault, therefore, rests not with the slave, but with the slave masters. Speaking about the degrading manner in which Dahomean captives were exhibited at the World's Columbian Exposition in 1893, Frederick Douglas articulated the issue in this way:

> Men talk of the Negro problem. There is no Negro problem. The problem is whether the American people have honesty enough, loyalty enough, honor enough, patriotism enough to live up to their own Constitution...During the war we were eyes to your blind, legs to your lame, shelter to the shelterless among your sons. Have you forgotten that now? Today we number 8,000,000 people. Today a desperate effort is being made to blacken the character of the Negro and to brand him a moral monster. In fourteen States of this Union wild mobs have taken the place of law. They hang, shoot, burn men of race without justice and without right. Today the Negro is barred out of almost every reputable and descent employment. We only ask to be treated as well as you treat the late enemies of your national life. We love this country and we want that you should treat us as well as you do those who love only part of it...Look at the progress the Negro has made in thirty years. We have come up out of Dahomey unto this. Measure the Negro. But not by the standard of the splendid Civilization of the Caucasian. Bend down and measure him—measure him from the depths out of which he has risen.[37]

Like the Dahomean Village at the World's Columbian Exposition, the *Clotilda* Africans remained an exhibition of man's inhumanity to man. But, their blackness, rather than being a badge of inferiority, is a mark of triumph. For, out of the bowels of slave ships they rose, and their descendants are, in the powerful words of Langston Hughes, "Still Here." The *Clotilda* Africans and their descendants are microcosmic illustrations of this fact.

Like millions of Africans, Cudjo and his shipmates lived exemplary lives in America, despite the tragic circumstances that brought them to the United States. With no prospects for returning to West Africa, the *Clotilda* captives resolved to make a life for themselves in Alabama. They were serious people who believed in "living right," according to their moral convictions and core African cultural values. Although the *Clotilda* Africans were held captive in a foreign land, they refused to let their culture degenerate in the face of oppressive forces. In spite of it all, they established, and maintained, a respectable, viable community where they raised their own crops, developed strong families, and educated their children. They gave mutual aid to one another, and they loved, and protected, each other. Today, AfricaTown exists as a symbol of their resiliency that lives on in their descendants, who did not collapse under the weight of racial oppression. But, they survived on the strength, knowledge, and wisdom that they inherited from their West African forebears. That was, that is, and that must continue to be the African American way, forever guided by the unconquerable spirit of our ancestors.

Notes

CHAPTER 1: PRELUDE TO PERIL

1. Dara Graves, "Haley Sees No AfricaTown, S. [South] Africa link," *Mobile Press Register,* February 27, 1986.

2. Ron Colquitt, "Archbishop from Benin Keynotes Ritual: His Ancestors Sold Slaves to be Shipped Here," *Mobile Register,* February 24, 1986, pp. 1B–2B. See also Vivian Cannon, "Archbishop of Benin Arrives for AfricaTown Folk Festival," *Mobile Register,* February 19, 1986.

3. Patrick Manning, *Slavery, Colonialism and Economic Growth In Dahomey, 1640–1960* (London: Cambridge University Press, 1982), 29.

4. David Ross, "The Career of Domingo Martinez in the Bight of Benin 1833–64," *Journal of African History* 6, no. 1 (1965): 79.

5. Captain William Foster, "Last Slaver from U.S. to Africa. A.D. 1860," Captain Foster's Account (photocopy): 1–11. Special Collections, Public History and Genealogical Department, Mobile Public Library, Mobile, AL.

6. Emma Langdon Roche, *Historic Sketches of the South* (New York: Knickerbocker Press, 1914), and Zora Neale Hurston, "Cudjo's Own Story of the Last African Slaver," *Journal of Negro History* 12 (October 1927), did not delineate the *Clotilda* African's heterogeneous geographical and cultural origins for similar reasons. Roche and Hurston did not travel to Africa for the purpose of collecting primary data that would have allowed them to elucidate those origins with a high degree of specificity, although Hurston was correct in her subsequent claim that Cudjo was a Nigerian man. Sylviane Diouf, author of *Dreams of Africa in Alabama: The Slave Ship* Clotilda *and the Story of the Last Africans Brought to America* (New York: Oxford University Press, 2007), fails to provide cogent explanations of the *Clotilda* Africans' origins beyond what has been revealed by Natalie S. Robertson's "The African Ancestry of the Founders of AfricaTown, Alabama, 1859 to Present," published in 1996. Diouf relies too heavily on this source that represents Robertson's research in its preliminary phase, revised and copyrighted in 2005 as *Spirit of Our Ancestors: The Slave Ship* Clotilda *and the Making of AfricaTown.* Diouf claims to have traveled to Takon, located in the Republic of Benin, to investigate the origins of the *Clotilda* Africans, but she does not provide academically sound geographic, ethnographic, or historiographic baselines for selecting Takon as a place of origin. Furthermore, she does not provide photographic evidence, and she provides

minimal primary data, from Takon that she subsequently admits could not have been the *Clotilda* Africans' place of origin. Diouf does admit that she conducted the bulk of her research in the Schomburg Center for Research in Black Culture of the New York Public Library (Diouf, x), beginning in 1996. Relying too heavily on secondary sources, with minimal regard for primary data and indigenous perspectives at the scholarly and lay levels, on both sides of the Atlantic, can be, and often is, problematic for transatlantic, cross-cultural studies that examine the African origins of black peoples.

7. Mr. Richard Edwards, interview by author, AfricaTown, AL, February 25, 1995, handwritten. Mr. Edwards was 16 years of age when he met Hurston, who collected folk material from him. See Zora Neale Hurston, *Every Tongue Got to Confess: Negro Folk-tales from the Gulf States,* ed. Carla Kaplan (New York: Harper Collins, 2001), 136, 262.

8. Hurston received this fellowship from the Association for the Study of Negro Life and History, founded by Dr. Carter G. Woodson. Lillie P. Howard, *Zora Neale Hurston* (Boston: Twayne Publishers, 1980), 21.

9. Zora Neale Hurston, "What White Publishers Won't Publish," in *I Love Myself When I Am Laughing...And Then When I Am Looking Mean and Impressive,* ed. Alice Walker (New York: The Feminist Press, 1979): 173.

10. When Mr. Richard Edwards told me that he met Zora Neale Hurston in his work camp in 1927, he remembered her well, but he forgot to mention that she had collected a folk saying from him entitled "The Hottest Day" in which he said, "I seen it so hot till you had to feed the hens cracked ice to keep them from laying hard-boiled eggs." Hurston, *Every Tongue Got to Confess,* 262. Mr. Edwards has crossed over into ancestorhood.

11. Zora Neale Hurston, *Dust Tracks on a Road* (Philadelphia: J.B. Lippincott, 1942), 49.

12. Hurston, "Cudjo's Own Story," 648–63.

13. Zora Neale Hurston, "The Last Slave Ship," *American Mercury* 58 (1944): 351–58; Howard, *Zora Neale Hurston,* 32. Hurston also included a considerable amount of ethnographic material collected from Cudjo in an unpublished work called "Barracoon: The Story of the Last 'Black Cargo,'" Box 164–186, File #1, typescript of unpublished mss., Moorland-Spingarn Manuscript Collection, Howard University.

14. Hurston, *Dust Tracks,* 63.

15. Ibid., 65, 67.

16. "Plateau Negro Remembers Capture in Jungle Lands: 'Kazoola,' Last of Cargo of Slaves Brought to America and Sold in Mobile , Has Vivid Recollection of Past Events." *Mobile Register,* September 29, 1929.

17. J. Ki-Zerbo, "The Living Tradition," in *General History of Africa I: Methodology and African Prehistory,* ed. J. Ki-Zerbo (Berkeley: University of California Press, 1990), 71. See also Mary Nooter Roberts and Allen F. Roberts, eds., *Memory: Luba Art and the Making of History* (New York: The Museum of African Art/Prestel: Munich, 1996), 17–28.

18. Ibid., 29.

19. Henry Romeyn, "Little Africa: The Last Slave Cargo Landed in the United States." This article contains information on the voyage of the *Clotilda,* as well as some ethnographic data that was collected via interviews with the *Clotilda* Africans. *Southern Workman* (publication of Hampton Normal and Agricultural Institute) 26, no. 1 (January 1897): 14–17.

CHAPTER 2: VOYAGE OF THE SLAVER *CLOTILDA*

1. *Slave Trade Act of 1807.* "Documents on Slavery." The Avalon Project at Yale Law School. Available at http://www.yale.edu.

2. Daniel P. Mannix, *Black Cargoes: A History of the Atlantic Slave Trade, 1518–1865* (Associated Publishers, Inc., 1962), 197.

3. Donald G. Nieman, *Promises To Keep: African-Americans and the Constitutional Order, 1776 to the Present* (New York: Oxford University Press, 1991), 13.

4. Ralph Ketchum, "The American Presidency." Grolier Encyclopedia. Available at http://www.gi.grolier.com.

5. Paul Jennings authored the first White House memoir entitled "Paul Jennings: A Colored Man's Reminiscences of James Madison." Available at http://www.msstate.edu/Archives/History/USA/Afro-Amer/jennings.txt. See also William Seale, *The President's House: A History,* vol. 1 (White House Historical Association with the Cooperation of the National Georgraphic Society and Harry N. Abrams, 1986), 122.

6. Henry Steele Commager, ed., *Documents of American History* (New York: F.S. Crofts & Co., 1974), 141.

7. W.E.B. Du Bois, *The Suppression of the African Slave Trade to the United States of America, 1638–1870* (New York: Longmans, Green, and Company, 1904), 198.

8. Ibid., 110.

9. *Slave ships in Alabama: Message from the President of the United States, transmitting the proceedings of the court and marshall of the U.States for the District of Alabama to the cargoes of certain slave ships, &c.* (Washington, DC: Printed by Gales & Seaton, 1826), 6. This is a rare book in the library collection of the Mariner's Museum. Newport News, VA.

10. Emma Langdon Roche, *Historic Sketches of the South* (New York: Knickerbocker Press, 1914), 69–72. See also "The Plateau Negro Remembers Capture in Jungle Lands: 'Kazoola,' Last of Cargo of Slaves Brought to American and Sold in Mobile, Has Vivid Recollection of Past Events," *Mobile Register,* September 29, 1929. See also "Capt. Wm. Foster. Commander of the Last American Slave Vessel Buried Yesterday." n.d. The transcript of information collected from Captain William Foster's wife, one day after his death, via an interview by a *Herald* reporter. Special Collections, Local History and Genealogical Department of the Mobile Public Library, Mobile, AL.

11. "Capt. Wm. Foster. Commander of the Last American Slave Vessel Buried Yesterday."

12. John R. Spears, *The American Slave-Trade: An Account of Its Origin, Growth and Suppression* (Port Washington, NY: Kennikat Press, Inc., 1900), 152.

13. Frederick C. Drake, "Secret History of the Slave Trade to Cuba Written by an American Naval Officer, Robert Wilson Schufeldt, 1861," *Journal of Negro History* 55, no. 3 (July 1970): 224.

14. Eric Williams, "Capitalism and Abolition," in *The Atlantic Slave Trade,* ed. David Northrup (Massachusetts: D.C. Heath and Company, 1994), 188. See also Harral E. Landry, "Slavery and the Slave Trade in Atlantic Diplomacy," *Journal of Southern History* 27, no. 2 (May 1961): 189–92, 205.

15. Williams, "Capitalism and Abolition," 188.

16. Ibid., 196.

17. U.S. Congress, Senate, *Correspondence Imputing Malpractices to the American Consul at Havana,* 26th Cong., 2nd sess.., Senate Document no. 125 (1841): 217.

18. Clifton Johnson, "The Amistad Case and Its Consequences in U.S. History," Amistad Research Center, available at http://www.tulane.edu.

19. Mannix, *Black Cargoes,* 208.

20. U.S. Congress, Senate, *Correspondence Imputing Malpractices To The American Consul at Havana,* 9–231.

21. Pierre Verger, *Trade Relations between the Bight of Benin and Bahia from the 17th to 19th Century* (Ibadan, Nigeria: Ibadan University Press, 1976), 372.

22. Ibid.

23. Warren S. Howard, *American Slavers and the Federal Law, 1837–1862* (Los Angeles: University of California Press, 1963), 33. See also *Facts and Observations Relative to the Participation of American Citizens in the African Slave Trade,* published by direction of a meeting representing the Religious Society of Friends in Pennsylvania, New Jersey, etc. (Philadelphia: Joseph & William Kite, Printers, 1841), available at http://amistad.mysticseaport.org/library, p. 13.

24. *New York Morning Herald,* October 8, 1839, 2. Available athttp://mysticseaport.org/library.

25. U.S. Congress, Senate, *Correspondence Imputing Malpractices to the American Consul at Havana,* 9–231.

26. Ibid., 140–41.

27. Ibid., 142.

28. Verger, *Trade Relations between the Bight of Benin and Bahia,* 70.

29. J.A. Rogers, *Sex and Race,* vol. 2 (St. Petersburg, FL: Helga M. Rogers, 1968), 199.

30. Warren Fiske, "Jefferson Fathered Slave," *Virginia-Pilot,* November 1, 1998, A9. See also Charles L. Blockson, *Black Genealogy* (Baltimore: Black Classic Press, 1991), 106; and, J.A. Rogers, *Sex and Race,* vol. 2, 186n.

31. According to J.A. Rogers, "incest was common on plantations," and Jefferson Davis had sexual intercourse with his niece. See *Sex and Race,* vol. 2, 190–91.

32. Ibid.

33. See Dr. John L. Johnson, *500 Questions and Answers on the Black Presence in the Bible* (Chicago: Lushena Books, 2000).

34. Howard, *American Slavers and the Federal Law,* 34.

35. Louis Martin Sears, "Nicholas P. Trist, A Diplomat with Ideals," *Mississippi Valley Historical Review* 11, no. 1 (1924): 85–88.

36. *Grolier Encyclopedia* (Grolier Electronic Publishing, Inc., 1995).

37. Mannix, *Black Cargoes,* 199.

38. Spears, *The American Slave-Trade,* 81.

39. Du Bois, *The Suppression of the African Slave Trade,* 297.

40. Drake, "Secret History of the Slave Trade," 228.

41. "The Ostend Manifesto: Aix-La-Chapelle: October 18, 1854." Available at http://xroads.virginia.edu.

42. Ibid.

43. Nicholas Philip Trist Papers, Manuscripts Department, Library of the University of North Carolina at Chapel Hill. Available at http://cadmus.lib.unc.edu.

44. Sears, "Nicholas P. Trist, A Diplomat with Ideals," 89.

45. "Chronology on the History of Slavery, 1830 to the End." Available at http://innercity.org/holt/chron_1830_end.html.

46. Petition to Partition Real Estate Owned by J.M. and T. Meaher. Mobile Probate Court Archives. Pigeon Hole 185. File No. 38, 1884. See also Physical Features: Mobile and Suburbs (Map no. 12) in *Boudousquie's Directory for the City of Mobile* (1861), 188. Special Collections, Local History and Genealogical Department, Mobile Public Library, Mobile, AL.

47. Meaher Family Papers. Minnie Mitchell Archives, Mobile Historical and Perservation Society, Mobile, AL.

48. *Meaher v. Cox, Brainard & Co* (Appeal from the Chancery Court at Mobile), Supreme Court of Alabama,. January 1861 (LexisNexis, 2006).

49. Bert Neville, *Directory of River Packets in the Mobile-Alabama-Warrior-Tombigbee Trades, 1818–1932* (Selma, AL, 1962), 307. See also Caleb Curren, "The Wreck of the Orline St. John: With A General History of Steamboats in Southwest Alabama." *PAL Journal* (1998). Available at http://www.Archeologyinc.org/steamboats.html.

50. "Necrological: The Funeral of Captain Timothy Meaher." *Mobile Daily Register,* March 5, 1892, 4.

51. *Facts and Observations Relative to the Participation of American Citizens In the African Slave Trade. Published by Direction of a Meeting Representing the Religious Society of Friends in Pennsylvania, New Jersey, &c.* Philadelphia: Joseph & William Kite, Printers (1841). Available at http://amistad.mysticseaport.org/library, p. 8.

52. Harriet E. Amos, "Social Life in an Antebellum Cotton Port: Mobile, Alabama, 1820–1860" (PhD diss., Emory University, 1976), 351–52.

53. George M. Fredrickson, *The Black Image in the White Mind* (Hanover, NH: Wesleyan University Press, 1971), 78.

54. Frederick Bancroft, *Slave-Trading in the Old South* (New York: Ungar, 1967), 365–81.

55. Harvey Wish, "The Revival of the African Slave Trade in the United States," *Mississippi Valley Historical Review* 27 (March 1941): 571.

56. James Baldwin, *The Evidence of Things Not Seen* (New York: Holt, Rinehart, and Winston, 1985), 29–34. W.E.B. Du Bois was one of the first to observe that, "the discovery of personal whiteness among the world's peoples is a very modern thing—a nineteenth- and twentieth-century matter, indeed. The ancient world would have laughed at such a distinction. Today, we have changed all that, and the world in a sudden, emotional conversion had discovered that it is white and by that token, wonderful!" Du Bois, *Darkwater, Voices from Within the Veil* (New York, 1920), 29–30.

57. In antiquity, whites valued Blacks for cultural, intellectual, and sexual contrast. For an extended discussion of the social and sexual relations between "whites" and "blacks" before the codification of race and slavery, see Rogers, *Sex and Race*, vol. 1.

58. "An Act in addition to the Acts which prohibit the Slave Trade," January 13, 1859. Available at http://cdl.library.cornell.edu.

59. Du Bois, *The Suppression of the African Slave Trade,* 184–87.

60. *Afro-American Encyclopedia,* vol. 8 (Florida: Educational Book Publishers, Inc., 1974), 2398. See also Natalie S. Robertson, *Spirit of Our Ancestors: The Slave Ship* Clotilda *and the Making of AfricaTown* (Washington, DC: Library of Congress, 2005).

61. George Francis Dow, *Slave Ships and Slaving* (Salem, MA: Marine Research Society, 1927), 276–79.

62. Ibid., 277–78.

63. Spears, *The American Slave-Trade,* 198.

64. "Early Life In The Southwest—The Bowies." *DeBow's Review* 13, issue 4 (October 1852), 381.

65. Robert H. Smith, Collector of Customs at Mobile, to Jeremiah S. Black, Attorney General of the United States, December 21, 1858; National Archives II, College Park, MD.

66. Ibid.

67. Roche, *Historic Sketches,* 70.

68. S.H.M. Byers, "The Last Slave Ship," *Harper's Monthly Magazine* 63 (1906): 744. There is disagreement regarding where Meaher wagered the bet. Roche states that he made the bet while standing on a wharf (*Historic Sketches,* 71). Other sources state that he wagered the bet aboard his steamer *Roger B. Taney,* some of his wealthy passengers putting up various sums of money (see William H. Woodberry of Boston to Mr. Donaldson of Springhill, Alabama, October 20, 1890; Special Collections, Local History and Genealogical Department of the Mobile Public Library, Mobile, AL). See also "Last Cargo of Slaves: How a Ship Load of Negroes Were Imported in 1861. An Alabama Captain's Desperate but Successful Undertaking—One hundred and Sixty Slaves Landed—The Only Full-Blood African Colony in America," *Globe-Democrat,* November 26, 1890. This is a *Globe-Democrat* reporter's written account of his interview with Timothy Meaher. Special Collections, Local History and Genealogical Department of the Mobile Public Library, Mobile, AL).

69. "Circuit Court of the United States. In Admiralty. The United States of America, By Information versus The Schooner Wanderer and Cargo," in *The African Slave Trade And American Courts: The Pamphlet Literature,* Series V, vol. 2 (New York: Garland Publishing, 1988), 27, 59. See also Mannix, *Black Cargoes,* 281.

70. Wish, "The Revival of the African Slave Trade," 582.

71. In 1860, Nathaniel Gordon, captain of the slaver *Erie,* was overhauled with approximately 897 slaves in her hold. The Africans were transported to Liberia, where they were manumitted while Gordon was sent to New York, where he was tried as a pirate. The first trial miscarried. Gordon was retried and convicted of piracy on November 4, 1861. Proslavery advocates tried to have Gordon pardoned. Expectations for a pardon were high, since convicted smugglers regularly received pardons from Jefferson, Madison, and Monroe. Gordon was not pardoned, however. Refusing to take his place in American history as the first, and only, citizen to be hanged for smuggling Africans, Gordon attempted to commit suicide by poisoning. Botching the suicide attempt, he was hanged on February 21, 1862. Occurring 42 years after the Piracy Act was implemented, however, Gordon's execution can only be viewed as an affectation

rather than as a genuine attempt to deter Americans who had profited from smuggling for half a century after the Constitution prohibited new importations in 1808. Gordon himself had participated in several smuggling ventures before 1860. For an extensive discussion of Gordon's exploits, see Hugh Thomas, *The Slave Trade: The Story of the Atlantic Slave Trade: 1440–1870* (New York: Touchstone, 1997).

72. Mannix, *Black Cargoes,* 267.

73. *Afro-American Encyclopedia,* 2401.

74. Meaher Family Papers, Minnie Mitchell Archives, The Mobile Historical and Preservation Society, Mobile, AL.

75. "Necrological: Death of Captain Tim Meaher, The Venerable Steamboat Man," *Mobile Daily Register,* March 4, 1892. See also "Last Cargo of Slaves: How a Ship Load of Negroes Were Imported in 1861."

76. Original registry for the schooner *Clotilda,* Register of Vessels, Entry No. 26, November 19, 1855. National Archives. Washington, DC. This information is cross-referenced with the Record of Registers, 1854–1857 (No. 13), Bureau of Navigation, Department of Commerce, National Archives.

77. "The Foster Family," The Island Register, Prince Edward Island's Premier Genealogy Home Page, http://www.islandregister.com.

78. Ibid.

79. *American Lloyds' Registry of American and Foreign Shipping* (New York: E.& G.W. Blunt, 1862), 395.

80. Register of Vessels, Entry No. 32, August 27, 1857; National Archives, Washington, DC.

81. Register of Vessels, February 1860; National Archives. Washington, DC

82. "Letterhead of Clarke & Murrell Insurance Agents," p. 1. Special Collections, Local History and Genealogical Department of the Mobile Public Library, Mobile, AL.

83. *American Lloyds' Registry of American and Foreign Shipping,* 395.

84. Henry Romeyn, "Little Africa: The Last Slave Cargo Landed in the United States." This article contains information on the voyage of the *Clotilda,* as well as some ethnographic data that was collected via interviews with the *Clotilda* Africans. *Southern Workman* (publication of Hampton Normal and Agricultural Institute) vol. 26, no. 1 (January 1897): 14.

85. Captain William Foster, "Last Slaver from U.S. to Africa. A.D. 1860." Captain Foster's Account (photocopy), p. 1. Special Collections. Local History and Genealogical Department of the Mobile Public Library, Mobile, AL.

86. *Daily Register* (Mobile, AL), November 9, 1858, 3.

87. Donald R. Wright, *African-Americans in the Colonial Era: From African Origins Through the American Revolution* (Illinois: Harlan Davidson, Inc., 1990), 88–90.

88. Captain Foster's Account, 1.

89. U.S. Congress, House, *Report of the Secretary of State in Reference to the African Slave Trade,* 36th Cong., 2d sess., 1860 (H. Doc. 7), 185.

90. Captain Foster's Account, 1.

91. W. Jeffrey Bolster, *Black Jacks: African American Seamen in the Age of Sail* (Cambridge, MA: Harvard University Press, 1997), 58–59.

92. Natalie S. Robertson, *Spirit of Our Ancestors: The Slave Ship* Clotilda *and the Making of AfricaTown* (Washington, DC: Library of Congress, 2005), 81–82. "Circuit Court of the United States. In Admiralty," 27, 59.

93. Captain Foster's Account, 1.

94. *British Parliamentary Papers. Correspondence with British Commissioners and other Representatives Abroad and with Foreign Ministers in England, Together with Reports from the Admiralty relative to the slave trade,* vol. 46 (Dublin: Irish University Press, 1969), 10.

95. Ibid., 96.

96. Drake, "Secret History of the Slave Trade," 222.

97. Romeyn, "Little Africa," 14.

98. Roche, *Historical Sketches of the South*, 84–85.

99. Captain Foster's Account, 1.

100. Ibid.

101. Ibid.

102. Ibid., 2.

103. Ibid.

104. Bolster, *Black Jacks,* 19.

105. Captain Foster's Account, 2.

106. Ibid., 3.

107. Ibid, 3.

108. Ibid., 3–4.

109. Spears, 225.

110. Dispatches From United States Consuls In Santiago, Cape Verde, 1851–1869 (Washington, DC: the National Archives). Microcopy No. T-434.

111. Captain Foster's Account, 4.

112. Roche, *Historic Sketches,* 85.

113. For an insightful, detailed description of various smuggling schemes, see Mannix, *Black Cargoes,* 199. See also Drake, "Secret History of the Slave Trade, 224.

114. Tracy Hollingsworth Lay, *The Foreign Service of the United States* (New York: Prentice-Hall, Inc., 1928), 15.

115. Roche, *Historic Sketches,* 85.

116. "Slave and Coolie Trade," House Executive Document, 34th Cong., 1st sess., no. 105, 19. Also, see the cases concerning the slavers *Advance* and *Rachel P. Brown* in Du Bois, *The Suppression of the African Slave Trade,* 296.

117. Captain Foster's Account, 4.

CHAPTER 3: THE DAHOMEAN DIMENSION

1. Captain William Foster, "Last Slaver from U.S. to Africa. A.D. 1860." Captain Foster's Account (photocopy), pp. 4–5. Special Collections, Public History and Genealogical Department of the Mobile Public Library. Mobile, AL.

2. Ibid.

3. Maurice Ahanhanzo Glélé, *Le Danxome: Du Pouvoir Aja à la Nation Fon* (Paris: Nubia, 1974), 40, 88–89.

4. Ibid.

5. John Henrik Clarke and Yosef ben-Jochannan, *New Dimensions in African History* (New Jersey: Africa World Press, 1991), 30.

6. Pierre Verger, *Trade Relations between the Bight of Benin and Bahia from the 17th to 19th Century* (Ibadan, Nigeria: Ibadan University Press, 1976), 141.

7. "The Last Slave Ships." Mel Fisher Maritime Heritage Society, Inc. (2002), http://www.melfisher.com

8. Ibid., 44–47.

9. David Ross, "The Career of Domingo Martinez in the Bight of Benin 1833–64," *Journal of African History* 6, no. 1 (1965): 79.

10. W.J. Argyle, *The Fon of Dahomey: A History and Ethnography of the Old Kingdom* (Oxford: Clarendon Press, 1966), 81–82.

11. Jean Pliya, *Histoire de Mon Pays* (Cotonou, Republic of Benin: Libraire Notre-Dame, 1993), 75.

12. Basil Davidson, *Black Mother: The Years of Our African Slave Trade: Precolonial History, 1450–1850* (Boston: Little, Brown, & Co., 1961), 63.

13. Glélé, *Le Danxome,* 41.

14. David Ross, "The Dahomean Middleman System, 1727–c. 1818." *Journal of African History* 28 (1987): 366.

15. For an extended etymological analysis of the name, see B. Clochard, ed., *Ouidah: Petite Anthologie Historique* (Cotonou, Republic of Benin: L'Imprimerie Industrielle Nouvelle Presse, 1993), 15–16.

16. Supreme Chief Dah Akolemin Dossou Agadja Kakanakou, interview by author, Village of Zoungboji, Republic of Benin, July 2, 1994, tape recording.

17. View the films *Cooley High* and *Dead Presidents* as contemporary points of reference.

18. Supreme Chief Dah Akolemin Dossou Agadja Kakanakou, interview, July 2, 1994. The inclusion of the name Agadja in the Supreme Chief's name signifies his political connection to the king who designated Zoungboji as a military garrison, installing Kakanakou's royal ancestors to oversee the political affairs of the village.

19. Ibid.

20. Chief Lohotogbe nongloakou Gankpe, interview by author, Village of Zoungboji, Whydah, Republic of Benin, July 7, 1994, tape recording.

21. Patrick Manning, *Slavery, Colonialism and Economic Growth in Dahomey, 1640–1960* (London: Cambridge University Press, 1982), 81.

22. Stephen D. Behrendt, "Markets, Transaction Cycles, and Profits: Merchant Decision Making in the British Slave Trade," *William and Mary Quarterly* 58, no. 1 (January 2001): 21. Available at http://www.historycooperative.org.

23. Richard Burton, *A Mission to Gelele King of Dahome* (London: Routledge and Kegan Paul, 1966), 46.

24. Ibid.

25. Miss Martine Françoise De Souza, interview by author, Whydah, Republic of Benin, July 2, 1994, tape recording.

26. Chief Lohotogbe nongloakou Gankpe, interview, July 7, 1994.

27. Captain Foster's Account, 5.

28. Ibid.

29. Ibid. For additional evidence of this customary mode of transportation, see Clochard, *Ouidah*, 47.

30. Burton, *A Mission to Gelele King of Dahome*, 70.

31. Glélé, *Le Danxome*, 137.

32. Ibid.

33. Captain Foster's Account, 6.

34. Ibid.

35. Glélé, *Le Danxome*, 137; Argyle, *The Fon of Dahomey*, 73.

36. Glélé, *Le Danxome*, 143; Argyle, *The Fon of Dahomey*, 77.

37. Glélé, *Le Danxome*, 143; Argyle, *The Fon of Dahomey*, 77. See also Natalie S. Robertson, *Spirit of Our Ancestors: The Slave Ship* Clotilda*and the Making of Africa*Town (Washington, DC: Library of Congress, 2005).

38. Captain Foster's Account, 6.

39. Verger, *Trade Relations between the Bight of Benin and Bahia*, 147.

40. Argyle, *The Fon of Dahomey*, 104–5. See also Rosemary Arnold, "A Port of Trade: Whydah on the Guinea Coast," in *Trade and Market in the Early Empires*, ed. Karl Polanyi and others (Glencoe, IL: The Free Press and The Falcon's Wing Press, 1957), 167.

41. Verger, *Trade Relations between the Bight of Benin and Bahia*, 179, 187.

42. Pliya, *Histoire de Mon Pays*, 75.

43. Glele, *Le Danxome*, 137.

44. Argyle, *The Fon of Dahomey*, 73; Glélé, *Le Danxome*, 137.

45. Argyle, *The Fon of Dahomey*, 68–69; Glélé, *Le Danxome*, 137.

46. Captain Foster's Account, 7.

47. Ibid.

48. Robin Law, "'The Common People Were Divided': Monarchy, Aristocracy and Political Factionalism in the Kingdom of Whydah, 1671–1727," *International Journal of African Historical Studies* 23, no. 2 (1990): 209.

49. Pliya, *Histoire de Mon Pays*, 106.

50. Mr. Dagbo Hounon, Supreme Chief of Vodun for the Republic of Benin, interview by author, Whydah, August 26, 1994, handwritten.

51. V. Y. Mudimbe, *The Invention of Africa: Gnosis, Philosophy, and the Order of Knowledge* (Bloomington: Indiana University Press, 1988), 172–73.

52. It is not a coincidence that shrines and celebrations dedicated to Black Christs and Black Madonna-and-child figures can be found in Asia, the Phillipines, Peru, Mexico, and Europe.

53. For an image of Pope Jean Paul II kneeling and kissing the feet of a Black Christ, see Ashra Kwesi, *Christianity, The Stolen Religion From Africa*, Part I, 120 min., VHS (1995), produced and distributed by Kemetnu Productions, Inc., Dallas, TX.

54. Clochard, *Ouidah*, 56.

55. As I traveled through Allada (Benin) in 1994, the local people were erecting a memorial to L'Ouverture.

56. John Hope Franklin and Alfred A. Moss, Jr., *From Slavery to Freedom: A History of African Americans,* 8th ed. (Boston: McGraw Hill, 2000), 102.

57. Captain Foster's Account, 7.

58. Arnold, "A Port of Trade: Whydah on the Guinea Coast," 170–71.

59. Patrick Manning, "Slave Trade, 'Legitimate' Trade, and Imperialism Revisited: The Control of Wealth in the Bights of Benin and Biafra," in *Africans in Bondage: Studies in Slavery and the Slave Trade,* ed. Paul E. Lovejoy (Madison, WI: African Studies Program, 1986), 219. See also John C. Yoder, "Fly and Elephant Parties: Political Polarization in Dahomey, 1840–1870," *Journal of African History* 15 (1974): 431.

60. Although the members of this household prefer the French spelling of their name, referring to themselves as De Souza rather than Da Souza, they are descendants of Francisco Felix Da Souza. Miss Martine Francoise De Souza, interview by author, Whydah, Republic of Benin, July 4, 1994, tape recording.

61. Ibid.

62. Vincent B. Thompson, *The Making of the African Diaspora in the Americas, 1444–1900* (England: Longman Group, 1987), 95–98.

63. Ibid.

64. Captain Foster's Account, 7–8.

65. Daniel P. Mannix, *Black Cargoes: A History of the Atlantic Slave Trade, 1518–1865* (Associated Publishers, Inc., 1962), 198.

66. Zora Neale Hurston, "Barracoon: The Story of the Last 'Black Cargo.'" Box 164–186. File #1. Typescript of unpublished mss. Moorland-Spingarn Manuscript Collection, Howard University, Washington, DC.

67. Captain Foster's Account, 8.

68. Zora Neale Hurston, "The Last Slave Ship," *American Mercury* 58 (1944): 356.

69. Supreme Chief Akolemin Kakanakou, interview, July 2, 1994.

70. Zora Neale Hurston, "Cudjo's Own Story of the Last African Slaver," *Journal of Negro History* 12 (October 1927): 657; see also Hurston, "Barracoon," 57–58.

71. Emma Langdon Roche, *Historic Sketches of the South* (New York: Knickerbocker, 1914), 82–83.

72. Hurston, "The Last Slave Ship," 354; and Hurston, "Cudjo's Own Story," 656–57.

73. Roche, *Historic Sketches,* 113–14.

74. Hurston, "Cudjo's Own Story," 655.

75. Booker T. Washington, "The First and Last Slave-Ship," chap. in *The Story of the Negro: The Rise of the Race From Slavery* (New York: Doubleday, Page & Company, 1909), 104.

76. "Last Slave Ship Sunk Here Raised: Colony of Negroes Who Came Over on the Krotiley [*Clotilda*] Alive At Plateau," n.d. Special Collections, Local History and Genealogical Department of the Mobile Public Library, Mobile, AL.

77. For more information on this topic, consult William D. Piersen, "White Cannibals, Black Martyrs: Fear, Depression, and Religious Faith as Causes of Suicide Among New Slaves." *Journal of Negro History* 62, no. 2 (1977): 152.

78. Captain Foster's Account, 8.

79. Hurston, "Barracoon," 58.

80. Captain Foster's Account, 8–9.

81. Ibid, 9.

82. Henry Romeyn, "Little Africa: The Last Slave Cargo Landed in the United States." This article contains information on the voyage of the *Clotilda*, as well as some ethnographic data that was collected via interviews with the *Clotilda* Africans. *Southern Workman* (publication of Hampton Normal and Agricultural Institute) vol. 26, no. 1 (January 1897): 14–17.

83. Ibid.

CHAPTER 4: ATLANTIC PASSAGE

1. Captain William Foster, "Last Slaver from U.S. to Africa. A.D. 1860." Captain Foster's Account (photocopy), pp. 9–10. Special Collections, Local History and Genealogical Department of the Mobile Public Library, Mobile, AL.

2. Ibid., 10.

3. Pierre Verger, *Trade Relations Between the Bight of Benin and Bahia from the 17th To 19th Century* (Ibadan, Nigeria: Ibadan University Press, 1976), 586.

4. John R. Spears, *The American Slave-Trade: An Account of Its Origin, Growth, and Suppression* (New York: Charles Scribner's Sons, 1900), 108–9.

5. Henry Romeyn, "Little Africa: The Last Slave Cargo Landed in the United States," contains information on the voyage of the *Clotilda*, as well as some ethnographic data that was collected via interviews with the *Clotilda* Africans. *Southern Workman* (publication of Hampton Normal and Agricultural Institute) 26, no. 1 (January 1897): 14–17.

6. Manifest of the *Clotilda*, pp. 1–2. Special Collections, Local History and Genealogical Department of the Mobile Public Library, Mobile, AL.

7. William H. McNeill, *Plagues and People* (New York: Anchor Press/Doubleday, 1976), 177, 208–18. See also Joseph C. Miller, *Way of Death: Merchant Capitalism and the Angolan Slave Trade 1730–1830* (Madison: University of Wisconsin Press, 1988).

8. Zora Neale Hurston, "Cudjo's Own Story of the Last African Slaver," *Journal of Negro History* 12 (October 1927): 658.

9. For more information regarding the extent to which Africans committed suicide to avoid enslavement, see William D. Piersen, "White Cannibals, Black Martyrs: Fear, Depression, and Religious Faith as Causes of Suicide among New Slaves," *Journal of Negro History* 62, no. 2 (1977): 147–59.

10. Emma Langdon Roche, *Historic Sketches of the South* (New York: Knickerbocker Press, 1914), 89.

11. Ibid., 82.

12. Captain Foster's Account, 10.

13. Ibid.

14. Spears, *The American Slave-Trade*, 38.

15. Captain Foster's Account, 11.

16. Ibid.

17. "Last Cargo of Slaves: How a Ship Load of Negroes Were Imported in 1861. An Alabama Captain's Desperate but Successful Undertaking—One hundred and Sixty Slaves Landed—The Only Full-Blood African Colony in America," *Globe-Democrat*, November 26, 1890. This is a *Globe-Democrat* reporter's written account of his interview with Timothy Meaher. Special Collections, Local History and Genealogical Department of the Mobile Public Library, Mobile, AL.

18. Captain Foster's Account, 11–12.

19. Ibid., 12.

20. Roche, *Historic Sketches*, 97. In instances in which Roche does not refer to a Meaher by his first name, it is thought that she is referring to Tim.

21. Ibid., 94. See also "Last Cargo of Slaves: How a Ship Load of Negroes Were Imported in 1861"; and Henry C. Williams, *AfricaTown, U.S.A.* (Mobile, AL: American Ethnic Science Society, 1981), 22.

22. Captain Foster's Account, 11.

23. Mable Dennison, *Biographical Memoirs of James Dennison* (Boynton Beach, FL: Futura Printing, Inc., 1984), 29. For additional information regarding the experiences of Black male slaves as crewmen, captains, and pirates, see W. Jeffrey Bolster, *Black Jacks: African-American Seamen in the Age of Sail* (Cambridge, MA: Harvard University Press, 1997), 131–33.

24. Captain Foster's Account, 11. See also Henry C. Williams, *A History of Mobile County Training School* (Mobile, AL: privately printed, 1977), 4. In several cases, smugglers burned their slave ships because the excrement that remained in their holds constituted incriminating evidence. See Daniel P. Mannix, *Black Cargoes: A History of the Atlantic Slave Trade, 1518–1865* (Associated Publishers, Inc., 1962), 229.

25. Bert Neville, *Directory of River Packets in the Mobile-Alabama-Warrior-Tombigbee Trades, 1818–1932* (Selma, AL, 1962), 79, 81. Courtesy of the Library at the Mariners' Museum, Newport News, VA.

26. List of Accounts in Petty Ledger. Code MISC, Book F, pp. 372–77, 1856, Mobile Probate Court Archives.

27. Federal Census, Slave Schedule, Southern Division, County of Mobile, July 5, 1860, Schedule 2. See also Erwin Craighead, *Mobile: Fact and Tradition* (Mobile, AL: The Powers Printing Company, 1930), 358.

28. Craighead, *Mobile: Fact and Tradition*, 358.

29. USA-Presidents.Info—James Buchanan Fourth State of the Union Address. Available at http://www.usa-presidents.info.

30. *United States v. William Foster,* Summons. United States District Court, Southern District of Alabama, Mixed Case Files, 1820–1860, Summons n. 2621. Special Collections, Local History and Genealogical Department of the Mobile Public Library, Mobile, AL.

31. "Capt. Wm. Foster, Commander of the Last American Slave Vessel Buried Yesterday," n.d. The transcript of information collected from Captain William Foster's wife, one day after his death, via an interview by a *Herald* reporter. Special Collections, Local History and Genealogical Department of the Mobile Public Library, Mobile, AL.

32. *United States v. Jno. M. Dabney,* Writ of Seizure. U.S. District Court, Southern District of Alabama. Mixed Case Files, 1820–1860. Box 46, Writ #2619. Mobile Municipal Archives. Mobile, AL.

33. Ibid.

34. *United States v. Burns Meaher.* Writ of Seizure. United States District Court, Southern District of Alabama. Final Record Book, 1859–1860. Mobile Municipal Archives. Mobile, AL.

35. *United States v. William Foster and Richard Sheridan.* United States District Court, Southern District of Alabama. Mixed Case Files, 1820–1860. Summons and Complaint #3516. Box 51. Special Collections, Local History and Genealogical Department of the Mobile Public Library. Mobile, Alabama.

36. The two summons were signed on April 2 and 4, 1860; they were issued on August 7; and, they were handed to Foster on October 28.

37. Subpoena issued to Anatol Rabby and Joseph Laurendine. Richard Eames, Edwin Eames, D.J. Bryant, Emmanuel Bryant, and Richard Rivers to serve as witnesses in *United States vs. Wm Foster and Richard Sheridan.*

38. Clarke County, Alabama, "Largest Slaveholders from 1860 Slave Census Schedules and Surname Matches for African Americans on 1870 Census," available at http://www.freegenealogy.rootsweb.com/~ajac/alclarke.htm.

39. "Last Cargo of Slaves: How a Ship Load of Negroes Were Imported in 1861."

40. Executed on December 18 and 19, 1860, these subpoena are located in a file of Documents regarding the *Clotilda* case. Special Collections, Local History and Genealogical Department of the Mobile Public Library, Mobile, AL.

41. U.S. District Court, Southern District of Alabama, Minute Book, 1859–1861. Mobile Historical Society, Mobile, AL.

42. "Last Cargo of Slaves: How a Ship Load of Negroes Were Imported in 1861."

43. Christine Jordan, "Justice Campbell—Last of the Jacksonians," The Supreme Court Historical Society Publications. Digitized volumes from the Society's collections are available at http://www.supremecourthistory.org.

44. Campbell Family Papers, Manuscript Department Library of the University of North Carolina at Chapel Hill. Available at http://www.lib.unc.edu.

45. "Justice John Archibald Campbell: Concurring Opinion, March 6, 1857," in Paul Finkelman, *Dred Scott v. Sanford: A Brief History with Documents* (New York: Bedford Books, 1997), 92.

46. Thad Holt Jr., "The Resignation of Mr. Justice Campbell," *The Alabama Review* 12, no. 2 (April 1959): 114n.

47. Circuit Court of the United States. Southern District of Alabama. Spring Term 1860. *United States vs. Horatio N. Gould; U.S. vs. T.V. Bordnax. The Mobile Register.* Thursday Morning, 19 April 1860. The National Archives of the United States. RG 60. See also Natalie S. Robertson, *Spirit of Our Ancestors: The Slave Ship* Clotilda *and the Making of AfricaTown* (Washington, DC: Library of Congress, 2005).

48. Ibid.

49. Oath of judgeship taken by William Giles Jones, in the presence of R.B. Owens, United States Commissioner, February 13, 1860. National Archives of the United States. RG 60.

50. Craighead, *Mobile: Fact and Tradition,* 358.

51. *United States v. Jno M. Dabney,* writ of seizure. U.S. District Court, Southern District of Alabama. Mixed Case Files, 1820–1860. Box 46, Writ # 2619. Mobile Municipal Archives. Mobile, AL.

52. Manifest of the *Clotilda,* pp. 1–2. Special Collections, Local History and Genealogical Department of the Mobile Public Library, Mobile, AL.

53. "Last Cargo of Slaves: How a Ship Load of Negroes Were Imported in 1861."

54. Ibid.

55. See *Ewing v. Sanford,* Supreme Court of Alabama, June 1851; decided 19 Ala. 605; 1851 Ala. LEXIS 132. Lexis Nexis Academic Search.

56. Craighead, *Mobile: Fact and Tradition,* 358.

57. John W. DuBose, *Alabama's Tragic Decade* (Birmingham, AL: Webb Brook Company, 1940), 256n.

58. *Last Will and Testament of William Giles Jones,* Mobile Probate Court Archives. Pigeon Hole 398. Files 38 through 41 (1857), 3.

59. Ibid.

60. Ibid., 4.

61. Ibid., 5.

62. Jones served as trustee for Philip A. Aylet in the purchase of these Black men, women, and children who were included in the sale of 1,280, known as at Bozarge Tract, located in Bayou La Batre and belonging to John Nash and J. Valvarte. "Trust Sale of Land and Negroes at Auction." *Mobile Daily Register,* December 1, 1857.

63. Slave sale, MISC Book G (1858), 11; Mobile Probate Court Archives.

64. Slave loan, MISC Book D (1843), 438; Mobile Probate Court Archives.

65. "Necrological: Death of Captain Tim Meaher, the Venerable Steamboat Man," *Mobile Daily Register,* March 4, 1892.

66. List of Dismissed Cases, Minute Book, 1836–61; 1865–66. Mobile Municipal Archives, Mobile, AL.

67. *Foster v. Holly,* Supreme Court of Alabama, June 1861; decided 38 Ala. 76; 1861 Ala. LEXIS 13.

68. William Giles Jones to President James Buchanan (letter of resignation of judgeship), January 12, 1861. National Archives of the United States, RG 60.

69. http://www2.law.cornell.

70. Official Bond. Book 1, Page 307.1. Mobile Probate Court Archives (1861).

71. "Capt. Wm. Foster, Commander of the Last American Slave Vessel Buried Yesterday." See also Amnesty Oaths File 37, pp. 291, 293, and 149 (1868), for James Meaher, Tim Meaher, and Cade M. Godbold respectively, Mobile Probate Court Archives.

72. "U.S. Supreme Court. The Gray Jacket, Appeal from the District Court of the United States for the Eastern District of Louisiana. December Term, 1866. 72 U.S. 342 (1866)." Full text of the case is available at http://www.justia.us/us/72/342/case.html.

73. Ibid., 2.

74. Ibid.

75. Ibid., 3.

76. Ibid.

77. Ibid., 4–5.

78. Ibid., 5.

79. Ibid.

80. Ibid., 16.

81. Ibid., 2.

82. "Last Cargo of Slaves: How a Ship Load of Negroes Were Imported in 1861."

CHAPTER 5: IN THE JAWS OF THE LION

1. Zora Neale Hurston, "The Last Slave Ship," *American Mercury* 58 (1944): 357. See also Emma Langdon Roche, *Historic Sketches of the South* (New York: Knickerbocker Press, 1914), 101–2; and Addie E. Pettaway, *AfricaTown, U.S.A.: Some Aspects of Folklife and Material Culture of an Historic Landscape* (Wisconsin Department of Public Instruction, 1985), 5.

2. Roche, *Historic Sketches*, 101–2.

3. Federal Census Slave Schedule, Southern Division, County of Mobile, July 5, 1860.

4. Roche, *Historic Sketches*, 97.

5. Ibid., 101–2.

6. Mrs. Lorna Woods, interview by author, Mobile, AL, March 1, 1994, tape recording.

7. "History of Cudjoe Lewis," a brief statement written by James M. Lewis, 73 years of age, grandson of Cudjoe Lewis, and son of Alex Lewis (of Montgomery, AL) November 29, 1968. Special Collections, Local History and Genealogical Department of the Mobile Public Library. Mobile, AL. See also Hurston, "The Last Slave Ship," 357.

8. Mechal Sobel, *Trabelin' On: The Slave Journey to an Afro-Baptist Faith* (Westport, CT: Greenwood Press, 1979), 26–27.

9. Ibid., 28–29.

10. Darold D. Wax, "Preferences For Slaves In Colonial America." *Journal of Negro History* 58, no. 4 (October 1973): 391–92.

11. See Charles L. Blockson, *Black Genealogy* (Baltimore, MD: Black Classic Press, 1991), 134–35. See also Sobel, *Trabelin' On*, 26–28.

12. Zora Neale Hurston, "Cudjo's Own Story of the Last African Slaver." *Journal of Negro History* 12 (1927): 649.

13. Hurston, "The Last Slave Ship," 351–58.

14. Patrick Manning, *Slavery, Colonialism and Economic Growth in Dahomey, 1640–1960* (London: Cambridge University Press, 1982), 30.

15. Roche, *Historic Sketches*, 88. Diouf describes Cudjo's map as "highly problematic and unreliable" (*Dreams of Africa in Alabama*, 40). However, the map's meaning, and its

value, can only be deduced after being subjected to a contextual analysis of Dahomey's slave-raiding activities in the middle of the nineteenth century, relative to New Oyo as a source of captives.

16. S.H.M. Byers, "The Last Slave Ship." *Harper's Monthly Magazine* 63 (1906): 743. Byers traveled to AfricaTown where he interviewed Cudjo and his wife, Albine, who told him that they had originated in Whinney. However, Diouf is unaware of the fact that Gossalow is distortion of the name Kazoola, one of Cudjo's African names. She describes Gossalow as "a man" with an identify that is separate from Cudjo when, in fact, they are one in same person (*Dreams of Africa in Alabama,* 36).

17. Pierre Verger, "The Yoruba High God—a Review of the Sources." *ODU* 2, no. 2 (January 1966): 39.

18. J.A. Atanda, *The New Oyo Empire: Indirect Rule and Change in Western Nigeria, 1894–1934* (New York: Humanities Press, 1973), 25.

19. E.A. Ayandele, "The Yoruba Civil Wars and the Dahomean Confrontation," in *Nigerian Historical Studies* (London: Frank Cass, 1979), 55.

20. A.I. Asiwaju, "A Note On The History of Sabe," *Lagos Notes and Records: University of Lagos Bulletin of African Studies,* 4 (January 1973): 26.

21. Ibid.

22. E. Geoffrey Parrinder, *The Story of Ketu: An Ancient Yoruba Kingdom* (Ibadan, Nigeria: Ibadan University Press, 1956), 88–90.

23. Ibid.

24. Ibid., 50.

25. Guerres du Roi Glele, Archives IFAN, DAKAR–XVIII a, a list of wars, obtained from the Archives Nationale Du Benin. Porto Novo, Republic of Benin.

26. J.A. Atanda, "Dahomean Raids On Oke Ogun Towns," *The Historia: Journal of the University of Ibadan Historical Society* 3 (April 1966): 2.

27. S.O. Babayemi, "Upper Ogun: An Historical Sketch," *African Notes* 6, no. 2 (1970), 72.

28. R.O. Lasisi, , "Oyo-Yoruba and Ilorin Relations in the 19th Century," in *Readings in Nigerian History and Culture: Essays in Memory of Professor J.A. Atanda,* ed. G.O. Oguntomisin and S. Ademola Ajayi (Ibadan, Nigeria: Hope Publications, 2002), 255

29. Roche, *Historic Sketches,* 80. See also Hurston, "Cudjo's Own Story," 655.

30. Hurston, "Cudjo's Own Story," 649.

31. C.K. Meek, *The Northern Tribes of Nigeria,* vol. 1 (London: Oxford University Press, 1925), 123–24.

32. http://lime.weeg.uiowa.edu/~africart/toc/people/Yoruba. See also R.E. Dennett, *Nigerian Studies or the Religious and Political System of the Yoruba* (London: Frank Cass & Co. Ltd., 1968), 141.

33. S.A. Agboola, "The Traditional Significance of Yam in Yorubaland in Pre-Colonial Times," *Nigerian Agricultural Journal* (1968): 59, 60.

34. 'Deji Ogunremi, "Foundations of the Yoruba Economy in the Pre-Colonial Era," in *Culture and Society In Yorubaland,* ed. 'Deji Ogunremi and 'Biodun Adediran (Ibadan, Nigeria: Rex Charles Publication, 1998), 117.

35. Hurston, "Cudjo's Own Story," 649.

36. Olatunji Ojo, "Slavery, Farm Slaves, and Agriculture in Nineteenth Century Ibadan," *Nigerian Journal of Economic History* 2 (1999): 139, 140–41.

37. Hurston, "Cudjo's Own Story," 655.

38. M.A. Jabbar and M.L. Diedhiou, "Does Breed Matter to Cattle Farmers and Buyers? Evidence from West Africa," p. 4. Available athttp://www.ilri.cgiar.org.

39. Ibid., 651–53.

40. Ibid., 653.

41. Sylvain C. Anignikin, "De la Traite Negriere au Defi du Developpement: Reflexion sur les Conditions de la Paix Mondiale," paper presented at the international symposium Routes des L'Esclave, Ouidah, Republic of Benin. September 1–5, 1994, 3. See also Karl Polanyi et al., eds., *Trade and Market in the Early Empires* (Glencoe, IL: The Free Press and The Falcon's Wing Press, 1957), 138.

42. P.O. Olatunbosun, *History of West Africa, from A.D. 1000 to the Present Day, in a Current Perspective* (Ilesha, Nigeria: Fatiregun Press & Publishing Company, 1976), 117. See also Natalie S. Robertson, *Spirit of Our Ancestors: The Slave Ship* Clotilda*and the Making of AfricaTown* (Washington, DC: Library of Congress, 2005).

43. Ibid., 115–16.

44. Tundi Tella, *Isaga: A Victim of the Egba Dahomey Military Confrontations, 1862–1951* (Ibadan, Nigeria: International Publishers Limited, 1998), 30.

45. Ayandele, "The Yoruba Civil Wars and the Dahomean Confrontation," 43. See also Jean Pliya, *Histoire de Mon Pays* (Cotonou, Republic of Benin: Libraire Notre-Dame, 1993), 87.

46. I.A. Akinjogbin, interview by author at his residence in Ibadan, Oyo State, Nigeria, June 14, 2003, handwritten.

47. Edna G. Bay, "Servitude and Worldly Success in the Palace of Dahomey," in *Women and Slavery In Africa*, ed. Claire C. Robertson and Martin A. Klein (Madison: University of Wisconsin Press, 1983), 351.

48. Robert B. Edgerton, "Warrior Women: The Amazons of Dahomey and the Nature of War." Available at http://orion.oac.uci.edu, p. 16.

49. Richard Burton, *Mission to Gelele King of Dahome* (London: Routledge and Kegan Paul, 1966), 261n.

50. Byers, "The Last Slave Ship," 743.

51. Hurston, "The Last Slave Ship," 353.

52. Hurston, "Barracoon," 49.

53. Hurston, "The Last Slave Ship," 351. See also "Plateau Negro Remembers Capture in Jungle Lands: 'Kazoola,' Last of Cargo of Slaves Brought to America and Sold in Mobile, Has Vivid Recollection of Past Events," *Mobile Register*, September 29, 1929.

54. The 1880 census for the County of Mobile lists Cudjo as being 45 years of age, suggesting he was 25 when he was smuggled into Mobile 20 years earlier.

55. Angela Davis, "Attacking the Prison Industrial Complex," transcript from September 22, 1998. Available at http://www.Time.com.

56. Maryland State Archives (African-American Record Descriptions). Available at http://www.mdarchives.state.md.us.

57. Hurston, "The Last Slave Ship," 354.

58. Hurston, "Barracoon," 47.

59. Ibid.

60. Hurston, "The Last Slave Ship," 353.

61. Maurice Ahanhanzo Glélé, *Le Danxome: Du Pouvoir Aja à la Nation Fon* (Paris: Nubia, 1974), 203.

62. Hurston, "Barracoon," 49.

63. Ibid.

64. Ibid.

65. Ibid.

66. Akintunde Akinyemi, "The Social Responsibilities of the Yoruba Royal Bards." *Ife* 4 (1993): 28–36. See also Laoye I, Timi of Ede, "Yoruba Drums." *ODU: Journal of the University of Ile-Ife* 7 (March 1959): 5. Drums and drumming were outlawed in various parts of the New World, because Africans used drumming and other forms of music to communicate with, and inform, each other. Africans were always more intelligent than assumed by their masters, who paid a price for underestimating their intelligence.

67. For culturally relevant analyses of this title, see Ayi Kwei Armah, *KMT: In the House of Life* (Popenguine, Senegal: PER ANKH, 2003).

68. S.O. Babayemi, "Oyo Palace Organization: Past and Present," *African Notes* 10, no. 1 (1986): 4–5.

69. Ikudefùn, interview by author, Afin, Oyo town, Oyo State, Nigeria, June 18, 2003, tape recording.

70. Ibid.

71. F. Olu. Okediji and F.A. Okediji, "The Sociological Aspects of Traditional Yoruba Names and Titles." *ODU: University of Ife Journal of African Studies* 3, no. 1 (July 1966): 69.

72. Ibid., 70.

73. Alhaji R.O. Oladipo, principal private secretary of Alafin Adeyemi III, interview by author, Afin, Oyo, Oyo State, June 18, 2003, handwritten.

74. I had the honor of presenting my research before Wole Soyinka at Gorée Institute in Senegal, as a participant in the inaugural UNCF/Mellon Faculty Seminar entitled "Gods, Knowledge, and Modernity," facilitated by Soyinka. July 18, 2002.

75. Prince Ganiyu Ojo, interview by author, Afin, Oyo town, Oyo State, Nigeria, June 18, 2003, handwritten.

76. J.F. Ade Ajayi and Robert Smith, *Yoruba Warfare in the Nineteenth Century* (Ibadan, Nigeria: Ibadan University Press, 1964), 87.

77. Ibid.

78. Babayemi, "Oyo Palace Organization," 19.

79. Ibid.

80. Hurston, "The Last Slave Ship," 351.

81. Babayemi, "Oyo Palace Organization," 19.

82. Samuel Johnson, *The History of the Yorubas: From the Earliest Times to the Beginning of the British Protectorate* (Lagos, Nigeria: C.M.S. Bookshops, 1956), 70.

83. Babayemi, "Oyo Palace Organization," 19.

84. Ibid.

85. Ibid.

86. Obakayeja, interview by author, Afin, Oyo town, Oyo State, Nigeria, May 22, 2004, handwritten.

87. Babayemi, "Oyo Palace Organization," 19–20. See also Ajayi and Smith, *Yoruba Warfare in the Nineteenth Century,* 92n.

88. S. Goddard, "Town-Farm Relationships in Yorubaland: A Case Study from Oyo," *Africa* 35, no. 1 (1965): 23.

89. Prince Ganiyu Ojo, interview, June 18, 2003.

90. Johnson, *History of the Yorubas,* 362–63.

91. Hurston, "Barracoon," 47.

92. Ibid., 69.

93. Johnson, *History of the Yorubas,* 61.

94. Hurston, "Barracoon," 50.

95. Johnson, *History of the Yorubas,* 69.

96. Ibid.

97. Hurston, "Cudjo's Own Story," 654.

98. Johnson, *History of the Yorubas,* 57.

99. Ibid., 61.

100. Hurston, "Barracoon," 39.

101. Obaloluwa, interview by author, Afin, Oyo, Oyo State, Nigeria, June 18, 2003, tape recording. See also Johnson, *History of the Yorubas,* 61.

102. Babayemi, "Oyo Palace Organization," 15.

103. Ikudefùn, interview by author, Afin, Oyo town, Oyo State, Nigeria, July 17, 2003, tape recording.

104. Hurston, "Barracoon," 42. See also Hurston, "Cudjo's Own Story," 652.

105. Alhaji Olatunde Iyanda , interview by author with the assistance of Olayinka Adekola, Monsifa Area, Oyo town, Oyo State, Nigeria, July 10, 2007, electronic mail.

106. Toyin Falola, *Yoruba Gurus: Indigenous Production of Knowledge in Africa* (New Jersey: Africa World Press, Inc., 1999), 88n. See also Johnson, *History of the Yorubas,* 131.

107. Hurston, "Barracoon," 40.

108. Ibid., 19.

109. Ibid.

110. Ona Olo kun Esin, interview by author, Afin, Oyo town, Oyo State, Nigeria, July 17, 2003, tape recording.

111. Okediji and Okediji, "The Sociological Aspects of Traditional Yoruba Names and Titles," 75.

112. Obakayeja, interview by author, Afin, Oyo town, Oyo State, Nigeria, June 18, 2003, tape recording. See also Babayemi, "Oyo Palace Organization," 17.

113. Roche, *Historic Sketches,* 124.

114. G.O. Oguntomisin, informal discussion with author, University of Ibadan, Oyo State, Nigeria, June 10, 2003, handwritten.

115. Johnson, *History of the Yorubas,* 106.

116. Falola, "Yoruba Warlords," 253.

117. Lasisi, "Oyo-Yoruba and Ilorin Relations," 259.

118. Bolanle Awe, interview by author, Bodija (Ibadan), Oyo State, Nigeria, June 24, 2003, handwritten.

119. Ojo, "Slavery, Farm Slaves and Agriculture in Nineteenth Century Ibadan," 147.

120. R.A. Olaoye, "The Traditional Cloth-Weaving Industry in Nigeria Before 1800," in *Readings in Nigerian History and Culture: Essays in Memory Of Professor J.A. Atanda,* ed. G.O. Oguntomisin and S. Ademola Ajayi (Ibadan, Nigeria: Hope Publications, 2002), 205. See also Walter Rodney, *How Europe Underdeveloped Africa* (Washington, DC: Howard University Press, 1982), 115.

121. "Weaving and Dying in Oyo Province." File number 1757, National Archives of Nigeria, Ibadan (January 1947): 400–405.

122. Hurston, "Cudjo's Own Story," 651.

123. Ibid.

124. Atanda, "Dahomean Raids On Oke Ogun Towns," 3.

125. G.O. Ogunremi, "Transportaion in Pre-Colonial Africa." *Tarikh* 10 (1992): 29.

126. R.O. Ajetunmobi, *Coastal Yorubaland of Nigeria, 1500–1900: Migrations, Settlements and Socio-political Development* (Raytel Communications Ltd., 2003), 80.

127. Hurston, "Barracoon," 42–46.

128. Ibid., 55.

129. Frederick E. Forbes, *The Dahomeans: Being the Journals of Two Missions to the King of Dahomey, and Residence at His Capital, in the Years 1849 and 1850,* vol. 1 (London: Longman, Brown, Creen and Longmans, 1851), 17.

130. Hurston, "The Last Slave Ship," 354.

131. Robin Law, "'My Head Belongs to the King.' On the Political and Ritual Significance of Decapitation in Pre-Colonial Dahomey." *Journal of African History* 30 (1989): 402–3.

132. Mr. Jean-Gauthier Amidi, interview by author,Musée Historique (Royal Palace) d'Abomey. Republic of Benin, August 28, 1994, handwritten.

133. Burton, *A Mission to Gelele King of Dahome,* 131.

134. Ayandele, "The Yoruba Civil Wars and the Dahomean Confrontation," 55.

135. Hurston, "Barracoon," 55. The terms "relatives and friends" were recorded by Hurston when describing those individuals who were decapitated during the raid on Whinney (Hurston, "Cudjo's Own Story," 656). Today, that tragedy is commemorated as the Feast of Relatives and Friends during the AfricaTown Folk Festival.

136. Roche, *Historic Sketches,* 82.

137. Dov Ronen, *Dahomey: Between Tradition and Modernity* (Ithaca, NY: Cornell University Press, 1975), 23.

138. Hurston, "Barracoon," 56.

CHAPTER 6: CENTRAL NIGERIA

1. R.A. Olaniyan and A.G. Adebayo, "Yoruba Intergroup Relations and Diplomacy," in *Culture and Society In Yorubaland,* ed. 'Deji Ogunremi and 'Biodun Adediran (Ibadan, Nigeria: Rex Charles Publication, 1998), 105.

2. ViaVoh Mobee, curator of the Mobee Family Museum, interview by author, Badagry, Nigeria, May 25, 2004, handwritten.

3. Ibid.

4. John Babatunde Ajose, Curator of the Badagry Heritage Museum, interview by author, 25 May 2004. Badagry, Nigeria. Handwritten.

5. Ibid.

6. Anthony I. Asiwaju, *West African Transformations: Comparative Impacts of French and British Colonialism* (Lagos, Nigeria: Malthouse Press Ltd., 2001), 12.

7. Dayo Senami, interpretive guide, Route of Slaves, interview by author, Badagry, Nigeria, May 25, 2004, handwritten.

8. Frederick E. Forbes, *The Dahomeans: Being the Journals of Two Missions to the King of Dahomey, and Residence at His Capital, in the Years 1849 and 1850,* vol. 1 (London: Longman, Brown, Creen and Longmans, 1851), 20.

9. Kola Folayan, "International Politics in a Frontier Zone: Egbado, 1833–63." *ODU: A Journal of West African Studies,* n.s., 8 (October 1972): 27–28.

10. Dayo Senami, interview, May 25, 2004. This information was reinforced by Olorundare G. Oguntomisin, an historian at the University of Ibadan, interview by author, Ibadan, Nigeria, June 9, 2003, handwritten. See also Olusegun Mobee, *History of Mobee Family of Badagry and Their Involvement in Slave Trade* (Lagos: Al-Rasaq & Company, 2001), v.

11. The indigenes executed Portuguese trader Ferman Gomes for selling a Badagrian into the slave trade. John Babatunde Ajose, curator of the Badagry Heritage Museum, interview by author, May 25, 2004, handwritten. See also *Trans-Atlantic Slave Trade: Exhibition Guide of the Badagry Heritage Museum* (Lagos, Nigeria: Lagos State Waterfront and Tourism Development Corporation, 2002), 20.

12. John Babatunde Ajose, interview, May 25, 2004.

13. Pierre Verger, *Trade Relations between the Bight of Benin and Bahia from the 17th to 19th Century* (Ibadan, Nigeria: Ibadan University Press, 1976), 6.

14. Martin R. Delany, Chief Commissioner, "Official Report of the Niger Valley Exploring Party" (New York: Thomas Hamilton, 1861). Available at http://www.hierographics.org.

15. See Natalie S. Robertson, *Spirit of Our Ancestors: The Slave Ship* Clotilda *and the Making of AfricaTown* (Washington, DC: Library of Congress, 2005).

16. J. Ki-Zerbo, "The Living Tradition," in *General History Of Africa I: Methodology and African Prehistory,* ed. J. Ki-Zerbo (Berkeley: University of California Press, 1990), 94.

17. Joseph Jemkur, interview by author, University of Jos, Nigeria, June 4, 2004, handwritten.

18. Sati Baba, secretary to the Traditional Council of Kaninkon, interview by author, Chiefdom of Kaninkon, Jema'a, Kaduna, Nigeria, June 5, 2004, handwritten.

19. Mallam Tanko Tete, Chief of Kaninkon, interview by author, Chiefdom of Kaninkon, Jema'a, Kaduna, Nigeria, June 5, 2004, handwritten.

20. Ibid.

21. Michael Mason, "Population Density and 'Slave Raiding'—The Case of the Middle Belt of Nigeria," *Journal of African History* 10, no. 4 (1969): 558.

22. M.G. Smith, *Government in Zazzau: A Study of Government in the Hausa Chiefdom of Zaria in Northern Nigeria from 1800 to 1950* (New York: Oxford University Press, 1960), 89, 93–94.

23. Mallam Tanko Tete, interview, June 5, 2004.

24. Smith, *Government in Zazzau*, 77.

25. Mallam Tanko Tete, interview, June 5, 2004.

26. Ibid.

27. Smith, *Government in Zazzau*, 93.

28. Dr. S.N. Sani, district head, interview by author, Chiefdom of Jaba, Fada District, Kaduna, Nigeria, June 6, 2004, handwritten.

29. Dr. John L. Johnson, *500 Questions and Answers on the Black Presence in the Bible* (Chicago: Lushena Books, 2000) 22–31, 95, 120, 129.

30. Ibid., 136. See also "Ugarit and the Bible," http://www.theology.edu.

31. Cheikh Anta Diop, *The African Origin of Civilization: Myth or Reality* (Chicago: Lawrence Hill Books, 1974), 109.

32. Ibid., 139. See also C.K. Meek, *The Northern Tribes of Nigeria* (London: Oxford University Press, 1925), 69–73.

33. Dr. S.N. Sani, interview, June 6, 2004.

34. Chief Emmanuel I. Galadima, head of the District of Sabon Gari Kwoi, interview by author, Chiefdom of Jaba, Fada District, Kaduna, Nigeria, June 6, 2004, handwritten.

35. Ibid.

36. Augustine Meaher (son of Timothy Meaher) to Mr. Donaldson (of Springhill, Alabama), November 10, 1890. Letter in the hand of Augustine Meaher. Special Collections. Local History and Genealogical Department of the Mobile Public Library. Mobile, Alabama.

37. Dr. S.N. Sani, interview, June 6, 2004.

38. Ibid.

39. Emma Langdon Roche, *Historic Sketches of the South* (New York: Knickerbocker Press, 1914), 75.

40. S.H.M. Byers, "The Last Slave Ship," *Harper's Monthly Magazine* 63 (1906): 743.

41. Harold G. Gunn, *Peoples of the Plateau Area of Northern Nigeria* (London: International African Institute, 1953), 76.

42. Tobias Nkom Wada (Agwam Takad I), interview by author, Fadan Attakar, Takad Chiefdom, Kaura Local Government Area, Kaduna, Nigeria, June 6, 2004, handwritten.

43. Tobias Nkom Wada (Agwam Takad I), *Takad Chiefdom: First Circle of Self-Determination* (Kaduna, Kual Prints Limited, 2003), 4.

44. Ibid.

45. Ibid.

46. Byers, "The Last Slave Ship," 743.

47. Tobias Nkom Wada (Agwam Takad I), interview, June 6, 2004.

48. Benedict Kanyip, Takad indigene, interview by author, October 20, 2005. Electronic Mail.

49. Tobias Nkom Wada (Agwam Takad I), interview, June 6, 2004.

50. Christopher Roy, "Hausa Information." Art and Life in Africa Online, http://www.uiowa.edu.

51. Joseph F. Jemkur, *Aspects of the Nok Culture* (Zaria: Ahmadu Bello University Press, Ltd., 1992), 12–13, 15.

52. Roche, *Historic Sketches,* 82.

53. Tobias Nkom Wada, (Agwam Takad I), interview, June 6, 2004.

54. Jemkur, *Aspects of the Nok Culture,* 13–14.

55. Ibid., 14.

56. Simon Yohanna, Registrar of Kaduna State College of Education, provided brief, but important, information regarding the Kataf region relative to slave-raiding activities in southern Kaduna.

57. Tobias Nkom Wada, the *Agwam* Takad I, interview by author, 6 June 2004, Fadan Attakar, Takad Chiefdom, Kaura Local Government Area, Kaduna, Nigeria. Handwritten

58. Martin R. Delany, Chief Commissioner, "Official Report of the Niger Valley Exploring Party" (New York: Thomas Hamilton, 1861). Available at www.hierographics.org.

59. Ibid.

60. Henry Romeyn, "Little Africa: The Last Slave Cargo Landed in the United States." This article contains information on the voyage of the *Clotilda,* as well as some ethnographic data that was collected via interviews with the *Clotilda* Africans. *Southern Workman* (publication of Hampton Normal and Agricultural Institute) 26, no. 1 (January 1897): 14–17.

61. Patrick Manning, "Merchants, Porters, and Canoemen in the Bight of Benin: Links in the West African Trade Network," in *The Workers of African Trade,* ed. C. Coquery-Vidrovitch (Beverly Hills, CA: Sage Publications, 1985), 56, 65.

62. Alhaji M. Mohammed, interview by author, Zuma Rock Nigerian Village, Suleja, Niger State, Nigeria, June 7, 2004,handwritten.

63. Mallam Shuaibu Na'Ibi and Alhaji Hassan, *The Gwari, Gade, and Koro Tribes* (Ibadan, Nigeria: University of Ibadan Press, 1969), 38n.

64. Chief Abdullahi S. Gani, interview by author (via translator Philip S. Joseph), Zuma-Chaci village, Suleja, Niger State, Nigeria, July 8, 2004, handwritten.

65. Roche, *Historic Sketches,* 127.

66. Ibrahim Adamu, a Gwari indigene, interview by author via Mr. Olayinka Adekola, Ibadan, Nigeria, May 18, 2005.

67. Ibid.

68. Seidu Akilu, a Gwari indigene and a Professor of City Polytechnic University, interview by author via Mr. Olayinka Adekola, Ibadan, Nigeria, June 14, 2007.

69. Na'Ibi and Hassan, *Gwari, Gade, and Koro Tribes,* 38.

70. Mason, "Population Density and 'Slave Raiding,'" 551n, 555, 561.

71. Seidu Akilu, interview, June 14, 2007.

72. Mason, "Population Density and 'Slave Raiding,'" 561.

73. Ibid., 558.

74. Booker T. Washington, "The First and Last Slave Ship," in *The Story of the Negro: The Rise of the Race From Slavery* (New York: Doubleday, Page & Company, 1909), 104.

75. Ibid.

76. For more information regarding his life, see Booker T. Washington, *Up From Slavery* (New York: Penguin Books, 1986).

77. Washington, "The First and Last Slave Ship," 104.

78. Ibid.

79. Asiwaju, *West African Transformations*, 14–20. See also Robert Smith, "The Alaafin in Exile: A Study of the Igboho Period in Oyo History." *Journal of African History.* 6, no. 1 (1965): 57–77; and J.S. Eades and Chris Allen, compilers, *Benin* (Oxford: Clio Press, 1996), xxvii.

80. Gwendolyn M. Carter, ed., *Five African States: Responses to Diversity* (New York: Cornell University Press, 1963), 162. See also Natalie S. Robertson, *Spirit of Our Ancestors: The Slave Ship* Clotilda *and the Making of AfricaTown* (Washington, DC: Library of Congress, 2005).

81. Jacques Lombard, *Stuctures de Type Feodal en Afrique Noire: Etude des Dynamismes Internes et des Relations Sociale Chez les Bariba du Dahomey* (Paris: Mouton & Co., 1965), 149.

82. Augustine Meaher to Mr. Donaldson (of Springhill, Alabama), November 10, 1890. Special Collections, Local History and Genealogical Department of the Mobile Public Library. Mobile, AL.

83. For more information about slave raids on Dassa, see Natalie S. Robertson, "The African Ancestry of the Founders of AfricaTown, Alabama, 1859–Present" (PhD diss., University of Iowa, 1996); see also Robertson, *Spirit of Our Ancestors.*

84. Robin Law, "Slave-Raiders and Middlemen, Monopolists and Free-Traders: The Supply Of Slaves for the Atlantic Trade in Dahomey c. 1715–1850." *Journal of African History* 30 (1989): 58.

85. Asiwaju, *West African Transformations,* 710.

86. J.A. Rogers, *World's Great Men of Color.* Vol. 2 (New York: Simon and Schuster, 1975), 24, 34, 79, 123.

87. J.A. Rogers, *Sex and Race.* vol. 1 (St. Petersburg, FL: Helga M. Rogers, 1968), 227.

88. Robin Law, "Royal Monopoly and Private Enterprise in the Atlantic Trade: The Case of Dahomey." *Journal Of African History* 18, no. 4 (1977): 561. See also E. Geoffrey Parrinder, *The Story of Ketu: An Ancient Yoruba Kingdom* (Ibadan, Nigeria: Ibadan University Press, 1956), 42.

89. Roche, *Historic Sketches,* 126.

90. Ibid., 86.

91. Ibid.

92. Ibid.

93. Josephine Lee Marshall, interview by author, AfricaTown, AL, March 14, 1994, tape recording.

94. Romeyn, "Little Africa," 14–17.

95. Rogers, *World's Great Men Of Color,* 391.

96. Ibid., 389.

97. Ibid., 390.

98. Ibid., 392–93.

99. Robert W. Rydell, *All the World's a Fair: Visions of Empire at American International Expositions, 1876–1916* (Chicago: University of Chicago Press, 1984), 61.

100. Ibid., 53, 60–71.

101. For more information, see Carl Sifakis, "Benga, Ota: The Zoo Man," in *American Eccentrics* (New York: Facts on File, 1884). See also Phillip V. Bradford and Harvey Blume, *Ota Benga: The Pygmy in the Zoo*, (New York: St. Martin's Press, 1992).

102. This quote was taken from a description of the video *The Life and Times of Sara Baartman—"The Hottentot Venus,"* available from a video list (New York: First Run Icarus Films, 2000), 3.

103. Ibid.

CHAPTER 7: THE FOUNDING OF AFRICATOWN

1. Emma Langdon Roche, *Historic Sketches of the South* (New York: Knickerbocker Press, 1914), 166.

2. Ibid., 123n.

3. Ibid., 124.

4. Recall that scene in *Beloved*, when Sethe takes *Beloved* in because she was a woman in need of assistance without realizing that *Beloved*, in the flesh or *in spirit*, was the child against whom she committed, or attempted to commit, infanticide. Her reappearance speaks volumes about the inseparable bond that continues to exist, though in an often times fragmented manner, between Black peoples.

5. Roche, *Historic Sketches*, 101–2. See also Erwin Craighead, *Mobile: Fact and Tradition* (The Powers Printing Company, 1930), 358; and "Death of Captain Tim Meaher, The Venerable Steamboat Man," *Mobile Daily Register*, March 4, 1892.

6. Hurston, "Barracoon," 62.

7. Roche, *Historic Sketches*, 101. See also Zora Neale Hurston, "Dust Tracks on a Road," in *Zora Neale Hurston: Folklore, Memoirs, and Other Writings*, ed. Cheryl A. Wall (New York: The Library of America, 1995), 710.

8. Hurston, "Barracoon," 62.

9. Runaway Slave Book I (1863), 148. Mobile Probate Court Archives.

10. Ibid., 63.

11. Ibid.

12. John Hope Franklin and Alfred A. Moss, *From Slavery to Freedom: A History of African Americas*, vol. 2 (New York: McGraw Hill, Inc., 1998), 199–200.

13. Jim Bishop, *The Day Lincoln Was Shot* (New York: Harper & Brothers, 1955), 70–71.

14. The FBI is investigating incidences in which hate mail has been sent to Black male athletes at the high school, college, and professional levels, demanding that they end their interracial relationships "or they're going to be castrated, shot or set on fire." Available at FOXSports.com.

15. "The Work of a Mob," in *The Crisis Reader,* ed. Kathryn Wilson (New York: Random House, Inc., 1999), 345–50. See also Jacqueline Jones Royser, ed. *Southern Horrors and Other Writings: The Anti-Lynching Campaign of Ida B. Wells, 1892–1900* (New York: Bedfore Books, 1997).

16. Donald v. United Klans of America: Michael Donald Lynching Case. Southern Poverty Law Center, http://www.splcenter.org.

17. Ibid.

18. "Report: Letter Calls Jeter 'Traitor to His Race.'" ESPN MLB Web page, http://www.espn.com.

19. Donald G. Nieman, *Promises To Keep: African-Americans and the Constitutional Order, 1776 to the Present* (New York: Oxford University Press, 1991), 60–61.

20. http://www.jimcrowhistory.org

21. Ibid.

22. Ibid. This antimiscegenation law was enacted in 1915.

23. Ella Barrett Ligon, "The White Woman and the Negro," contained in file labeled "Negroes in Mobile, Alabama." Minnie Mitchell Archives. Historic Mobile Preservation Society. Mobile, AL.

24. David M. Oshinsky, *"Worse Than Slavery": Parchman Farm and the Ordeal of Jim Crow Justice* (New York: Simon & Schuster, 1996), 43.

25. "PrisonAct: Convict-Leasing in Alabama." Available at http://www.prisonactivist.org.

26. Hurston, "Barracoon," 66.

27. Emma Langdon Roche, "Last Survivor of Slave Ship Deeply Grateful to God, Man," *Mobile Press Register,* August 13, 1935.

28. Hurston, "Barracoon," 70.

29. S.H.M. Byers, "The Last Slave-Ship," *Harper's Monthly Magazine* 113 (1906):

30. "Mobile—Its Past, Present, and Future," *De Bow's Review* 26, no. 1 (January 1859).

31. Miss Ivory Hill, interview by author, AfricaTown, AL, February 6, 1995, tape recording.

32. Miss Mary Pogue, interview by author, AfricaTown, AL, February 9, 1995, tape recording.

33. "Moses Grandy on Slavery and Social Control," in *From Timbuktu To Katrina: Readings in African-American History,* ed. Quintard Taylor Jr., vol. 1 (Boston: Thompson Wadworth, 2007), 54.

34. Roche, *Historic Sketches,* 114–15.

35. Hurston, "Barracoon," 69.

36. Roche, *Historic Sketches,* 114–15, 166.

37. Ibid.

38. Ibid. See also Addie E. Pettaway, *AfricaTown, USA: Some Aspects of Folklife and Material Culture of an Historic Landscape* (Wisconsin Department of Public Instruction, 1985), 3.

39. Henry C. Williams, *AfricaTown, U.S.A.* (Mobile, AL: American Ethnic Science Society, 1981), 28.

40. City Court of Mobile. October Term 1868 (23rd and 24th). Local History and Genealogical Department, Mobile Public Library. Mobile, AL. Archie and Toney (sometimes called Tommy) Thomas were members of the *Clotilda* cargo. However, their adoption of European names have obscured their West African identities. See also Natalie S. Robertson, *Spirit of Our Ancestors: The Slave Ship* Clotilda *and the Making of AfricaTown* (Washington, DC: Library of Congress, 2005).

41. Ibid.

42. Elizabeth D. Leonard, *Lincoln's Avengers: Justice, Revenge, and Reunion after the Civil War* (New York: W.W. Norton & Company, 2004), 56.

43. Mrs. Lorna Woods, interview by author, Mobile, AL, March 1, 1994, tape recording.

44. Thomas Buford to Jabez [Jaba] Chase, Horace Ely, Charley Lewis, Maggie Lewis, Matilda Ely, Lucy Wilson & Polly Shay, Deed Book 70 (1870), 244–45. Mobile Probate Court Archives.

45. Meaher to Allen, Deed Book 30 (1872), 643. Mobile Probate Court Archives.

46. Meaher to Kebee, Deed Book 30 (1872), 655. Mobile Probate Court Archives.

47. Wilson to Lewis, Deed Book 30 (1872), 601. Mobile Probate Court Archives.

48. Cudjoe Lewis to Mobile Light & RR Co. Deed Book. D. 113 (1904), p. 23.Mobile Probate Court Archives.

49. *Census Report for the County of Mobile* (1900), Special Collections, Local History and Genealogical Department, Mobile Public Library, Mobile, AL.

50. Hauser to Lewis, Deed Book 55 (1887), p. 160. Mobile Probate Court Archives

51. Samuel Johnson, *The History Of The Yorubas: From the Earliest Times to the Beginning of the British Protectorate* (Lagos, Nigeria: C.M.S. Bookshops, 1956), 96.

52. Frank Sikora, "Groups Tracing History of Last Slaves to Arrive," *Birmingham News*, March 26, 1980, 2A.

53. Henry Romeyn, "Little Africa: The Last Slave Cargo Landed in the United States." This article contains information on the voyage of the *Clotilda*, as well as some ethnographic data that was collected via interviews with the *Clotilda* Africans. *Southern Workman* (publication of Hampton Normal and Agricultural Institute) 26, no. 1 (January 1897): 14–17.

54. Hurston, "Barracoon," 15.

55. Emma Langdon Roche, "Last Survivor of Slave Ship Deeply Grateful To God, Man." *Mobile Press Register*, August 13, 1935.

56. Roche, *Historic Sketches*, 76, 104. See also Johnson, *History of the Yorubas*, 90.

57. Pettaway, *AfricaTown, USA*, 27.

58. Henry C. Williams, *AfricaTown, U.S.A.*, 36. See also Pettaway, *AfricaTown, USA*, 25.

59. For more information regarding these houses, and their possible connections to Yoruba architecture, see John Michael Vlach, *The Afro-American Tradition in Decorative Arts* (Cleveland, OH: Cleveland Museum of Art, 1978), 123–33.

60. Miss Ivory Hill, interview by author, Toulminville, AL, July 17, 2007, handwritten.

61. Hurston, "Barracoon," 71.

62. Ibid., 62

63. Romeyn, "Little Africa,." 16, 17.

64. Mrs. Lorna Woods, interview, March 1, 1994.

65. For more information regarding West African influences on Afro-American family structures, see Niara Sudarkasa, "African and Afro-American Family Structure: A Comparison," *The Black Scholar* (November–December 1980): 43–47.

66. Zora Neale Hurston, "Cudjo's Own Story of the Last African Slaver," *Journal of Negro History* 12 (October 1927): 652.

67. I.A. Akinjogbin, *Milestones and Concepts in Yoruba History and Culture* (Ibadan, Nigeria: Olu-Akin Publishers, 2002), 27.

68. *Census Report for the County of Mobile* (1880). Special Collections, Local History and Genealogical Department, Mobile Public Library. Mobile, AL.

69. Hurston, "Barracoon," 72.

70. *Census Report for the County of Mobile* (1880).

71. Ibid., 14–17.

72. Hurston, "Barracoon," 74.

73. Ibid., 39.

74. Hurston was the first to record the following African names for each child. I have provided more accurate spellings of each name, along with its Yoruba meaning. See "Barracoon," 74.

75. "Lee Family Reunion: The Old Homestead" (Mobile, AL: private collection of Mrs. Josephine Lee Marshall, 1991), 1.

76. Pettaway, *AfricaTown, USA*, 5. See also Chamba and Hales Wigerfall, marriage license, Mobile Probate Court Archives, CML Book 5 (1876), p. 172; Clara and Samuel Turner, marriage license, Mobile Probate Court Archives, CML Book 6 (1880), p. 432.

77. *Census Report for the County of Mobile* (1900).

78. Mrs. Josephine Lee Marshall, interview by author, AfricaTown, AL, March 14, 1994, tape recording.

79. Mable Dennison, *Biographical Memoirs of James Dennison* (Boynton Beach, FL: Futura Printing, Inc., 1984), 28.

80. Issac O. Delano, *Owe L'Esin Oro: Yoruba Proverbs: Their Meaning and Usage* (Ibadan, Nigeria: Oxford University Press, 1996), 47.

81. Pettaway, *AfricaTown, USA*, 13.

82. *Census Report for the County of Mobile* (1880).

83. Mrs. Josephine Lee Marshall, interview, March 14, 1994.

84. Henry Drewel, John Pemberton III, and Rowland Abiodun, *Yoruba: Nine Centuries of African Art* (New York: Center For African Art, 1989), 170.

85. N.A. Fadipe, *The Sociology of the Yoruba* (Ibadan, Nigeria: Ibadan University Press, 1970), 310.

86. Augustine Meaher (son of Timothy Meaher) to Mr. Donaldson (of Springhill, Alabama), November 10, 1890. Letter in the hand of Augustine Meaher. Special Collections, Local History and Genealogical Department of the Mobile Public Library, Mobile, AL.

87. Donald R. Wright, *African-Americans in the Colonial Era: From African Origins through the American Revolution* (Illinois: Harlan Davidson, Inc., 1990), 91.

88. Chris McFadyen, "Legacy of a 'Peculiar Institution.'" *Mobile Register* (1984): 4.

89. Miss Ivory Hill, interview, February 6, 1995.

90. Mrs. Lorna Woods, interview, March 1, 1994.

91. Mr. Spencer Williams, interview by author, AfricaTown, AL, February 25, 1994, tape recording.

92. Roche, *Historic Sketches*, 76–77.

93. Wole Soyinka, facilitator, "Gods, Knowledge, and Modernity," inaugural UNCF/Mellon Faculty Seminar, Gorée Institute, Senegal, July 18, 2002.

94. Mr. John C. Randolph, interview by author, AfricaTown, AL, March 14, 1994, tape recording.

95. McFadyen, "Legacy," 4.

96. John S. Mbiti, *Introduction to African Religion* (London: Heinemann Educational Books, 1991), 174.

97. Roche, *Historic Sketches*, 118.

98. Ibid., 77.

99. Ibid.

100. C.K. Meeks, *The Tribes of Northern Nigeria*, vol. 1 (London: Oxford University Press, 1925), 259–63.

101. *The State of Alabama v. Cudjoe Lewis*. City Court Criminal Minute Book 18 (1899–1902), 118. University of South Alabama Archives.

102. Diouf, *Dreams of Africa in Alabama*, 191.

103. Hurston, "Barracoon," 74.

104. *The State of Alabama v. Cudjoe Lewis*, 118.

105. *In the matter of the special venire in the case v. Cudjoe Lewis*. City Court Criminal Minute Book 18, (1899–1902), 112–13. University of South Alabama Archives.

106. David E. Alsobrook, "Mobile's Solitary Sentinel: U.S. Attorney William H. Armbrecht and the Richard Robertson Lynching Case of 1909." *Gulf South Historical Review* 20, no. 1 (2004): 7.

107. Ibid.

108. *Rules and Regulations for the Government of the Convict System of Alabama, Approved by The Board of Inspectors Of Convicts, March 3, 1886. Approved by the Governor March 22, 1886. Published by Order of the Board* (Montgomery, AL: Barrett & Co., State Printers, 1886), 24. Minnie Mitchell Archives, Historic Mobile Preservation Society, Mobile, AL.

109. *The State of Alabama v. Cudjoe Lewis*, 129.

110. *Rules and Regulations for the Government of the Convict System of Alabama*, Approved by The Board of Inspectors Of Convicts, March 3, 1886. Approved by the Governor March 22, 1886. Published by Order of the Board (Montgomery, AL: Barrett & Co., State Printers, 1886), 24. Minnie Mitchell Archives. Historic Mobile Preservation Society. Mobile, AL.

111. *Proceedings of the Annual Congress of the American Prison Association of the United States*, Nashville, November 16–20, 1889 (Washington, DC: American Correctional Association, 1963–c.1970), 115.

112. Ibid., 130.

113. Ibid., 111.

114. Petition for the pardon of Cudjo Lewis Jr., written on behalf of several citizens of Mobile, July 1901. Deposited in the Alabama Department of Archives and History, Montgomery.

CHAPTER 8: SPIRIT OF OUR ANCESTORS

1. David Eltis, *The Rise of African Slavery in the Americas* (Cambridge: Cambridge University Press, 1999), 65.

2. Addie E. Pettaway, *AfricaTown, USA: Some Aspects of Folklife and Material Culture of an Historic Landscape* (Wisconsin Department of Public Instruction, 1985), 15. Mr. Spencer Williams, interview by author, AfricaTown, AL, February 25, 1994, tape recording.

3. Mrs. Lorna Woods, interview by author, Mobile, AL, March 1, 1994, tape recording.

4. Mr. John C. Randolph, interview by author, AfricaTown, AL, March 14, 1994, tape recording.

5. Judith Wragg Chase, "Material Culture," in *Dictionary Of Afro-American Slavery,* ed. Randall M. Miller and John David Smith (New York: Greenwood Press, 1998), 457–58.

6. Mr. Henry C. Williams, local historian, interview by author, AfricaTown, AL, March 12, 1994, tape recording.

7. Babatunde Agiri, "Missionaries, Muslims, Warfare and Slavery in Ogbomoso in the 19th Century" (unpublished article that Agiri donated to author), 3.

8. Zora Neale Hurston, "Cudjo's Own Story of the Last African Slaver." *Journal of Negro History* 12 (October 1927): 650.

9. Mr. Spencer Williams, interview, February 25, 1994. Trapping is commonly associated with hunting among the Yoruba. For more information on this topic, see Deji Ogunremi, "Foundations of the Yoruba Economy in the Pre-Colonial Era," in *Culture and Society in Yorubaland,* ed. 'Deji Ogunremi and 'Biodun Adediran (Ibadan, Nigeria: Rex Charles Publication, 1998), 118.

10. Mr. John C. Randolph, interview, March 14, 1994.

11. Mrs. Lorna Woods, interview by author, Lewis' Quarters, AL, August 14, 2004, handwritten.

12. Mr. Spencer Williams, interview, February 25, 1994.

13. Israel Lewis III, interview by author, Mobile, AL, February 20, 1995, handwritten.

14. Hurston, "Barracoon," 25.

15. Thelma Shamburger, interview by author, AfricaTown, AL, February 6, 1995, tape recording.

16. Miss Ivory Hill, interview by author, AfricaTown, AL, February 6, 1995, tape recording.

17. Chris McFadyen, "Legacy of a 'Peculiar Institution,'" *Mobile Register* (1984): 4.

18. Kudẹ̈yfu, interview by author, Afin, Oyo town, Oyo State, Nigeria, July 17, 2003, tape recording.

19. Charles Porter, "African Bees Said Still in AfricaTown," *Inner City News,* September 20, 1986; see also McFadyen, "Legacy," 4.

20. Frank Sikora, "Groups Tracing History of Last Slaves to Arrive," *Birmingham News,* March 16, 1980, 2A.

21. Samuel Johnson, *The History of the Yorubas: From the Earliest Times to the Beginning of the British Protectorate* (Lagos, Nigeria: C.M.S. Bookshops, 1956),

22. F. Olu. Okediji and F. A. Okediji, "The Sociological Aspects of Traditional Yoruba Names and Titles." *ODU: University of Ife Journal of African Studies* 3, no. 1 (July 1966): 71. See also Johnson, *History of the Yorubas,* 84.

23. Emma Langdon Roche, *Historic Sketches of the South* (New York: Knickerbocker Press, 1914), 124.

24. Prince Ganiyu Ojo, interview by author, Afin, Oyo town, Oyo State, Nigeria, June 18, 2003, handwritten.

25. N. A. Fadipe, *The Sociology of the Yoruba* (Nigeria: Ibadan University Press, 1970), 148–49.

26. *Census Report for the County of Mobile* (1880), Special Collections, Local History and Genealogical Department of the Mobile Public Library, Mobile, AL.

27. Miss Ivory Hill, interview, February 6, 1995.

28. John Eisterhold, "Mobile: Lumber Center of the Gulf Coast," *The Alabama Review* 26, no. 2 (1973): 90–92.

29. Pettaway, *AfricaTown, USA,* 12.

30. *Cudjo Lewis v. The Louisville and Nashville Railroad Company.* Verdict for damages assessed at $650.00. January 1903. University of South Alabama Archives. See also The State of Alabama Judicial Department: *The Supreme Court of Alabama. Certificate of Reversal. November Term. 1904.* University of South Alabama Archives.

31. Pettaway, *AfricaTown, USA,* 4.

32. Ibid., 12.

33. Ibid.

34. Ibid.

35. Mr. Spencer Williams, interview, February 25, 1994.

36. Pettaway, *AfricaTown, USA,* 14.

37. Miss Mary Pogue, interview by author, AfricaTown, AL, February 9, 1995, tape recording.

38. Thelma Shamburger, interview, February 6, 1995.

39. McFadyen, "Legacy," 4.

40. Mrs. Josephine Lee Marshall, interview by author, AfricaTown, AL, March 14, 1994, tape recording.

41. Miss Mary Pogue, interview, February 9, 1995.

42. Ibid.

43. Mrs. Vernetta Henson, interview by author, Mobile, AL, July 19, 2007, handwritten.

44. Mr. John Peoples, interview by author, AfricaTown, AL, February 24, 1995, handwritten.

45. Fadipe, *Sociology of the Yoruba,* 299.

46. McFadyen, "Legacy," 4.

47. Ibid.

48. Beverly Robinson, "Africanisms and the Study of Folklore," in *Africanisms in American Culture*, ed. Joseph E. Holloway (Bloomington: Indiana University Press, 1990), 220.

49. Miss Martine F. De Souza, interview by author, Whydah, Republic of Benin, August 16, 1994, tape recording.

50. William Grimes, *Ethno-Botany of the Black Americans* (St. Claire Shores, MI: Scholarly Press, Inc., 1976), 123–24.

51. Pettaway, *AfricaTown, USA*, 21–22.

52. Anthony D. Buckley, *Yoruba Medicine* (Oxford: Clarendon Press, 1985), 192.

53. Loudell F. Snow, *Walkin' over Medicine* (Boulder, CO: Westview Press, 1993), 158. See also Buckley, *Yoruba Medicine*, 47, 59.

54. Pettaway, *AfricaTown, USA*, 20–21. The *Clotilda* Africans developed this medicine in conjunction with Reverend Edward Williams, who was an herbalist and a resident of Magazine Point. Poke-salad is used as an astringent throughout African America (Snow, *Walkin' over Medicine*, 77).

55. Leonard E. Barrett, *Soul-Force: African Heritage in Afro-American Religion* (Garden City, NY: Anchor Press, 1974), 28.

56. Ibid., 91.

57. S.H.M. Byers, "The Last Slave-Ship," *Harper's Monthly Magazine* 113 (1906): 743.

58. A.J.N. Tremearne, "Notes on the Kagoro and Other Nigerian Head-Hunters," *Journal of the Royal Anthropological Institute* 42 (1912): 147. See also Natalie S. Robertson, *Spirit of Our Ancestors: The Slave Ship* Clotilda *and the Making of AfricaTown* (Washington, DC: Library of Congress, 2005).

59. Melville J. Herskovits, *Dahomey: An Ancient West African Kingdom*, vol. 1 (New York: J.J. Augustin, 1938): 262.

60. Ibid.

61. Roche, *Historic Sketches*, 114. See also Robertson, *Spirit of Our Ancestors*.

62. Henry C. Williams, *A History of Mobile County Training School* (Mobile, AL: privately printed, 1977), 5; Roche, *Historic Sketches*, 117n; Roche, "Last Survivor of Slave Ship Deeply Grateful To God, Man," *Mobile Press Register*, August 13, 1935.

63. John S. Mbiti, *Introduction to African Religion* (London: Heinemann Educational Books, 1991), 174.

64. In contemporary Nigeria, the name Sango incites a different kind of fear in many Yoruba peoples who have been taught, mainly through their British-influenced educational systems, to reject their indigenous deities as evil beings while Britons and other peoples are trafficking African artifacts as "primitive art." In other words, the very things that Africans are being told to reject are the things that are being confiscated and marketed by foreigners for capital gain. This is one of the destructive outcomes of Eurocentric education and religion.

65. Roche, *Historic Sketches*, 80.

66. Herskovits, *Dahomey*, vol. 2, 152.

67. Ibid., 156–57.

68. George Brandon, "Sacrificial Practices in Santeria, an African-Cuban Religion in the United States," in *Africanisms In American Culture*, 123.

69. E. Bolaji Idowu, *Olodumare: God in Yoruba Belief* (Original Publications, 1999), 89.

70. Paul Radin, *God Struck Me Dead: Religious Conversion Experience and Autobiographies of Negro Ex-slaves* (Nashville, TN: Social Science Institute, Fisk University, 1945), 27–30.

71. Roche, *Historic Sketches*, 124.

72. John Pemberton III, "The Oyo Empire," in *Yoruba: Nine Centuries Of African Art and Thought*, ed. Henry Drewal, John Pemberton III, and Rowland Abiodun (New York: The Center for African Art, 1989), 168. Yoruba horsemen and Fon amazons wore haversack bands in the same fashion.

73. Idowu, *Olodumare*, 118.

74. Olo kun Esin, interview by author, Afin, Oyo town, Oyo State, Nigeria, July 17, 2003, tape recording.

75. Ibid.

76. Idowu, *Olodumare*, 16.

77. Ashra Kwesi, *Christianity, The Stolen Religion From Africa, Part I* 120 min., 1995, produced and distributed by Kemetnu Productions, Inc., Dallas, TX.

78. Hurston, "Cudjo's Own Story," 653.

79. Idowu, *Olodumare*, 103, 106.

80. "The Alabama Negro: 1863–1946," (Mobile, AL: The Gulf Informer Publishing Co., n.d.). University of South Alabama Archives.

81. Pettaway, *AfricaTown, USA*, 5.

82. Ibid., 8.

83. Ibid.

84. Ibid., 106.

85. McFadyen, "Legacy," 4.

86. Miss Ivory Hill, interview by author, Toulminville, AL, July 17, 2007, handwritten.

87. *Alabama: A Guide to the Deep South*, compiled by the workers of the Writer's Program of the Work Projects Adminstration in the state of Alabama (New York: Richard R. Smith, 1941), 359.

88. Hurston, "The Last Slave Ship," 358.

89. Roche, "Last Survivor of Slave Ship."

90. McFadyen, "Legacy," 4.

91. Mbiti, *Introduction to African Religion*, 142.

92. C. Eric Lincoln and Lawrence H. Mamiya, *The Black Church in the African American Experience* (Durham, NC: Duke University Press, 1990), 6–7.

93. Sterling Stuckey, *Slave Culture: Nationalist Theory and the Foundations of Black America* (New York: Oxford University Press, 1987), 11–14.

94. Pettaway, *AfricaTown, USA*, 10.

95. Mechal Sobel, *Trabelin' On: The Slave Journey to an Afro-Baptist Faith* (Westport, CT: Greenwood Press, 1979), 143.

96. Miss Ivory Hill, interview, February 6, 1995.

97. Henry Romeyn, "Little Africa: The Last Slave Cargo Landed in the United States." This article contains information on the voyage of the *Clotilda,* as well as some ethnographic data that was collected via interviews with the *Clotilda* Africans. *Southern Workman* (publication of Hampton Normal and Agricultural Institute) 26, no. 1 (January 1897): 14–17.

98. Ibid.

99. Jimcrowhistory.org.

100. Hurston, "Barracoon," 75.

101. Henry C. Williams, *A History Of Mobile County Training School,* 7–8

102. Henry C. Williams, interview, March 12, 1994.

103. Ibid.

104. W.E.B. Du Bois, "The Negro Since 1900," in *W.E.B. Du Bois: A Reader,* ed. Meyer Weinberg (New York: Harper & Row, 1970), 89.

105. Henry C. Williams, *A History of Mobile County Training School,* 8.

106. Ibid.

107. Ibid.

108. Henry C. Williams, interview, March 12, 1994.

109. Mr. John C. Randolph, interview by author, March 14, 1994, AfricaTown, AL, tape recording.

110. Alain Locke, *The New Negro* (New York: A. and C. Boni, 1925), 245.

111. Jack Berry, *West African Folktales* (Evanston, IL: Northwestern University Press, 1991), xxiii.

112. Ibid., 200.

113. Robert Russa Moton, *Finding a Way Out: An Autobiography.* Documenting the American South. Available at http://www.docsouth.unc.edu.

114. Earl G. Graves, *How to Succeed in Business Without Being White* (New York: Harper Business, 1997), 35.

115. Israel Lewis III, interview by author, Mobile, AL, February 20, 1995, handwritten.

116. Roche, "Last Survivor," n.p.

117. "Famous Ex-Slave Dies Here with Ambition Unrealized," *Mobile Register,* July 27, 1935.

118. *Certificate of Death. Cudjo Lewis.* (1935). Alabama Center for Health Statistics. African-American Vertical Files; "Lewis, Cudjo" (folder #2), University of South Alabama Archives.

119. Hurston, "Barracoon," 76.

120. Ibid., 77.

121. Ibid., 86.

122. Ibid., 73.

123. Ibid., 91–92.

124. Cujo Lewis to Thomas L. Dawson, Deed Book 189 (1920), 418. Mobile Probate Court Archives.

125. Cudjo Lewis to Mobile County, Deed Book 212 (1926), 424. Mobile Probate Court Archives.

126. *Joe Lewis's Petition to become Administrator of Cudjo Lewis's Estate.* Administrative Account. Book 150 (1936), p. 607. Mobile Probate Court Archives.

127. Ibid.

128. *Estate of Cudjo Lewis.* Book 285 (1939), 227–45. Mobile Probate Court Archives.

129. Ibid.

130. Merlin N. Hanson, "Burial of the Last Slave." *Globe*, p. 60. Slavery-Clothilde File, Minnie Mitchell Archives, Historical Mobile Preservation Society, Mobile, AL.

131. Ibid., 58.

132. Ibid., 60.

133. Israel Lewis III, interview by author, Prichard, AL, July 19, 2007, handwritten.

134. Ibid.

135. "Honoring Cudjo Lewis: America's Last Piece of African 'Black Ivory.'" *Literary Digest*, November 21, 1931, 36.

136. "Famous Ex-Slave Dies Here with Ambition Unrealized."

CHAPTER 9: CROSSROADS

1. Natalie S. Robertson to Augustine Meaher III, June 14, 2007, certified letter.

2. *Dred Scott, Plaintiff in Error, v. John F.A. Sanford.* December Term, 1856. Available at Web site of the Touro Law Center, 1995–2004, http://www.tourolaw.edu.

3. *Charge to Grand Jury—Fugitive Slave Law,* Case No. 18,261, Circuit Court, S.D. New York 30 F. Cas. 1007; 1851 U.S. App. LEXIS 376; 1 Blatchf. 635 April, 1851. Available through Lexis-Nexis Academic Search.

4. "Congress Approves Task Force To Honor Slaves Who Built The U.S. Capitol." *Jet,* June 2005, 20.

5. *See Section 6 of the Slave Trade Act of 1807,* "Documents on Slavery," The Avalon Project at Yale Law School, available at http://www.yale.edu.

6. "Bank of the United States." *The Columbia Encyclopedia,* 6th ed., 2001–5. http://www.Bartleby.com.

7. *Fleckner, Plaintiff in Error, v. The President, Directors, and Company of the Bank of The United States, Defendants in Error,* U.S. Supreme Court, decided February 28, 1823. Available through LexisNexis Academic Search, http://libweb.hamptonu.edu.

8. *Bank of the United States v. Smith.* Available through LexisNexis Academic Search, http://libweb.hamptonu.edu.

9. Ibid.

10. Public Sales, *Branch Bank at Montgomery vs. L.D. Hallonquist, James G. Birney,* May 1, 1844, in Original Documents #98, Slavery/Receipts/Bills of Sale for Slaves, Minnie Mitchell Archives, Historic Mobile Preservation Society, Mobile, AL.

11. *Wills & Co. v. The Planters' & Merchants' Bank of Mobile,* Supreme Court of Alabama, January 1851. Available through LexisNexis Academic Search, http://libweb.hamptonu.edu.

12. *Dunn & Wife et al. v. The Bank of Mobile et al.* Available through LexisNexis Academic Search, http://libweb.hamptonu.edu.

13. "A List of John P. Broun's Negroes, To be sold on the 4th day of January 1859," in Original Documents #98, Slavery/Receipts/Bills of Sale for Slaves.

14. Ibid.

15. "City Taxes For 1858," City of Mobile, in Original Documents #98. Slavery/Receipts/Bills of Sale for Slaves.

16. Douglas A. Blackmon, "From Alabama's Past, Capitalism and Racism in a Cruel Partnership—Till 1928, Companies "Leased" Convicts, Most of Them Black and Many Doomed—Sent to the Mines for 'Gaming,'" *Wall Street Journal,* July 16, 2001.

17. *Rules and Regulations for the Government of the Convict System of Alabama, Approved by The Board of Inspectors Of Convicts, March 3, 1886. Approved by the Governor March 22, 1886. Published by Order of the Board* (Montgomery: Barrett & Co., State Printers, 1886), 31–39. Minnie Mitchell Archives, Historic Mobile Preservation Society, Mobile, AL.

18. "Wachovia Completes Research." Available at http://www.wachovia.com. See also "Wachovia Corporation Admits Ties To Slavery; Apologizes," *Jet* (June 2005), 22.

19. "JP Morgan Chase & Co. Apologizes for Predecessor Banks Accceptance of Slaves as Collateral," *Jet* (February 2005), 14.

20. *Deadria Farmer-Paellmann, Plaintiff, v. FleetBoston Financial Corporation, Aetna Inc., CSX, and Their predecessors, successors and/or assigns, and Corporate Does Nos. 1–1000,* available at http://www.FindLaw.com.

21. Ibid.

22. Ibid.

23. "Power of Attorney to Receive Payments from Compensation Bonds Issued as a Result of the 1848 Emancipation of the Slaves, 1854–56," Box 732, ¼ inch, entry 334 [MISSING], National Archives.

24. District of Columbia Emancipation Act. April 16, 1862. Available at http://teachingamericanhistory.org.

25. Ibid.

26. Supreme Court Historical Society Web site, http://www.supremecourthistory.org

27. Caldwell Delaney, *Craighead's Mobile* (Mobile, AL: The Haunted Book Shop, 1968), 189.

28. "Breaking The Silence: Learning about the Trans-Atlantic Slave Trade: Slave Routes: United Kingdom," http://www.antislavery.org.

29. "Slave Trade Suit Targets Lloyd's, U.S. Companies; Seeks $2B in Comp." *Paper Money* 1, no. 11, April 6, 2004. Available athttp://www.globalpapermoney.org.

30. "Historical Note," Lexis-nexis.com, p. 10. The *Mary* is thought to be the first slave ship to sail from Rhode Island in 1736. She deposited a cargo of Africans in the West Indies. The Browns resumed participation in the slave trade in 1759. For more information, consult the Rhode Island Historical Society at http://www.rihs.org.

31. Ibid., p. 7. Some of Brown's vessels, such as the slaver *Hope,* were opium traders. See http://www.danbyrnes.com.

32. *Deadria Farmer-Paellmann, Plaintiff, v. FleetBoston Financial Corporation, Aetna Inc., CSX, and Their predecessors, successors and/or assigns, and Corporate Does Nos. 1–1000,* available at http://www.FindLaw.com. See Kate Zernike, "Slave Traders in Yale's Past Fuel Debate on Restitution," *New York Times,* August 13, 2001. See also Paras

D. Bhayani, "Beneath the Ivy: A Legacy of Chains," available at http://www.the crimson.com.

33. Daniel P. Mannix, *Black Cargoes: A History of the Atlantic Slave Trade, 1518–1865* (Associated Publishers, Inc., 1962), 162–63.

34. James B. Farr, *Black Odyssey: The Seafaring Traditions of Afro-Americans* (New York: Peter Lang, 1989), 31.

35. Sam Hodges, "What Others Are Doing," *Press Register,* January 12, 1999. http://www.al.com.

36. "Meaher Industrial Sites: First Choice of World Class Companies," http://www.firstchoicesties.com.

37. Robert W. Rydell, ed., *The Reason Why the Colored American Is Not in the World's Columbian Exposition* (Chicago: University of Illinois Press, 1999), xxxii.

Bibliography

MONOGRAPHS

Ajayi, J.F. Ade, and Robert Smith. *Yoruba Warfare in the Nineteenth Century.* Ibadan, Nigeria: Ibadan University Press, 1964.

Ajetunmobi, R.O. *Coastal Yorubaland of Nigeria, 1500–1900: Migrations, Settlements and Socio-political Development.* Raytel Communications Ltd., 2003.

Akinjogbin, I.A. *Milestones and Concepts in Yoruba History and Culture* Ibadan, Nigeria: Olu-Akin Publishers, 2002.

Alabama: A Guide to the Deep South. Compiled by the Workers of the Writer's Program of the Work Projects Adminstration in the State of Alabama. New York: Richard R. Smith, 1941.

Argyle, W.J. *The Fon of Dahomey: A History and Ethnography of the Old Kingdom.* Oxford: Clarendon Press, 1966.

Armah, Ayi Kwei *KMT: in the House of Life.* Popenguine, Senegal: PER ANKH, 2003.

Arnold, Rosemary. "A Port of Trade: Whydah on the Guinea Coast." In *Trade and Market in the Early Empires,* edited by Karl Polanyi et al. Glencoe, IL: The Free Press & The Falcon's Wing Press, 1957.

Asiwaju, Anthony I. *West African Transformations: Comparative Impacts of French and British Colonialism.* Lagos, Nigeria: Malthouse Press Ltd., 2001.

Atanda, J.A. *The New Oyo Empire: Indirect Rule and Change in Western Nigeria 1894–1934.* New York: Humanities Press, 1973.

Ayandele, E.A. "The Yoruba Civil Wars and the Dahomean Confrontation." In *Nigerian Historical Studies* (London: Frank Cass, 1979), 55.

Baldwin, James. *The Evidence Of Things Not Seen.* New York: Holt, Rinehart, and Winston, 1985.

Bancroft, Frederick. *Slave-Trading in the Old South.* New York: Ungar, 1967.

Barrett, Leonard E. *Soul-Force: African Heritage in Afro-American Religion.* Garden City, NY: Anchor Press, 1974.

Bay, Edna G. "Servitude and Worldly Success in the Palace of Dahomey." In *Women and Slavery in Africa,* edited by Claire C. Robertson and Martin A. Klein. Madison: University of Wisconsin Press, 1983.

Bergerson, Aurther N., Jr. *Confederate Mobile.* Jackson: University of Mississippi Press, 1991.

Berry, Jack. *West African Folktales.* Evanston, IL: Northwestern University Press, 1991.

Blockson, Charles L. *Black Genealogy.* Baltimore: Black Classic Press, 1991.

Bolster, W. Jeffrey. *Black Jacks: African American Seamen in the Age of Sail.* Cambridge, MA: Harvard University Press, 1997.

Brandon, George. "Sacrificial Practices in Santeria, an African-Cuban Religion in the United States." In *Africanisms in American Culture,* edited by Joseph E. Holloway. Bloomington: Indiana University Press, 1990.

Buckley, Anthony D. *Yoruba Medicine.* Oxford: Clarendon Press, 1985.

Burton, Richard. *A Mission to Gelele King of Dahome.* London: Routledge and Kegan Paul, 1966.

Carter, Gwendolyn M., ed. *Five African States: Responses to Diversity.* New York: Cornell University Press, 1963.

Chase, Judith Wragg. "Material Culture." In *Dictionary of Afro-American Slavery,* edited by Randall M. Miller and John David Smith. New York: Greenwood Press, 1998.

Clochard, B., ed. *Ouidah: Petite Anthologie Historique.* Cotonou, Republic of Benin: L'Imprimerie Industrielle Nouvelle Presse, 1993.

Commager, Henry Steele, ed. *Documents of American History.* New York: F.S. Crofts & Co., 1974.

Craighead, Erwin. *Mobile: Fact and Tradition.* Mobile: The Powers Printing Company, 1930.

Davidson, Basil. *Black Mother: The Years of Our African Slave Trade: Precolonial History, 1450–1850.* Boston: Little, Brown, & Co., 1961.

Davis, G. *Pathfinder Geographies Book 1: Nigeria.* Nigeria: Longmans, 1963.

Delano, Issac O. *Owe L'Esin Oro: Yoruba Proverbs: Their Meaning and Usage.* Ibadan, Nigeria: Oxford University Press, 1996.

Dennett, R.E. *Nigerian Studies or the Religious and Political System of the Yoruba.* London: Frank Cass & Co. Ltd., 1968.

Dennison, Mable. *Biographical Memoirs of James Dennison.* Boynton Beach, FL: Futura Printing, Inc., 1984.

Diop, Cheikh Anta. *The African Origin of Civilization: Myth or Reality.* Chicago: Lawrence Hill Books, 1974.

Dow, George Francis. *Slave Ships and Slaving.* Salem: Marine Research Society, 1927.

Drewel, Henry, John Pemberton III, and Rowland Abiodun. *Yoruba: Nine Centuries of African Art.* New York: Center For African Art, 1989.

Du Bois, W.E.B. *Darkwater, Voices from Within the Veil.* New York, 1920.

———. "The Negro Since 1900." In *W.E.B. Du Bois: A Reader,* edited by Meyer Weinberg. New York: Harper & Row, 1970.

———. *The Suppression of the African Slave Trade to the United States of America, 1638–1870.* New York: Longmans, Green, and Company, 1904.

DuBose, John W. *Alabama's Tragic Decade.* Birmingham, AL: Webb Brook Company, 1940.

Eades, J.S., and Chris Allen, compilers. *Benin.* Oxford: Clio Press, 1996.

Fadipe, N. A. *The Sociology of the Yoruba.* Ibadan, Nigeria: Ibadan University Press, 1970.

Falola, Toyin. *Yoruba Gurus: Indigenous Production of Knowledge in Africa.* New Jersey: Africa World Press, Inc., 1999.

Forbes, Frederick E. *Dahomey and the Dahomans: Being the Journals of Two Missions to the King of Dahomey, and Residence at His Capital.* Volume 1. London: Longman, Brown, Green, 1851.

Franklin, John Hope, and Alfred A. Moss. *From Slavery to Freedom: A History of African Americas.* Volume 2. New York: McGraw Hill, Inc., 1998.

Glélé, Maurice Ahanhanzo. *Le Danxome: Du Pouvoir Aja à la Nation Fon.* Paris: Nubia, 1974.

Grimes, William. *Ethno-Botany of the Black Americans.* St. Claire Shores, MI: Scholarly Press, Inc.

Gunn, Harold G. *Peoples of the Plateau Area of Northern Nigeria.* London: International African Institute, 1953.

Howard, Warren S. *American Slavers and the Federal Law, 1837–1862.* Los Angeles: University of California Press, 1963.

Herskovits, Melville J. *Dahomey: An Ancient West African Kingdom.* Volume 1. New York: J.J. Augustin, 1938.

Howard, Lillie P. *Zora Neale Hurston.* Boston: Twayne Publishers, 1980.

Hurston, Zora Neale. "What White Publishers Won't Publish." In *I Love Myself When I Am Laughing...And Then When I Am Looking Mean and Impressive,* edited by Alice Walker. New York: The Feminist Press, 1979.

———. *Every Tongue Got to Confess: Negro Folk-tales from the Gulf States,* edited by Carla Kaplan. New York: Harper Collins 2001.

———. *Dust Tracks on a Road.* Philadelphia: J.B. Lippincott, 1942.

———. "Dust Tracks on a Road," in *Zora Neale Hurston: Folklore, Memoirs, and Other Writings,* edited by Cheryl A. Wall. New York: Library of America, 1995.

Idowu, E. Bolaji. *Olodumare: God in Yoruba Belief.* Original Publications, 1999.

Johnson, Dr. John L. *500 Questions and Answers on the Black Presence in the Bible.* Chicago: Lushena Books, 2000.

Johnson, Samuel. *The History of the Yorubas: From the Earliest Times to the Beginning of the British Protectorate.* Lagos, Nigeria: C.M.S. Bookshops, 1956.

Ki-Zerbo, J. "The Living Tradition." In *General History Of Africa I: Methodology and African Prehistory,* edited by J. Ki-Zerbo. Berkeley: University of California Press, 1990.

Lasisi, R.O. "Oyo-Yoruba and Ilorin Relations in the 19th Century." In *Readings in Nigerian History and Culture: Essays in Memory of Professor J.A. Atanda,* edited by G.O. Oguntomisin and S. Ademola Ajayi. Ibadan, Nigeria: Hope Publications, 2002.

Lay, Tracy Hollingsworth. *The Foreign Service of the United States.* New York: Prentice-Hall, Inc., 1928.

Leonard, Elizabeth D. *Lincoln's Avengers: Justice, Revenge, and Reunion after the Civil War* New York: W.W. Norton & Company, 2004.

Lincoln, C. Eric, and Lawrence H. Mamiya. *The Black Church in the African American Experience.* Durham, NC: Duke University Press, 1990.

Locke, Alain. *The New Negro.* New York: A. and C. Boni, 1925.

Lombard, Jacques. *Stuctures de Type Feodal en Afrique Noire: Etude des Dynamismes Internes et des Relations Sociale Chez les Bariba du Dahomey*. Paris: Mouton & Co., 1965.

Manning, Patrick. *Slavery, Colonialism and Economic Growth in Dahomey, 1640–1960*. London: Cambridge University Press, 1982.

———. "Merchants, Porters, and Canoemen in the Bight of Benin: Links in the West African Trade Network." In *The Workers of African Trade*, edited by C. Coquery-Vidrovitch. Beverly Hills, CA: Sage Publications, 1985.

———. "Slave Trade, 'Legitimate' Trade, and Imperialism Revisited: The Control of Wealth in the Bights of Benin and Biafra." In *Africans In Bondage: Studies in Slavery and the Slave Trade*, edited by Paul E. Lovejoy. Madison: African Studies Program, University of Wisconsin Press, 1986.

Mannix, Daniel P. *Black Cargoes: A History of the Atlantic Slave Trade, 1518–1865*. Associated Publishers, Inc., 1962.

Mbiti, John S. *Introduction to African Religion*. London: Heinemann Educational Books, 1991.

McNeill, William H. *Plagues and People*. New York: Anchor Press/Doubleday, 1976.

Meek, C.K. *The Northern Tribes of Nigeria*. Volume 1. London: Oxford University Press, 1925.

Miller, Joseph C. *Way of Death: Merchant Capitalism and the Angolan Slave Trade 1730–1830*. Madison: University of Wisconsin Press, 1988.

Mobee, Olusegun. *History of Mobee Family of Badagry and Their Involvement in Slave Trade*. Lagos: Al-Rasaq & Company, 2001.

Mudimbe, V.Y. *The Invention of Africa: Gnosis, Philosophy, and the Order of Knowledge*. Bloomington: Indiana University Press, 1988.

Na'Ibi, Mallam Shuaibu, and Alhaji Hassan, *The Gwari, Gade, and Koro Tribes*. Ibadan, Nigeria: Ibadan University Press, 1969.

Neville, Bert. *Directory of River Packets in the Mobile-Alabama-Warrior-Tombigbee Trades, 1818–1932*. Selma, AL: 1962. Courtesy of the Library at The Mariners' Museum, Newport News, VA.

Nieman, Donald G. *Promises to Keep: African-Americans and the Constitutional Order, 1776 to the Present*. New York: Oxford University Press, 1991.

Ogunremi, Deji. "Foundations of the Yoruba Economy in the Pre-Colonial Era," in *Culture and Society in Yorubaland*, edited by 'Deji Ogunremi and 'Biodun Adediran. Ibadan, Nigeria: Rex Charles Publication, 1998.

Olaoye, R.A. "The Traditional Cloth-Weaving Industry In Nigeria Before 1800," in *Readings In Nigerian History and Culture: Essays in Memory of Professor J.A. Atanda*, edited by G.O. Oguntomisin and S. Ademola Ajayi. Ibadan: Hope Publications, 2002.

Olatunbosun, P.O. *History of West Africa, from A.D. 1000 to the Present Day, in a Current Perspective*. Ilesha, Nigeria: Fatiregun Press & Publishing Company, 1976.

Oshinsky, David M. *"Worse Than Slavery": Parchman Farm and the Ordeal of Jim Crow Justice*. New York: Simon & Schuster, 1996.

Parrinder, E. Geoffrey. *The Story of Ketu: An Ancient Yoruba Kingdom*. Ibadan, Nigeria: Ibadan University Press, 1956.

Pettaway, Addie E. *AfricaTown, USA: Some Aspects of Folklife and Material Culture of an Historic Landscape.* Wisconsin Department of Public Instruction, 1985.

Pliya, Jean. *Histoire de Mon Pays.* Cotonou, Republic of Benin: Libraire Notre-Dame, 1993.

Roberts, Mary Nooter, and Allen F. Roberts, eds. *Memory: Luba Art and the Making of History.* New York: The Museum of African Art/Prestel: Munich, 1996.

Robinson, Beverly. "Africanisms and the Study of Folklore." In *Africanisms In American Culture,* edited by Joseph E. Holloway. Bloomington: Indiana University Press, 1990.

Roche, Emma Langdon. *Historic Sketches of the South.* New York: Knickerbocker Press, 1914.

Rodney, Walter. *How Europe Underdeveloped Africa.* Washington, DC: Howard University Press, 1982.

Rogers, J.A. *Sex and Race,* 2 vols. St. Petersburg, FL: Helga M. Rogers, 1968.

———. "Behanzin Hossu Bowelle—The King Shark." In *World's Great Men of Color,* Vol. 1. New York: Simon & Schuster, 1996.

———. *World's Great Men Of Color.* Volume 2. New York: Simon & Schuster, 1946.

Ronen, Dov. *Dahomey: Between Tradition and Modernity.* Ithaca, NY: Cornell University Press, 1975.

Royser, Jacqueline Jones, ed. *Southern Horrors and Other Writings: The Anti-Lynching Campaign of Ida B. Wells, 1892–1900.* New York: Bedford Books, 1997.

Rydell, Robert W. *All the World's a Fair: Visions of Empire at American International Expositions, 1876–1916.* Chicago: University of Chicago Press, 1984.

———. *The Reason Why the Colored American Is Not in the World's Columbian Exposition.* Chicago: University of Illinois Press, 1999.

Seale, William. "The President's House: A History." Vol. 1. White House Historical Association with the Cooperation of the National Georgraphic Society and Harry N Abrams, 1986.

Sellers, James Benson. *Slavery in Alabama* Birmingham: University of Alabama Press, 1950.

Sobel, Mechal. *Trabelin' On: The Slave Journey to an Afro-Baptist Faith.* Westport, CT: Greenwood Press, 1979.

Sobel, Robert, and John Raimos, eds. *Biographical Directory of the Governors of the United States, 1789–1978.* Vol. 2. Connecticut: Meckler Books, 1978.

Smith, M.G. *Government in Zazzau: A Study of Government in the Hausa Chiefdom of Zaria in Northern Nigeria from 1800 to 1950.* New York: Oxford University Press, 1960.

Snow, Loudell F. *Walkin' over Medicine* Boulder, CO: Westview Press, 1993.

Spears, John R. *The American Slave-Trade: An Account of Its Origin, Growth And Suppression.* New York: Charles Scribner's Sons, 1900.

Stuckey, Sterling. *Slave Culture: Nationalist Theory and the Foundations of Black America.* New York: Oxford University Press, 1987.

Tella, Tundi. *Isaga: A Victim of the Egba Dahomey Military Confrontations, 1862–1951.* Ibadan, Nigeria: International Publishers Limited, 1998.

Thomas, Hugh. *The Slave Trade: The Story of the Atlantic Slave Trade: 1440–1870.* New York: Touchstone, 1997.

Thompson, Vincent B. *The Making of the African Diaspora in the Americas, 1444–1900.* England: Longman Group, 1987.

Trans-Atlantic Slave Trade: Exhibition Guide of the Badagry Heritage Museum. Lagos, Nigeria: Lagos State Waterfront and Tourism Development Corporation, 2002.

Verger, Pierre. *Trade Relations between the Bight of Benin and Bahia from the 17th to 19th Century.* Ibadan, Nigeria: Ibadan University Press, 1976.

Vlach, John Michael. *The Afro-American Tradition in Decorative Arts.* Cleveland, OH: Cleveland Museum of Art, 1978.

Wada, Tobias Nkom (Agwam Takad I). *Takad Chiefdom: First Circle of Self-Determination.* Kaduna: Kual Prints Limited, 2003.

Washington, Booker T. "The First and Last Slave-Ship." Chapter in *The Story of the Negro: The Rise of the Race from Slavery.* New York: Doubleday, Page & Company, 1909.

Williams, Henry C. *AfricaTown, U.S.A.* Mobile, AL: American Ethnic Science Society, 1981.

———. *A History of Mobile County Training School.* Mobile, AL: privately printed, 1977.

Wilson, Kathryn, ed., *The Crisis Reader.* New York: Random House, Inc., 1999.

Wright, Donald R. *African-Americans in the Colonial Era: From African Origins through the American Revolution.* Illinois: Harlan Davidson, Inc., 1990.

JOURNAL ARTICLES

Agboola, S.A. "The Traditional Significance of Yam in Yorubaland in Pre-Colonial Times." *Nigerian Agricultural Journal* (1968): 59–65.

Alsobrook, David E. "Mobile's Solitary Sentinel: U.S. Attorney William H. Armbrecht and the Richard Robertson Lynching Case of 1909." *Gulf South Historical Review* 20, no. 1 (2004): 7–27.

Asiwaju, A.I. "A Note On The History of Sabe." *Lagos Notes and Records: University of Lagos Bulletin of African Studies* 4 (January 1973): 17–29.

Atanda, J.A. "Dahomean Raids on Oke Ogun Towns." *The Historia: Journal Of the University of Ibadan Historical Society* 3 (April 1966): 1–13.

Babayemi, S.O. "Oyo Palace Organization: Past and Present." *African Notes* 10, no. 1 (1986): 5–24 .

———."Upper Ogun: An Historical Sketch." *African Notes* 6, no. 2 (1970): 72–84.

Byers, S.H.M. "The Last Slave Ship." *Harper's Monthly Magazine* 63 (1906): 742–46.

Drake, Frederick C. "Secret History of the Slave Trade to Cuba Written by an American Naval Officer, Robert Wilson Schufeldt, 1861," *Journal of Negro History* 55, no. 3 (July 1970): 218–35.

"Early Life in the Southwest—The Bowies." *DeBow's Review* 13, no. 4 (October 1852): 381.

Eisterhold, John. "Mobile: Lumber Center of the Gulf Coast." *The Alabama Review* 26, no. 2 (1973): 83–104.

Falola, Toyin. "The Yoruba Toll System: Its Operation and Abolition." *Journal of African History* 30 (1989): 69–88.

Folayan, Kola. "International Politics in a Frontier Zone: Egbado, 1833–63." *ODU: A Journal of West African Studies*, n.s., 8 (October 1972): 3–32.

Goddard, S. "Town-Farm Relationships in Yorubaland: A Case Study from Oyo." *Africa* 35, no. 1 (1965): 21–29.

Holt, Thad. "The Resignation of Mr. Justice Campbell." *The Alabama Review* 12, no. 2 (April 1959): 105–18.

Hurston, Zora Neale. "Cudjo's Own Story of the Last African Slaver." *Journal of Negro History* 12 (October 1927): 648–63.

———. "The Last Slave Ship." *American Mercury* 58 (1944): 351–58.

Laoye I, Timi of Ede. "Yoruba Drums." *ODU: Journal of the University of Ile-Ife.* 7 (March 1959): 5–14.

Landry, Harral E. "Slavery and the Slave Trade in Atlantic Diplomacy," *Journal of Southern History* (May 1961): 184–207.

Law, Robin. "'The Common People Were Divided': Monarchy, Aristocracy and Political Factionalism In The Kingdom of Whydah, 1671–1727," *The International Journal of African Historical Studies* 23, no. 2 (1990): 201–29.

———. "'My Head Belongs to the King.' On the Political and Ritual Significance of Decapitation in Pre-Colonial Dahomey." *Journal of African History* 30 (1989): 399–415.

———. "Royal Monopoly and Private Enterprise in the Atlantic Trade: The Case of Dahomey." *Journal Of African History* 18, no. 4 (1977): 555–77.

———. "Slave-Raiders and Middlemen, Monopolists and Free-Traders: The Supply of Slaves for the Atlantic Trade in Dahomey c. 1715–1850." *Journal of African History* 30 (1989): 45–68.

Mason, Michael. "Population Density and 'Slave Raiding'—The Case of the Middle Belt of Nigeria." *Journal of African History* 10, no. 4 (1969): 551–64.

"Mobile—Its Past, Present, and Future." *De Bow's Review* 26, no. 1 (January 1859): 81–82.

Ogunremi, G.O. "Transportation in Pre-Colonial Africa." *Tarikh* 10 (1992), 29.

Ojo, Olatunji. "Slavery, Farm Slaves, and Agriculture in Nineteenth Century Ibadan." *Nigerian Journal of Economic History* 2 (1999): 136–54.

Okediji, F. Olu, and F.A. Okediji, "The Sociological Aspects of Traditional Yoruba Names and Titles." *ODU: University of Ife Journal of African Studies* 3, no. 1 (July 1966): 64–79.

Piersen, William D. "White Cannibals, Black Martyrs: Fear, Depression, and Religious Faith as Causes of Suicide Among New Slaves." *Journal Of Negro History* 62, no. 2 (1977): 147–59.

Romeyn, Henry. "Little Africa: The Last Slave Cargo Landed in the United States." *Southern Workman* (publication of Hampton Normal and Agricultural Institute) 26, no. 1 (January 1897): 14–17.

Ross, David. "The Career of Domingo Martinez in the Bight Of Benin 1833–64." *Journal of African History* 6, no. 1 (1965): 79–90.

———. "The Dahomean Middleman System, 1727–c. 1818." *Journal of African History* 28 (1987): 357–75.

Sears, Louis Martin. "Nicholas P. Trist, A Diplomat with Ideals." *Mississippi Valley Historical Review,* 11, no. 1 (1924): 85–98.

Sifakis, Carl "Benga, Ota: The Zoo Man." *American Eccentrics* New York: Facts on File, 1884).

Smith, Robert. "The Alaafin in Exile: A Study of the Igboho Period in Oyo History." *Journal of African History* 6, no. 1 (1965): 57–77.

Sudarkasa, Niara. "African and Afro-American Family Structure: A Comparison." *The Black Scholar* (November–December 1980): 43–47.

Tremearne, A.J.N. "Notes on the Kagoro and Other Nigerian Head-Hunters." *Journal of the Royal Anthropological Institute* 42 (1912): 136–200.

Verger, Pierre. "The Yoruba High God—a Review of the Sources." *ODU* 2, no. 2 (January 1966): 19–40.

Wax, Darold D. "Preferences for Slaves in Colonial America." *Journal of Negro History* 58, no. 4 (October 1973): 371–401.

Wish, Harvey. "The Revival of the African Slave Trade in the United States." *Mississippi Valley Historical Review* 27 (March 1941): 569–88.

Yoder, C. "Fly and Elephant Parties: Political Polarization in Dahomey, 1840–1870." *Journal of African History* 15 (1974): 417–32.

NEWSPAPER ARTICLES

Cannon, Vivian. "Archbishop of Benin Arrives for AfricaTown Folk Festival." *Mobile Register,* February 19, 1986.

Colquitt, Ron. "Archbishop from Benin Keynotes Ritual: His Ancestors Sold Slaves to Be Shipped Here." *Mobile Register,* February 24, 1986, 1B–2B.

The Daily Register (Mobile, AL), November 9, 1858, 3.

"Famous Ex-Slave Dies Here With Ambition Unrealized." *Mobile Register,* July 27, 1935.

Fiske, Warren. "Jefferson Fathered Slave." *The Virginia-Pilot,* November 1, 1998, A9.

Graves, Dara. "Haley Sees No AfricaTown, S. Africa link." *Mobile Press Register,* February 27, 1986, n.p.

Hoffman, Roy. "Voyage of the Clotilda." *Mobile Register,* November 9, 2002, 1B, 6B.

McFayen, Chris. "Legacy of a 'Peculiar Institution.'" *Mobile Register,* 1984, 4.

"Necrological: Death of Captain Tim Meaher, The Venerable Steamboat Man," *Mobile Daily Register,* March 4, 1892.

"Necrological: The Funeral of Captain Timothy Meaher." *Mobile Daily Register,* March 5, 1892.

"The Plateau Negro Remembers Capture in Jungle Lands: 'Kazoola,' Last of Cargo of Slaves Brought to American and Sold in Mobile, Has Vivid Recollection of Past Events," *Mobile Register,* September 29, 1929.

Porter, Charles. "African Bees Said Still in AfricaTown." *Inner City News,* September 20, 1986.

Roche, Emma Langdon. "Last Survivor of Slave Ship Deeply Grateful to God, Man." *Mobile Press Register,* August 13, 1935.

Sikora, Frank. "Groups Tracing History of Last Slaves to Arrive." *Birmingham News.* March 16, 1980, 2A.

INTERVIEWS

Ajose, John Babatunde, Curator, Badagry Heritage Museum. Interview by author, May 25, 2004. Handwritten.

Akinjogbin, I. A. Interview by author at his residence in Ibadan, June 14, 2003, Oyo State, Nigeria. Handwritten.

Amidi, Jean-Gauthier. Interview by author, Musée Historique (Royal Palace) d'Abomey, Republic of Benin, August 28, 1994. Handwritten.

Awe, Bolanle. Interview by author, Bodija (Ibadan), Oyo State, Nigeria, June 24, 2003. Handwritten.

Baba, Sati, Secretary to the Traditional Council of Kaninkon. Interview by author, Chiefdom of Kaninkon, Jema'a, Kaduna, Nigeria, June 5, 2004. Handwritten.

De Souza, Martine Françoise. Interview by author, Whydah, Republic of Benin, July 2, 1994. Tape recording.

———. Interview by author, Whydah, Republic of Benin, July 4, 1994. Tape recording.

———. Interview by author, Whydah, Republic of Benin, August 16, 1994. Tape recording.

Edwards, Richard. Interview by author, AfricaTown, Alabama, February 25, 1995. Handwritten.

Galadima, Chief Emmanuel I, Head of the District of Sabon Gari Kwoi. Interview by author, Chiefdom of Jaba, Fada District, Kaduna, Nigeria, June 6, 2004. Handwritten.

Gankpe, Chief Lohotogbe nongloakou. Interview by author, Village of Zoungboji, Whydah, Republic of Benin, July 7, 1994. Tape recording.

Henson, Vernetta. Interview by author, Mobile (Crichton), Alabama, July 19, 2007. Handwritten.

Hill, Ivory. Interview by author, AfricaTown, Alabama, February 6, 1995. Tape recording.

———. Interview by author, Toulminville, Alabama, July 17, 2007. Handwritten.

Hounon, Dagbo, Supreme Chief of Vodun for the Republic of Benin. Interview by author, Whydah, August 26, 1994. Handwritten.

Ikudefùn, Ilari. Interview by author, Aafin, New Oyo, Oyo State, Nigeria, June 18, 2003. Tape recording.

———. Interview by author, Aafin, New Oyo, Oyo State, Nigeria, July 17, 2003. Tape recording.

———. Interview by author, Aafin, New Oyo, Oyo State, Nigeria, May 22, 2004. Handwritten.

Jemkur, Joseph. Interview by author, University of Jos, Nigeria, June 4, 2004. Hand-written.

Iyanda, Alhaji Olatunde. Interview by author with the assistance of Olayinka Adekola, Monsifa Area, Oyo, Oyo State, Nigeria, July 10, 2007. Electronic mail.

Kakanakou, Supreme Chief Dah Akolemin Dossou Agaja. Interview by author, Village of Zoungboji, Republic of Benin, July 2, 1994. Tape recording.

Kanyip, Benedict, Takad indigene. Interview by author, October 20, 2005. Electronic mail.

Lewis, Israel, III. Interview by author, Mobile, Alabama, February 20, 1995. Handwritten.

———. Interview by author, Prichard, Alabama, July 19, 2007. Handwritten.

Marshall, Josephine Lee. Interview by author, AfricaTown, Alabama, March 14, 1994. Tape recording.

Mobee, ViaVoh, Curator, Mobee Family Museum. Interview by author, Badagry, Nigeria, May 25, 2004. Handwritten.

Mohammed, Alhaji M. Interview by author, Zuma Rock Nigerian Village, Abuja, Nigeria, June 7, 2004. Handwritten.

Obakayeja, Ilari. Interview by author, Aafin, New Oyo, Oyo State, Nigeria, June 18, 2003. Tape recording.

———. Interview by author, Aafin, New Oyo, Oyo State, Nigeria, May 22, 2004. Handwritten.

Ojo, Ganiyu, Prince. Interview by author, Aafin, New Oyo, Oyo State, Nigeria, June 18, 2003. Handwritten.

Oladipo, Alhaji R.O., principal private secretary of Alaafin Adeyemi III. Interview by author, Aafin, Oyo, Oyo State, June 18, 2003. Handwritten.

Oguntomisin, Olorundare G. Interview by author, Ibadan, Nigeria, June 9, 2003. Handwritten

Ona Olo kun Esin. Interview by author, Aafin, New Oyo, Oyo State, Nigeria, July 17, 2003. Tape recording.

Peoples, John. Interview by author, AfricaTown, Alabama, February 24, 1995. Handwritten.

Pogue, Mary. Interview by author, AfricaTown, Alabama, February 9, 1995. Tape recording.

Randolph, John C. Interview by author, AfricaTown, Alabama, March 14, 1994. Tape recording.

Sani, Dr. S.N., district head. Interview by author, Chiefdom of Jaba, Fada District, Kaduna, Nigeria, June 6, 2004. Handwritten.

Seidu Akilu, a Gwari indigene and a professor of City Polytechnic University, interview by author via Mr. Olayinka Adekola, Ibadan, Nigeria, June 14, 2007. Electronic mail.

Senami, Dayo, interpretive guide, Route of Slaves. Interview by author, May 25, 2004, Badagry, Nigeria.Handwritten.

Shamburger, Thelma. Interview by author, AfricaTown, Alabama, February 6, 1995. Tape recording.

Tete, Mallam Tanko, Chief of Kaninkon. Interview by author, Chiefdom of Kaninkon, Jema'a, Kaduna, Nigeria, June 5, 2004. Handwritten.

Wada, Tobias Nkom, the *Agwam* Takad I. Interview by author, Fadan Attakar, Takad Chiefdom, Kaura Local Government Area, Kaduna, Nigeria, June 6, 2004. Handwritten.

Williams, Henry C., Historian. Interview by author, AfricaTown, Alabama, March 12, 1994. Tape recording.

Williams, Spencer. Interview by author, AfricaTown, Alabama, February 25, 1994. Tape recording.

Woods, Lorna. Interview by author, Mobile, Alabama, March 1, 1994. Tape Recording.

———. Interview by author, Lewis' Quarters, Alabama, August 14, 2004. Handwritten.

SPECIAL COLLECTIONS

Augustine Meaher (son of Timothy Meaher) to Mr. Donaldson (of Springhill, Alabama), November 10, 1890. Letter in the hand of Augustine Meaher. Special Collections, Local History and Genealogical Department of the Mobile Public Library, Mobile, Alabama.

"CAPT. WM. FOSTER: Commander of Last American Slave Vessel Buried Yesterday." Special Collections, Local History and Genealogical Department of the Mobile Public Library, Mobile, Alabama.

"City Taxes For 1858."City of Mobile. Original Documents #98. Slavery/Receipts/Bills of Sale for Slaves. Minnie Mitchell Archives. Historic Mobile Preservation Society. Mobile, Alabama.

Dispatches From United States Consuls In Santiago, Cape Verde, 1851–1869. Microcopy No. T-434, National Archives, Washington, DC.

Foster, Captain William. "Last Slaver from U.S. to Africa. A.D. 1860." Captain Foster's Account (photocopy): 1–11. Special Collections, Local History and Genealogical Department of the Mobile Public Library, Mobile, Alabama.

Guerres Du Roi Glele. Archives IFAN. Dakar-XVIII a. A list of wars found in the Archives Nationale Du Benin. Porto Novo, Republic of Benin.

"History of Cudjoe Lewis," a brief statement written by James M. Lewis, 73 years of age, grandson of Cudjoe Lewis, and son of Alex Lewis (of Montgomery, Alabama), November 29, 1968. Special Collections, Local History and Genealogical Department of the Mobile Public Library, Mobile, Alabama.

"Last Cargo of Slaves: How a Ship Load of Negroes Were Imported in 1861. An Alabama Captain's Desperate but successful Undertaking—One hundred and Sixty Slaves Landed—The Only Full-Blood African Colony in America," *Globe-Democrat,* November 26, 1890. This is a *Globe-Democrat* reporter's written account of his interview with Timothy Meaher. Special Collections, Local History and Genealogical Department of the Mobile Public Library, Mobile, Alabama.

"Last Slave Ship Sunk Here Raised: Colony of Negroes Who Came Over on the Krotiley [*Clotilda*] Alive At Plateau," n.d. Special Collections, Local History and Genealogical Department of the Mobile Public Library,, Mobile, Alabama.

"A List of John P. Broun's Negroes, To be sold on the 4th day of January 1859." Original Documents #98. Slavery/Receipts/Bills of Sale for Slaves. Minnie Mitchell Archives, Historic Mobile Preservation Society, Mobile, Alabama.

Manifest of the *Clotilda,* pp. 1–2. Special Collections, Local History and Genealogical Department of the Mobile Public Library, Mobile, Alabama.

Meaher Family Papers. Minnie Mitchell Archives, Mobile Historical and Perservation Society, Mobile, Alabama.

Oath of Judgeship taken by William Giles Jones, in the presence of R.B. Owens, United States Commissioner. February 13, 1860. National Archives of the United States. RG 60.

Physical Features: Mobile and Suburbs (Map No. 12) in *Boudousquie's Directory for the City of Mobile* (1861), 188. Special Collections, Local History and Genealogical Department of the Mobile Public Library, Mobile, Alabama.

Public Sales. *Branch Bank at Montgomery vs. L.D. Hallonquist, James G. Birney.* May 1, 1844. Original Documents #98. Slavery/Receipts/Bills of Sale for Slaves. Minnie Mitchell Archives, Historic Mobile Preservation Society, Mobile, Alabama.

Radin, Paul. *God Struck Me Dead: Religious Conversion Experience and Autobiographies of Negro Ex-slaves* (Nashville: Social Science Institute, Fisk University, 1945), 27–30. Peabody Collection. William R. and Norma B. Harvey Library, Hampton University, Hampton, Virginia.

Rules and Regulations for the Government of the Convict System of Alabama, Approved by the Board of Inspectors of Convicts, March 3, 1886. Approved by the Governor March 22, 1886. Published by Order of the Board (Montgomery, AL: Barrett & Co., State Printers, 1886), 24. Minnie Mitchell Archives, Historic Mobile Preservation Society, Mobile, Alabama.

Slave ships in Alabama: Message from the President of the United States, transmitting the proceedings of the court and marshall of the U. States for the District of Alabama to the cargoes of certain slave ships, &c. (Washington, DC: Printed by Gales & Seaton, 1826). Special Collections, Mariner's Museum, Newport News, Virginia.

"Weaving and Dying In Oyo Province." File number 1757. National Archives of Nigeria, Ibadan (January 1947): 400–5.

William Giles Jones to President James Buchanan. Letter of resignation of judgeship, January 12, 1861. National Archives of the United States. RG 60.

William H. Woodberry of Boston to Mr. Donaldson of Springhill, Alabama, October 20, 1890. Special Collections, Local History and Genealogical Department of the Mobile Public Library, Mobile, Alabama.

GOVERNMENT DOCUMENTS, PROBATE RECORDS, LEGAL CASES, SUBPOENA, AND WRITS

Amnesty Oaths File 37, pp. 291, 293, and 149 (1868) for James Meaher, Tim Meaher, and Cade M. Godbold respectively. Mobile Probate Court Archives.

Bank of Mobile v. Meagher & Co. Supreme Court of Alabama, January 1859. Decided. 33 Ala. 622; 1859 Ala. LEXIS 56. Available at http://www.lexisnexis.com.

Charge To Grand Jury – Fugitive Slave Law. Case No. 18,261 Circuit Court, S.D. New York 30 F. Cas. 1007; 1851 U.S. App. LEXIS 376; 1 Blatchf. 635April, 1851. Lexis-Nexis Academic Search.

Charles Collins et al v. N.B. Trist et al. No. 941. Supreme Court of Louisiana, New Orleans, May 1868. Decided. 20 La. Ann. 348; 1868 La. LEXIS 105. Available at http://www.lexisnexis.com.

Circuit Court of the United States. In Admiralty. The United States of America, By Information versus The Schooner Wanderer and Cargo, in *The African Slave Trade and American Courts: The Pamphlet Literature*. Series V, volume 2 (New York: Garland Publishing, 1988), 27, 59

Circuit Court of the United States. Southern District of Alabama. Spring Term 1860. *The United States vs. Horatio N. Gould; U.S. vs. T.V. Bordnax. The Mobile Register,* Thursday Morning, April 19, 1860. The National Archives of the United States. RG 60.

Cudjoe Lewis to Mobile Light & RR Co. Deed Book. D. 113 (1904), p. 23. Mobile Probate Court Archives.

Cudjo Lewis to Mobile County. Deed Book 212 (1926), 424. Mobile Probate Court Archives.

Cudjo Lewis v. The Louisville and Nashville Railroad Company. Verdict for damages assessed at $650.00. January 1903. University of South Alabama Archives.

Cujo Lewis to Thomas L. Dawson. Deed Book 189 (1920), p. 418. Mobile Probate Court Archives.

Ewing v. Sanford. Supreme Court of Alabama, June 1851. Decided 19 Ala. 605; 1851 Ala. LEXIS 132. Lexis-Nexis Academic Search.

Foster v. Holly. Supreme Court of Alabama, June 1861. Decided 38 Ala. 76; 1861 Ala. 13 . Available at http://www.lexisnexis.com.

Hauser to Lewis. Deed Book 55 (1887), 160. Mobile Probate Court Archives.

Last Will and Testament of William Giles Jones. Pigeon Hole 398. Files 38 through 41, 1857. Mobile Probate Court Archives.

List of Accounts in Petty Ledger. Code MISC, Book F, pp. 372–77, 1856. Mobile Probate Court Archives.

Meaher to Allen. Deed Book 30 (1872), 643. Mobile Probate Court Archives.

Meaher to Kebee. Deed Book 30 (1872), 655. Mobile Probate Court Archives.

Official Bond. Book 1 (1861), p. 307.1. Mobile Probate Court Archives.

Petition to Partition Real Estate Owned by J.M. and T. Meaher. Mobile Probate Court Archives. Pigeon Hole 185. File No. 38, 1884.

Proceedings of the Annual Congress of the American Prison Association of the United States. Held in Nashville, November 16–20, 1889. Washington, DC: American Correctional Association, 1963–c.1970.

Register of Vessels, Entry No. 26, November 19, 1855. Original registry for the schooner *Clotilda.* National Archives. Washington, DC. This information is cross-referenced with the *Record of Registers, 1854–1857* (No. 13). Bureau of Navigation, Department of Commerce, National Archives, Washington, DC.

Register of Vessels, Entry No. 32, August 27, 1857. National Archives. Washington, DC.

Register of Vessels, February 1860. National Archives. Washington, DC

Rules and Regulations for the Government of the Convict System of Alabama, Approved by The Board of Inspectors Of Convicts, March 3, 1886. Approved by the Governor March 22, 1886. Published by Order of the Board. Montgomery: Barrett & Co., State Printers, 1886. Minnie Mitchell Archives. Historic Mobile Preservation Society. Mobile, Alabama.

Runaway Slave Book I, p. 148 (1863). Mobile Probate Court Archives.

"Slave and Coolie Trade." House Executive Document, 34th Cong., 1st sess., no. 105, 19.

Slave Loan. MISC Book D (1843), p. 438. Mobile Probate Court Archives.

Slave Sale. MISC Book G (1858), p. 11. Mobile Probate Court Archives.

State of Alabama Judicial Department: *The Supreme Court of Alabama. Certificate of Reversal. November Term. 1904.* University of South Alabama Archives.

The State of Alabama v. Cudjoe Lewis. City Court Criminal Minute Book 18 (1899–1902). University of South Alabama Archives.

United States v. Burns Meaher. Writ of Seizure. United States District Court, Southern District of Alabama. Final Record Book, 1859–1860. Mobile Municipal Archives. Mobile, Alabama.

United States v. Jno M. Dabney. Writ of Seizure. U.S. District Court, Southern District of Alabama. Mixed Case Files, 1820–1860. Box 46, Writ # 2619. Mobile Municipal Archives. Mobile, Alabama.

United States v. William Foster and Richard Sheridan. United States District Court, Southern District of Alabama. Mixed Case Files, 1820–1860. Summons #3516. Box 51. Special Collections, Local History and Genealogical Department of the Mobile Public Library. Mobile, Alabama.

United States v. William Foster. Summons. United States District Court, Southern District of Alabama, Mixed Case Files, 1820–1860, Summons # 2621. Special Collections, Local History and Genealogical Department of the Mobile Public Library. Mobile, Alabama.

U.S. Congress. House. *Report of the Secretary of State in Reference to the African Slave Trade.* 36th Cong., 2nd sess., 1860. H. Doc. 7, 185

U.S. Congress. Senate. *Correspondence Imputing Malpractices to the American Consul at Havana,* 26th Cong., 2d sess., 1841. S. Doc. 125, 217.

U.S. District Court, Southern District of Alabama. *List of Dismissed Cases. Minute Book, 1836–61; 1865–66.* Mobile Municipal Archives. Mobile, Alabama.

U.S. District Court, Southern District of Alabama. *Minute Book, 1859–1861.* Mobile Historical Society. Mobile, Alabama.

U.S. Supreme Court. *The Gray Jacket, Appeal from the District Court of the United States for the Eastern District of Louisiana. December Term, 1866.* 72 U.S. 342 (1866). Full text of case available at http://www.justia.us/us/72/342/case.html

Wilson to Lewis. Deed Book 30 (1872), 601. Mobile Probate Court Archives.

CENSUS REPORTS

Clarke County, Alabama. *Largest Slaveholders from 1860 Slave Census Schedules and Surname Matches for African Americans on 1870 Census.* Available at http://www.freegenealogy.rootsweb.com/~ajac/alclarke.htm.

Census Report for the County of Mobile (1880). Special Collections, Local History and Genealogical Department of the Mobile Public Library, Mobile, Alabama.

Census Report for the County of Mobile (1900) Special Collections, Local History and Genealogical Department of the Mobile Public Library, Mobile, Alabama.

ELECTRONIC DATABASES AND VISUAL MEDIA

"A Belle of the Fifties; Memoirs of Mrs. Clay, of Alabama, Covering Social and Political Life in Washington and the South 1853–66." Electronic edition. Available at http://docsouth.unc.edu/clay/clay/html.

"An Act in Addition to the Acts which Prohibit the Slave Trade." January 13, 1859. Available at http://cdl.library.cornell. edu.

Campbell Family Papers. Manuscript Department Library of the University of North Carolina at Chapel Hill. Available at http://www.lib.unc.edu.

"Chronology On The History Of Slavery, 1830 To The End." Available at http://innercity.org.

"Convict Leasing in Alabama." Available at http://www.prisonactivist.org.

Curren, Caleb. "The Wreck of the Orline St. John: With a General History of Steamboats in Southwest Alabama." *PAL Journal* (1998). Available at http://www.Archeologyinc.org/steamboats.html.

Davis, Angela. "Attacking the Prison Industrial Complex." Transcript from September 22, 1998. Available at http://www.Time.com.

Delany, Martin R., Chief Commissioner. "Official Report of the Niger Valley Exploring Party." New York: Thomas Hamilton, 1861. Available at http://www.hierographics.org.

Dred Scott, Plaintiff in Error, v. John F. A. Sanford. December Term, 1856. Web site of the Touro Law Center, © 1995–2004. Available at http://www.tourolaw.edu.

Edgerton, Robert B. "Warrior Women: The Amazons of Dahomey and the Nature of War." Available at http://orion.oac.uci.edu, p. 16.

Facts and Observations Relative to the Participation of American Citizens in the African Slave Trade. Published by Direction of A Meeting Representing The Religious Society of Friends In Pennsylvania, New Jersey, &c. Philadelphia: Joseph & William Kite, Printers, 1841. Available at http://amistad.mysticseaport.org.

"The Foster Family." The Island Register—Prince Edward Island's Premier Genealogy Home Page. http://www.islandregister.com.

Jabbar, M. A., and M. L. Diedhiou, "Does Breed Matter to Cattle Farmers and Buyers? Evidence from West Africa," p. 4. Available at http://www.ilri.cgiar.org.

Johnson, Clifton. "The Amistad Case and Its Consequences in U.S. History." Amistad Research Center at http://www.tulane.edu.

Jordan, Christine. "Justice Campbell—Last of the Jacksonians." The Supreme Court Historical Society Publications. Digitized volumes from the Society's collections. http://www.supremecourthistory.org.

Ketchum, Ralph. "The American Presidency." Grolier Encyclopedia. Available at http://www.gi.grolier.com.

The Life And Times Of Sara Baartman—"The Hottentot Venus." Video List (New York: First Run Icarus Films, 2000), 3.

Maryland State Archives (African-American Record Descriptions). Available at http://www.mdarchives.state.md.us.

New York Morning Herald. October 8, 1839, 2. Available at http://mysticseaport.org

Nicholas Philip Trist Papers, Manuscripts Department, Library of the University of North Carolina at Chapel Hill. Available at http://cadmus.lib.unc.edu.

"The Ostend Manifesto: Aix-La-Chapelle: October 18, 1854." Available at http://xroads.virginia.edu.

"Paul Jennings: A Colored Man's Reminiscences of James Madison." Available at http://www.msstate.edu.

Proceedings of the Annual Congress of the American Prison Association of the United States. Held in Nashville, November 16–20, 1889 (Washington, DC: American Correctional Association, 1963–c.1970), 111. Available at Google Book Search.

Roy, Christopher. "Hausa Information." Art and Life in Africa Online. Available at http://www.uiowa.edu.

Slave Trade Act of 1807."Documents on Slavery." The Avalon Project at Yale Law School. Available at http://www.yale.edu.

DISSERTATIONS AND OTHER UNPUBLISHED WORKS

Agiri, Babatunde. "Missionaries, Muslims, Warfare and Slavery in Ogbomoso in the 19th Century." Unpublished article obtained from author, p. 3.

Amos, Harriet E. "Social Life in an Antebellum Cotton Port: Mobile, Alabama, 1820–1860." PhD diss., Emory University, 1976.

Anignikin, Sylvain C. "De la Traite Negriere au Defi du Developpement: Reflexion sur les Conditions de la Paix Mondiale." Paper presented at the international symposium Routes Des L'Esclave, Ouidah, Republic of Benin, September 1–5, 1994, 3.

Hurston, Zora Neale. "Barracoon: The Story of the Last 'Black Cargo.'" Box 164–186. File #1. Typescript of unpublished mss. Moorland-Spingarn Manuscript Collection, Howard University, Washington, DC.

Index

About the Author

NATALIE S. ROBERTSON teaches at Hampton University and is the editor of *African American History in Transatlantic Perspective* (2000) and *The Ancient and Global Dimensions of Black History* (2005). She is also a Senior Scholar at the United States National Slavery Museum.